Pr

This book is dedicated to the unnamed driver of the Corporation refuse-collection van who helped me rake through a quarter of a ton of urban garbage to rescue the first set of interviews which had been inadvertently consigned to the university dustbins by over-zealous cleaners.

PRIMARY TEACHERS
talking

A STUDY OF TEACHING AS WORK

Jennifer Nias

London and New York

First published 1989
by Routledge
11 New Fetter Lane, London EC4P 4EE
Reprinted 1990

Transferred to Digital Printing 2004

Simultaneously published in the USA and Canada
by Routledge
a division of Routledge, Chapman and Hall, Inc.
29 West 35th Street, New York, NY 10001

Typeset by Pat and Anne Murphy, Highcliffe-on-Sea, Dorset

British Library Cataloguing in Publication Data

Nias, Jennifer, *1932–*
    Primary teachers talking: a study of teaching as work.
    1. Primary schools. Teaching.
    I. Title
    372.11'02
    0-415-01115-9

Library of Congress Cataloging in Publication Data
has been applied for
0-415-01115-9 Pb

Contents

Acknowledgements

I am very grateful to Muriel Last and Andrew Pollard for their helpful comments on draft chapters and to all those others who have offered encouraging or critical reflections on earlier versions of material contained in this book. Notwithstanding, any mistakes and misinterpretations which remain are my own.

Without the skill, perspicacity and long suffering of Angie Ashton and Fiona Weideking, this book would never have been written. I am very grateful to them both. I would also like to make appreciative acknowledgement of the assistance I received from the University of Liverpool during the early stages of the research reported here and, more recently, of the support I have been given by the teaching and non-teaching staff of the Cambridge Institute of Education.

Finally, but most importantly, I would like to thank the teachers who made this book possible and from whom I have learnt so much.

Chapters 3, 4, 5, and 6 include extracts from three previously published papers — 'Reference groups in primary teaching: talking, listening and identity' in S. Ball and I. Goodson (eds) 1985, *Teachers' Lives and Careers*, Lewes: Falmer Press; 'A more distant drummer: teacher development as the development of self' in L. Barton and S. Walker (eds) 1985, *Education and Social Change*, London: Croom Helm; 'Leadership styles and job satisfaction in primary schools' in T. Bush *et al.* (eds) 1980, *Approaches to School Management*, London: Harper & Row.

Parts of Chapters 1, 2, 5, 6, and 7 have also appeared in 'Teaching and the Self', *Cambridge Journal of Education*, 17: 1987; 'The definition and maintenance of self in primary teaching', *British Journal of Sociology of Education*, 5: 1984; 'Commitment and motivation in primary school teachers', *Educational Review*, 33: 1981; 'Teacher satisfaction and dissatisfaction: Herzberg's two-factor hypothesis revisited', *British Journal of Sociology of*

Education, 2: 1981; 'Learning and acting the role: in-school support for primary teachers', *Educational Review*, 36: 1984. I am grateful to the publishers for permission to use them here.

Introduction

We all think we know what it is to have been a pupil. Accounts of that experience abound — fictional, autobiographical, historical, anthropological, poetic, and prosaic. Tangentially there is a substantial literature relating to teachers, much of it filtered through the writers' own memories of fear, humiliation, confusion, unhappiness or, more rarely, self-confidence and success. Some autobiographies and biographies also document the experience of being a teacher and in some of them, teachers (or sympathetic observers) have written accounts of their work. Many of these make good reading; they are touching, humorous, gently-barbed, and evangelical (of a particular educational style or mode). Less appealing to the general public is the mounting literature on teachers written by sociologists and teacher educators. This falls into three categories: books which are directly or indirectly about the classroom work of teachers; those which consider teachers in staffrooms and classrooms as part of case studies of schools; and those which focus on teachers' lives and careers. All of them draw to a greater or lesser extent upon interviews with teachers or on notes of staffroom talk, some on classroom observation. Yet very few attempt to portray, as much as any outsider can, an insider's account of teaching. Moreover, with very few exceptions, books and articles published in the past 20 years in England, North America and Australia have been about secondary schools. Primary teachers have been given little opportunity to speak for themselves.

Two books (Gibson, 1973; Huggett, 1986) and the analysis of an open-ended questionnaire survey (Primary School Research and Developmental Group, 1986) do give verbatim accounts by English teachers, some of them primary. These accounts begin to present a living picture of what teaching is like for those who practise it. None of them is, however, set within a theoretical framework which might provide practitioners, parents and decision-makers

1

with a more generalized understanding of primary teachers and the ways in which they experience their work. Nor does any of them consider how teachers or their thinking might change over time.

The purpose of this book is to fill that gap. Using interviews with, and a few written accounts by practising teachers, I have attempted to present an account of primary teaching as work, from the perspective of its practitioners. My justification, if one is needed, is that neither pupils' nor adult observers' accounts can fully capture the lived realities of teaching as an occupation; that can be done only by allowing teachers to voice their own thoughts and feelings. Inevitably, however, any attempt to order their words imposes a false coherence upon the latter and, it can reasonably be argued, therefore presents a distorted picture of the messy, uncertain complexity which is teaching. In response, I can say only that, first, no one's efforts to organize another's thoughts can ever be fully free of distortion but that, second, if teachers themselves recognize their own truths in what I have said, that is validation enough.

This book is, then, addressed first to primary teachers, in the hope that it will help them to understand and come to terms with themselves as professional workers and to use that understanding as a basis for trying to change what they do not like about themselves and their working lives. It is also addressed to teacher educators who prepare teachers for their work or help them on in-service courses, to parents and governors whose growing responsibilities for schools make it imperative that they understand what teaching is like as work, and to the politicians and administrators whose decisions are daily contributing to a crisis of confidence and morale within the profession.

Its argument is presented in two parts. Part I argues that one can best understand how primary teachers construe the notion of work and their developing relationship to it by grasping the importance that they attach to a sense of personal identity: they exist as people before they become teachers and their work calls for a massive investment of their 'selves'. Chapter 1 explains the notion of 'self', why it is important to primary teachers in England and Wales and how the 'self' is conceptualized in symbolic interactionism, Freudianism and self-psychology. Using symbolic interactionism as a framework, Chapter 2 examines how primary teachers in their early years see themselves and Chapter 3 shows, with particular emphasis to reference groups, how these aspects of the self-image are defended over time from peer and institutional pressures. Chapter 4 picks up the idea that teacher development is, at root, the development of the person who is the teacher. It has two main themes. First, not all teachers incorporate an occupational identity into their self-image; those who do not, either leave the profession or lose interest in it (some of them attempting to pursue parallel careers). Second, as these shifts in self-conception take place, teachers' personal concerns in relation to their work change, from preoccupation with survival and a search for occupational identification ('self' concerns) to the consolidation and extension of work-related skills ('task' concerns) and then to a search for greater influence ('impact' concerns) within what has now become a personally-selected profession.

Part II examines primary teachers' experience of work in the light of this progressive identification with (or rejection of) their daily occupation. Chapters 5 and 6 look at what they like and dislike about their work, Chapters 7 and 8 at the experience of teaching as an occupation requiring contact with adults as well as children, a topic which has until very recently been almost entirely neglected. Chapter 9 picks up the themes of tension and paradox which emerge in these chapters and proposes that the central skill of primary teaching is the ability to find and maintain a balance among them all. In the Conclusion (Chapter 10), I attempt a synthesis of these themes, with particular emphasis upon recent economic and political changes which affect the profession.

Throughout, I have mentioned these changes when they seem particularly relevant to a certain point or issue. However, I have not paid much attention to them in general until the Conclusion. Despite the actual and likely impact of these changes upon primary teachers, the main preoccupation of the latter is their work and particularly the children for whose early education they are responsible. Since this book sets out to explore and explain teachers' professional experience, it would be a distortion of that experience to present my account of it as a polemic. Yet no responsible commentator can ignore the radical changes contained in the Education Acts of 1986 and 1988 and those imposed by the financial settlement of 1986/7, or can overlook the effect of all these developments upon morale and motivation among primary and middle school teachers.

There are other aspects of the context in which teachers work which are not examined (except in passing, in Chapters 1 and 9). In particular, I have not set out to explore the social structures in which teaching is set, its cultural characteristics or historical roots, or the social contexts of individual schools. In other words, this book does not address teaching as a sociological or historical phenomenon. In one sense, of course, this cannot be true, because the teachers whose experience is reported are themselves the product of social, political, economic, biographical, and historical forces. So, accepting but not examining the historically located nature of the evidence, I have attempted to present the subjective reality of teachers' working lives during early and mid-career, in the belief that what their accounts reveal about teaching as work transcends, though is not unaffected by, many of the particularities of time and place.

Similarly, many readers will notice an absence of any overt emphasis upon gender. This may seem strange in a book written by a woman about a profession which is numerically dominated by women. Once again, however, this gap is deliberate; I have specifically mentioned gender-related issues only when teachers themselves have raised them (i.e. generally in relation to the distribution of power within school staffs and therefore to promotion). What did not emerge from my evidence was support for such stereotypes as 'women find emotional satisfaction in working with children' and 'men enjoy organization'. Indeed, I have throughout been at pains to point out, by indicating the gender of speakers whenever it seemed relevant, that, for instance, men become just as attached to their pupils as women do, and women are as interested in organizing and influencing their colleagues as men are; in short, that simplistic sexist notions do not stand up to examination. But although I have drawn attention, when it seems appropriate, to matters in which gender does seem to play a part (e.g. in definitions of 'career'), I have not examined my evidence from a consciously feminist perspective, believing that I could most effectively reflect the world of teachers of both sexes by speaking of their delights, anxieties and preoccupations, not by imposing my own upon them. Of course, to avoid directly addressing the gender implications of what these teachers said is to ignore the possibility that they and I are the victims of false consciousness. I have chosen to raise this concern but not to pursue it further.

It is a further reflection upon the society in which I and these teachers live that all the participants in this study are white and all speak English as a first language. About a third had taught or were teaching in areas where many of their pupils were non-native English speakers or were of minority ethnic origin, but very few raised racism, in their schools or communities or in society at large, as a personal or professional concern. Once again, their silence is reflected in the structure and content of the book.

Further, there is an apparent inconsistency in my work. To stress that primary teaching is a personal activity, imbued with and shaped by the beliefs, values, personalities and perspectives of particular practitioners, is, in one sense, to argue that no generalizations can do justice to the variety which characterizes even the smallest staff-room. However, as I studied the testimony of these teachers, I became aware of patterns. They had similar views of themselves, they spoke of their job satisfactions and dissatisfactions in the same kinds of terms, they experienced life in classrooms and staffrooms in common ways, developed along parallel paths and at analogous rates, registered similar emotions when they discussed pupils, colleagues, head teachers, parents. In short, as they talked about teachers, pupils and teaching they revealed a paradox: what they had in common was their individuality or, to put it another way, it was their persistent self-referentialism which made it possible to construct a generalized picture of their experience. Aspects of the 'self' repeatedly emerged as central to the experience of these teachers, even though each 'self' was different.

Methodology, analysis and use of evidence

This book is based upon the personal accounts of teachers who trained in one-year Post Graduate Certificate in Education (PGCE) courses for work in infant, junior and middle schools. Ninety-nine of them were first interviewed in 1975–1977. Just over two-thirds had attended, over five years, a course of which I was tutor. The remainder were a random sample who between them had attended similar courses at seven universities, polytechnics or colleges of education. Altogether there were thirty men and sixty-nine women, the balance of sexes in each group being roughly the same.

I knew all the members of the first group very well, and three-quarters of them had been in touch with me between the time that their course had ended and my enquiry began. Few of the second group knew me previously. I found that members of both groups were not only equally keen to talk to a neutral but interested out-sider about their professional lives, but that all of them were free (sometimes to the point of indiscretion) in their comments. Twenty-two members drawn from both groups also kept a diary for one day a week for one term, and the perspectives revealed in these accounts were very similar across groups.

I contacted all members of each group by telephone or letter. Six of the first group did not wish to be included in the project. The remaining forty-three of the first group and all of the second group gave their prior consent, and I visited them in their schools (in many different parts of England). I spent roughly half a day with each of them in their classes, making unstructured observations, which I subsequently noted down before each interview. I also visited in their own homes twenty of the first group who had left teaching and six people who were teaching but whom I could not visit in school. I had long telephone conversations with a further eight from the first group (six at were at home, two teaching outside England). Many interviews of those in the first group were completed in the pub or in members' homes. All of those in the second group took place at school. All talked equally freely, whether inside or outside their places of work.

The purpose of the school visit was to provide a background against which I could interpret subsequent interview data and not to undertake any formal observations. Afterwards I conducted semi-structured interviews, taking rapid notes in a personal shorthand and using a very loose interview schedule, framed in terms of broad key-questions. The main purposes of the latter were to encourage teachers to reflect very broadly upon their experiences of teaching in all the schools in which they had worked and upon their plans for the future. Respondents were encouraged to give long and, if they wished, discursive replies and I often used supplementary questions. The shortest of the interviews took 1½ hours, the longest 5 hours; most took about 3 hours. The diaries were chiefly used to flesh out individual accounts of perspective and practice.

Before the first interviews, I also contacted by letter, telephone, or visits, about 70 per cent of the head teachers of any school in which any of my interviewees had taught during the previous 10 years. The purpose of these conversations was to cross-check factual information and sometimes statements of opinion, and to provide an institutional context for teachers' replies. They have not been a primary source of evidence for this book.

A further fifty interviews took place in 1985 (most of them with people first interviewed 10 years before). This second set was different from the first in a number of respects. It took place 10 years later in what can loosely be termed 'mid-career' for most of the group. I did not talk to the head teachers of interviewees, nor, in general, visit their classrooms. Interviews were shorter; the shortest was about 50 minutes, the longest about 3 hours. About two-thirds were tape-recorded; for the remaining third I took rapid notes and wrote up a summary as soon as possible thereafter. In both cases, transcripts or summaries were sent to individuals for validation, with the suggestion (of which only three took advantage) that they delete anything they did not want me to use, and with assurances of confidentiality.

The biggest difference of all, however, is that the second group were much more obviously self-selected than the first. About 6 months before the second interviews I wrote to all those I had earlier interviewed, asking for their movements to date and whether they would be willing to talk to me again. I also wrote to fifteen people who had qualified in 1976 or 1977, too late for my original enquiry, but whom I knew were still teaching. Fifty-four of the first group replied, all but three saying they would be ready to meet me (these three were all men, still teaching in the same school or neighbourhood in which they had been 10 years earlier). Thirteen of the second group replied affirmatively. Although I knew by word of mouth what had happened to twenty-nine out of the forty-five people who did not reply (four were in primary schools, three were teaching outside primary schools, thirteen were raising families, nine were in other careers including educational psychology), I had no way of knowing whether the four who were still teaching but had not replied had not done so because they did not receive my letter or because they did not wish to talk about their work, perhaps because they were unhappy in it. Most of those who replied were succeeding, in career terms, or were enthusiastically resuming a career after childrearing. Thus the second set of evidence on which I have drawn is heavily biased. With few exceptions it reflects the experience of successful and committed teachers who had been working for between 9 and 18 years (though in the case of married women returners, the years worked varied from 5 to 12). What it does not represent is the experiences of those mid-career teachers who may be ready or anxious to change jobs or occupations but are unable to do so. By contrast, the views of such teachers are represented in the first interviews.

For the second interviews I decided to visit only those who were still working in infant, junior or middle schools. In the course of these interviews I also talked to one special-school teacher (a woman), three secondary teachers (two men and one woman), two adult education tutors (both women), five college lecturers (two men, three women), one adviser (a woman) and three mothers who had recently given up teaching. Altogether, I conducted fifty interviews (two of them by telephone), during industrial action by teachers in the spring term of 1985. I had been PGCE tutor to all but two of those who replied to my original letter and several had (intermittently) kept in touch with me. All of the fifty had taught 4–13-year-olds (the approximate age range for which they trained) at some point, and thirty-six (thirteen men, twenty-three women) were still doing so. Only three (two still teaching) spoke with lasting distaste of the experience. Because only a very few at the time of either interview were teaching, or had taught, in middle schools, I have spoken throughout the book of 'primary schools'. This term should be understood to refer to schools for children in the 4–13 age range, in many different types of phase organization, but predominantly catering for children in the 4–11 or 7–11 age groups, since most of my interviewees had experience of these types of school. There were seventeen men, thirty-three women, five head teachers (four men), seven deputy heads (of whom five were women), eight women doing part-time or supply work.

I left the choice of place to individuals; twenty-four chose their place of work, and I met the rest in pubs or in their own homes. The venue did not appear to affect the freedom with which they spoke. Interviews were semi-structured, following a loosely framed set of questions, and took place at times convenient to individuals. The main foci of my questions were: motivation; job satisfaction and dissatisfaction; professional, personal and career development; personal experience of and reflections upon teaching; and the place of work in life and future career plans. I also encouraged people to talk about any other aspect of their work or career.

It will be apparent that I ended up with a formidable amount of material — hand-written notes, transcripts or validated summaries of interviews, teachers' written accounts — collected over 10 years. This had the advantage that patterns among the responses appeared fairly readily and could be internally checked and validated; I had no shortage of corroborative evidence and, in consequence, have often been able to generalize with some confidence about my findings, as far as they relate to graduates who trained for 1 year. In the absence of further evidence it is a matter of speculation whether they also apply to teachers with a longer pre-service education.

Analysing the huge mass of evidence which I accumulated did, however, present problems, especially since I had not asked my broad questions in a standard order. Therefore, I sometimes had to sift relevant information from discussion of unrelated topics. In general, I used a thematic approach, allowing the themes to emerge whenever possible from the words of speakers (i.e., using 'grounded theory', Glaser and Strauss, 1967). For example, it was teachers' own testimony that alerted me to the importance of 'commitment', to their need for 'stimulation', to the enthusiasm they felt when 'a child's face lights up'. Themes were also suggested by the weight of evidence: it was this, for instance, that drew my attention to the frustration engendered by large classes or by poor communication within schools, to the pleasures of children's company, to the existence of reference groups and, above all, to the importance of self-image. Where it seems useful (as in the last two instances) I have used labels drawn from social psychology or sociology to 'name' phenomena which teachers knew existed but had not conceptualized or made explicit.

Having decided on a possible organizing theme, I proceeded in an orthodox manner (Hammersley and Atkinson, 1983; Burgess, 1984). I progressively re-sorted the evidence, refining the categories which appeared from it, looking for contradictions and using these to help in the process of clarification. Only when categories were 'saturated' (that is, when new evidence contributed nothing further to my understanding of them) did I assume that they represented teachers' realities in honest ways (which I hoped they themselves would recognize as reflecting their own worlds). It is, after all, one of the main purposes of qualitative research to provide 'a language for speaking about that which is not normally spoken about' (Hargreaves, 1978, p. 19). If this book enables primary teachers to conceptualize their daily experience, to reflect upon it and to discuss it with others, inside and outside the profession, it will have fulfilled my main aim.

Nevertheless, my interpretations of the experiences that teachers reported in their interviews, and (to a much lesser extent) in their diaries, remain, in the last resort, that of an outsider rather than an insider. Although they were tested in conversation with teachers as they evolved, the generalizations presented here are mine. Consequently, I am responsible for any errors or misinterpretations.

Selecting from the evidence for the purposes of presentation (given the constraints of book-length and the need to balance the reader's likely interest in abstractions on the one hand and living detail on the other) has been a constant headache. For the most part, I have set myself an arbitrary limit of three or four illustrative comments for any given point and have pared these down to essentials. The reader is asked to accept that the evidence I have presented has been painstakingly sifted from nearly 150 lengthy interviews, 22 diaries and several letters, and that I have omitted much more data than I have included.

I indicated at the start of this introduction that the book was arranged in two parts. In Part I, to which I now turn, I explore the connections which appear to exist between teachers' 'selves' and their work, in the first two decades of their professional lives. Part II (Chapters 5–9) uses the ideas put forward in Chapters 1–4 to present a fuller account of the nature of teaching as work. Chapter 10 attempts to synthesize the arguments from Parts I and II and makes particular reference to recent political and economic changes in the status of the teaching profession.

Part one

Chapter one

Teaching and the self

The claim that teaching is a personal activity is often advanced as a reason why it cannot be systematically taught to others or fully brought into the public domain. Yet this claim is seldom explicated or justified, to the detriment of mutual understanding among people inside and outside the profession. So, in this chapter, I show that to be a teacher in the primary (and in some instances, the middle) schools of England is to work in a historically determined context that encourages individualism, isolation, a belief in one's own autonomy and the investment of personal resources. Each of these conditions stresses the importance in teaching of the teacher as a person, as distinct from, though not as opposed to, the teacher as the possessor of occupational knowledge and skills. In other words, the self is a crucial element in the way teachers themselves construe the nature of their job. In turn, this directs attention to theoretical formulations of the self, a hypothetical construct which has been explored by, among others, poets, philosophers, psychologists, social psychologists and sociologists. Here, I focus upon the sociological and psychological perspectives provided by symbolic interactionism, Freudianism, and self-psychology, and in particular upon the nature of the self as 'me' and the self as 'I'.

Teaching as an individual activity

Unique and interpersonal

Most obviously, teaching is a personal activity because the manner in which each teacher behaves is unique. Teaching, like learning, has a perceptual basis. The minute-by-minute decisions made within the shifting, unpredictable, capricious world of the class-room and the judgements teachers reach when they are reflecting on their work depend upon how they perceive particular events, behaviours, materials, and persons. In turn, these perceptions are determined by schemata ('persistent, deep-rooted and well-organized classifications of ways of perceiving, thinking and behaving' which are also 'living and flexible', Vernon 1955: 181) or basic assumptions ('schemata . . . organised in more generalised, vague or ill-defined patterns', Abercrombie 1969: 64) which help us to order and make sense of the world around us. Schemata and assumptions are learned; they are slowly built up as, from birth, we develop and exercise the skill of seeing (or hearing, smelling, tasting, touching). They are modified by experience and activity. Since no two people have the same life experiences, we all learn to perceive the world and ourselves as part of it in different ways. So teachers, as people, 'see' and interpret their pupils and the latter's actions and reactions according to perceptual patterns which are unique to themselves. No matter how pervasive particular aspects of a shared social or occupational culture may be or how well individuals are socialized into it, the attitudes and actions of each teacher are rooted in their own ways of perceiving the world.

This biological explanation for teachers' individualism exists side by side with a persistent historical tradition which emphasizes the teacher's personality. In his study of elementary schoolteachers in the USA, Lortie (1975: 79) pointed to an unchallenged orthodoxy, that 'personal predispositions are not only relevant but, in fact, stand at the core of becoming a teacher', and Connell (1985) noted the same with Australian secondary teachers. In the United Kingdom similar views have been expressed, not only by academics (Woods 1981; Pollard 1985; Sikes *et al.*, 1985) but also by Her Majesty's Inspectorate and the Department of Education and Science. *The New Teacher in School* (DES 1982: 6.2) claimed: 'HMI found that the personal qualities of the teachers were in many cases the decisive factor in their effectiveness. A similar view was put forward by schools'; and the government White Paper *Teaching Quality* (DES 1983: 1.26) argued: 'Personality, character and commitment are as important as the specific knowledge and skills that are used in the day to day tasks of teaching'. Small wonder, then, that practitioners themselves perpetuate a largely unquestioned assumption that 'what gets taught is the teacher'.

This stress upon personality is encouraged by allegiance to philosophical traditions which see the personal relationship between teacher and learner as central to the educational process. Two centuries ago Rousseau wrote *Emile*, a prescriptive account of the education of one child by his tutor. On to this Romantic preoccupation with the individual, practising educationalists grafted the Christian tradition — expressed by Froebel and Pestalozzi as respect and concern for the whole child and by Buber as the 'I–thou' relationship (in which the teacher as a person becomes a resource for the self-activated development of the learner). Today many primary school teachers still see the personai relationship which they have with individual children not just as a means of establishing control and increasing motivation but also as the means by which education itself takes place (see, e.g. Lieberman and Miller 1984; Woods 1987a; Nias 1988).

Moreover, throughout their professional education and socialization, teachers are led to believe that they are capable of 'knowing' not just one child, but all the pupils in their care (Alexander 1984). When Kay Shuttleworth set up the first teacher training college in England at St John's, Battersea, he took many of his ideas from Pestalozzi's work in Switzerland. Among them were the notions that teaching should be inspired by love and that teachers should therefore live and work among their pupils. This aspiration was itself drawn partially from Froebel's metaphysical concern for the centrality of unity and wholeness and his consequent belief that education should be an organic process, free of artificial and damaging divisions. Teachers socialized into this tradition tend to identify with their classes, to talk of themselves in relationship to their pupils as 'we'. They tacitly believe that their personal relationship is with the whole class, not just one child.

Isolation and autonomy

The centrality of the personal relationship between teacher and pupils is further emphasized by the solitary nature of much primary teaching. Until recently, the architectural design of most English primary schools has unquestioningly followed the tradition, established in urban elementary schools in the nineteenth century, that instruction is best carried out in 'box' classrooms occupied by one teacher and a group of thirty to forty children. These classrooms are cut off from one another, though they are usually linked by a corridor, a staircase, or, in older schools, a central hall. In addition, windows are often placed so that it is difficult for passing teachers to see into one another's rooms. The isolation imposed by architecture has helped to foster an occupational context from which teachers learn to expect that much of their working lives will be spent with children not adults; teaching will be not only private but lonely (Lieberman and Miller 1984).

Further, initial teacher education provides students with relatively few chances to observe their more experienced colleagues in action and, except in open plan schools, the latter seldom see one another teaching. This lack of opportunity to 'sit by Nellie' encourages students and probationers to feel that they must survive by their own efforts and to believe in an occupational *rite de passage* which equates the establishment of competence with suffering. As many have argued (notably Lortie 1975; Hargreaves 1980), teachers have little opportunity or incentive to develop shared professional knowledge or a collegial sense of the 'state of the art'. As a result, in teaching as in social work (England 1986), there is a widespread belief in the intuitive basis of all professional action. Teacher education, experience, and conventional wisdom continually underline the uniqueness of the individual, the specificity of context and the primacy of the person.

These tendencies have been encouraged by the relative freedom from political control which primary teachers have until recently taken for granted (although, as Broadfoot and Osborn (1986) point out, in a comparative study of French and English teachers, the latter's freedom is restricted in practice by the power of their head teachers). For much of the past hundred years, teachers in Britain have felt that it was their responsibility to make far-reaching decisions about the curriculum and teaching methods used in their classes, to the point that there is little continuity, communication or agreement between classes in some schools. Indeed, as Alexander (1984) points out, the more immersed teachers become in their own classes, the freer head teachers are to exercise leadership over the whole school, unchallenged by any demand from their staff for co-operative planning or decision-making. Teachers often learn to depend upon their own knowledge, interests and preferences in making pedagogic and curriculum decisions. Indeed, this freedom from external constraints and collegial influence is, for some teachers, one of the main attractions of the job (though others deplore the sense of incoherence which it sometimes gives to their work, Nias 1980).

A sense of autonomy in matters of curriculum and pedagogy is closely related to the ideological freedom which most British primary teachers enjoy. This is particularly important because few of them are satisfied with imparting only knowledge or skills to their pupils. Rather, they have always been chosen, or have selected themselves, in part for their concern with religious, moral, political, or social values (Rich 1933; Tropp 1957; Floud 1962). The study by Ashton *et al.* (1975) of primary teachers' aims, found that the majority thought that aims relating to social and moral education were more important than those which were concerned with intellectual, physical, or aesthetic education, while Lortie (1975), Lacey (1977), Woods (1981; 1984), Connell (1985), Sikes *et al.* (1985), and Smith *et al.* (1986) have all highlighted the continuing existence within the profession of individuals with strong dedication to religious, political or humanitarian ideals. Kay Shuttleworth's vision of a band of 'intelligent Christian men entering on the instruction of the poor with religious devotion to their work' (quoted in Rich 1933) is still, *mutatis mutandis*, a recognizable one in many schools.

However, as studies such as those by Hartley (1985) demonstrate, there is little agreement, even within single schools, on which moral or educational values should be transmitted. Indeed, given the different social and curricular traditions (Blyth 1967) which have shaped the primary system and into which its teachers are socialized, it would be surprising if there were. Educational writers such as Alexander (1984), Kelly (1986), and Delamont (1987) have drawn attention to the persistence of this plurality, arguing that conflicting views of the nature of knowledge, and thus of teaching and learning, still bedevil primary schools. The epistemological confusion which such authors describe, does, however, allow those teachers and head teachers who have a coherent philosophy to pursue it with relative impunity. Despite recent political developments, the English system still offers plenty of scope to individuals who wish to propagate particular views of the educational process.

Teachers' freedom to make many of the decisions which closely affect their work and to select within broad limits the values which they seek to transmit, has also been protected in the past few decades by attempts to define teaching as a profession and therefore to regard it as self-governing. Although political decisions taken between 1986 and 1988 have undermined these efforts in England and Wales, habits of autonomy are likely to die hard. Teachers will probably go on expecting to enjoy large measures of personal choice and discretion in matters relating to the conduct of their classrooms.

Personal investment

Finally, there are some teachers who, consciously or unconsciously, reduce the boundaries between their occupational and other lives. For them, teaching is very 'inclusive' (Argyris 1964), i.e., it absorbs much of their time and energy and makes use of many of their talents, skills or abilities. For such people, teaching is particularly personal in the double sense that it draws upon interests and capacities which might, in other occupations, be reserved for non-work activities and that it allows little space for the development of alternative lives. Indeed, the more demanding it becomes of imagination, insight, problem-solving, and professional skills, the more it offers an outlet for creative potential, thereby reducing individuals' need to seek the latter elsewhere. Similarly, when teaching is conceptualized as a relationship between two or more people, rather than as an instrumental activity, it becomes possible for teachers to find personal and emotional satisfactions within their working lives rather than outside them.

The fact that teaching as an occupation is potentially 'inclusive' is compounded by the chronic scarcity of resources from which it suffers. By definition, no teacher ever has enough time, energy and material resources to meet all the learning and personal demands of a large class of young children. To this shortage are now added recent expenditure cuts at both local and national levels. Yet as an occupation, teaching has a bottomless appetite for 'commitment' (i.e. 'a readiness to allocate scarce personal resources', Lortie 1975: 189). As a result, teachers are easily trapped. The more they identify with their jobs, the greater the satisfaction they receive from their personal relationship with individuals and classes, and the more outlet they find in their work for varied talents and abilities, the greater the incentive that exists for them to invest their own personal and material resources in their teaching. They are, in short, beset by the double paradox that the personal rewards to be found in their work come only from self-investment in it and that when the cost of the latter is too high, the rewards are also reduced. The 'hidden pedagogy of survival' (Woods 1979) brings teachers little satisfaction.

Individual teachers

Primary teaching is, then, an activity which for psychological, philosophical and historical reasons can be regarded as individualistic, solitary and personal, inviting and, in some senses, requiring a high level of self-expenditure. As Pollard (1982) has shown, although primary teachers do work under common structural constraints they perceive them differently and react to them individually, making personal meanings (shaped by their personalities, biographies, and work contexts) out of similar situations and reacting to them in ways which have meaning for them (see also Woods 1987b). It follows that any understanding of primary teachers' actions and reactions must be based upon knowledge of them as people.

However, this line of thinking leads into poorly charted territory. Surprisingly, an occupation which has for nearly 200 years attached great importance to the idea of knowing and catering for the individual child has paid little formal attention to the concept of the individual teacher. Particular primary teachers have attracted some largely unflattering attention from fiction writers (see, for example, Biklen, 1986a), but very little from academics or from teachers themselves. There have been a few attempts (notably Elbaz 1983; Bussis *et al.* 1976; Brown and McIntyre 1986; Calderhead 1987 — in Canada, the USA, Scotland, and England, respectively) to examine the professional or craft knowledge of individuals, to portray their 'ideologies' (Hartley 1985) or personal constructs (Ingvarson and Greenway 1984), or to record their feelings (Hannam *et al.* 1971; Huggett 1986; Spencer 1986). One or two life histories exist (e.g. Aspinwall 1986) but, apart from the follow-up study undertaken by Smith *et al.* (1986) into the staff of an innovative American elementary school, there has so far been no work on individuals' lives and careers comparable to that carried out by Sikes *et al.* (1985) or Connell (1985) on English and Australian secondary teachers. Individuals feature in the school studies of King (1978), Berlak and Berlak (1981) and Pollard (1985), but their opinions and activities are treated as if they were representatives of groups or sub-cultures. Moreover, studies such as these make more use of observation than of interviews. In short, few attempts have been made to portray the subjective reality of teaching from the standpoint of, or in the words of, teachers themselves.

Notions of self

To emphasize the personal nature of teaching is also to draw attention to the importance of the 'self'. Yet, although terms such as 'self-concept', 'identity', 'self-esteem', 'the ideal self' have multiplied in educational writings, they are, like the notion of the 'self' itself, hypothetical constructs which do not refer to anything tangible or directly observable. Any choice of explanatory system for them is therefore to some extent arbitrary.

Symbolic interactionism: the self as 'me'

One such system which offers many productive insights is symbolic interactionism, a set of ideas primarily associated with two Americans, Charles H. Cooley and George H. Mead. Although the psychologist William James made the distinction in the 1890s between 'I' and 'me', it was Cooley (1902, 1983 edn) who argued that through interaction with people to whose behaviour we attach symbolic meanings we learn to take other people's perspectives and so to see ourselves as we think they see us. In doing so we come to have an awareness of ourselves as objects. Mead (1934) elaborated this idea, claiming that the self can be an object to itself (that is, 'I' (*ego*) can observe, be aware of and think about 'me' (*alter*)). We experience ourselves in the same ways that we experience the people and things with which we come in contact. More than that, by interacting (or talking, as Mead argued) with others, we become aware of the attitudes they hold towards us and this in turn shapes the way we see ourselves. Our 'selves' are inescapably social. Deprived of interaction with others we would have no sense of self, for 'selves can only exist in definite relationships with other selves' (Mead 1934: 164).

This is not to claim that all interactions are equally important in determining the way we see ourselves. Social psychologists now generally accept that 'significant others' (the idea, though not the term, was coined by Cooley) have a particularly powerful effect upon our self-concept. For, as Cooley (1902, 1983 edn: 175) argues: 'In the presence of one whom we feel to be of importance, there is a tendency to enter into and adopt, by sympathy, his judgment of myself.' Mead built upon this idea when he introduced the concept of the 'generalised other'. His suggestion was that, in time and through repeated interactions, we internalize the attitudes not just of particular people but also of organized social groups (e.g. churches, political parties, community groups, work forces). When we do this, we supplement with new influences the forms of internal regulation we have acquired through identification with significant others. Our behaviour as adults is therefore likely to vary not just in relation to the social context of which we are immediately a part but also according to the 'reference group' (Newcomb 1950) whom we have in mind in any particular situation. In other words, Mead set the scene for the development of the notion of 'multiple selves', each sustained and regulated by reference to different 'generalised others'.

'Situational selves' and 'substantial self'

Yet few social psychologists would wish to defend a totally situational view of the self. Katz (1960) suggested that each individual develops an inner self or core through contact with significant others. Writing as a biologist, Abercrombie (1969) put forward similar views, arguing that, at birth, individuals begin to develop assumptions about the world and themselves as part of it, through the processes of perception. The most potent schemata or assumptions (including those which are self-referential) are established by close physical contact between the infant and growing child and those who care for him/her. Because they are formed before the child can talk, and 'having been made non-verbally are very difficult to talk about' (Abercrombie 1969: 73), it is particularly hard for individuals to uncover the fundamental assumptions they have about themselves. These therefore remain relatively impervious to change.

Ball (1972) used the term 'substantial' to distinguish this inner core, which, he argued, is persistently defended and highly resistant to change. It comprises the most highly prized aspects of our self-concept and the attitudes and values which are salient to them. This idea, that we most strongly protect from challenge those attitudes which are expressive of self-defining values, finds support from other theoretical perspectives. Rogers (1982) argued from his experience as a psychotherapist and educationalist that individuals need to maintain consistent self-concepts and will reject new ideas which they do not perceive as compatible with their view of themselves. Festinger (1957), observing that people often find it psychologically uncomfortable to hold views which are mutually incompatible or to act in ways which are inconsistent with one or more of them, suggested that we resolve the resulting 'cognitive dissonance' by changing our views or actions so as to bring them into line with one another. Rokeach (1973) went further, claiming that the dissonances most likely to precipitate change in an individual arise not at the level of views but of beliefs and values. By implication, it is against dissonance in values or between values and actions that we most strongly protect ourselves. The group psychotherapist, Foulkes, was also of this opinion. He argued that 'the nuclear family imbues and impregnates the individual from his earliest phase of life and even before birth with the total value system of the culture of which this family is part' (Foulkes 1975: 60). We become habituated to the patterns of behaviour derived from these values and very skilled in their defence, to the extent that in new situations we try to recreate the relationships which sustain and perpetuate the values from which our view of ourselves derives. There is, then, support from different disciplines for the idea that we each develop a relatively impervious 'substantial self' which can be distinguished from our 'situational selves' and which incorporates those beliefs, values and attitudes which we feel to be most self-defining. This is not, however, to argue for a completely static view of the self. To be sure the substantial self is hard to reach even by reflexive activity (e.g. introspection and self-examination), and is well defended and difficult to change, in part because people develop situationally specific strategies to protect themselves from the need to alter the ways in which they perceive themselves.

Two further distinctions need to be made with respect to the self as 'me'. The first is between self-concept and self-esteem. It is easy to envisage circumstances under which people are not happy with or proud of the image which they have of themselves. Though the evidence is inconclusive (Hargreaves *et al.* 1975), it seems in general to support the idea that when there is a conflict between the two, people act so as to maintain a stable self-image, even though this image may not be the one they wish they had. This may be in part because self-perceivers have access to 'privileged information' (Hampson 1982: 192): that is, to knowledge of past and present experience which is denied to their partners in the interaction. Such knowledge may affect their perceptions of themselves and also of the messages being transmitted by their partners. The second is related: social psychologists often distinguish between people's image of themselves as they would like to be ('ideal') and as they think that they are ('real'). However, if one is guided by Thomas' (1931) well-known dictum that 'what people believe to be true is true in its consequences', this distinction becomes blurred. Unless people make it clear when they refer to themselves that they are making a distinction between their 'ideal' and 'real' selves, it may be helpful to assume that they have the latter in mind.

The self as 'I': Mead and Freud

So far, the discussion has been of the self as 'me'. Symbolic inter-actionists also conceptualize the self as 'I', the active subject which initiates and innovates as well as responding to the messages about 'me' that it receives from others. As a concept the self as subject is, however, even more elusive than that of the self as object because 'I' turns into 'me' as soon as the actor is self-conscious (i.e. as soon as their actions become the object of reflexive thought). As Mead said, 'The "I" of this moment is present in the "me" of the next moment . . . I cannot turn round quick enough to catch myself' (Mead 1934: 174).

Nevertheless the 'I' is important for two reasons. On the one hand, many people are intuitively aware of its existence as a deep sense of personal identity. Nearly a century ago, William James wrote, in a letter to his wife:

A man's character is discernible in the mental and moral attitude in which, when it came upon him, he felt himself most deeply and intensely active and alive. At such moments there is a voice inside which speaks and says, '*This* is the real me!'

(quoted in Erikson 1968: 19)

Although James does not offer a definition of the 'I' and his description contains no criteria for its recognition by anyone other than himself, his is an experience of which writers from diverse fields (ranging from poetry to psychology) are aware. On the other hand, we need to take note of its existence because it is:

> that part of the self which is relatively free of social constraints: it is impulsive and capable of inventing new ideas or meanings not sent in by the 'others'. It is that most private core of inner experience which has a degree of autonomy . . . The 'me' cannot be anything but conformist . . . [but when we realize] that in some respect we acted against the grain of society, such a realisation is awareness of the 'I' and its capacities.
>
> (Open University, D207, Course Team 1981)

In other words, Mead's notion of the 'ego' makes it possible for us to reject the concept of a self which is entirely the product of social conditioning.

But accepting that the self exists as subject as well as object brings us no closer to knowing how we should conceptualize or characterize the 'ego'. This may be in part because, as Holland (1977) has so clearly shown, attempts from Mead onwards to explain the social self have been unable (or unwilling) to come to terms with the powerful, instinctual forces of the human personality to which Freud drew attention over a century ago. Freud's analysis of personality structure afforded two hypothetical constructs — the super-ego (the controlling 'conscience' provided by internalized values) and the ego (the conscious actor in touch with the daily realities of living) — which fitted in relatively well with the idea of a socially constructed self. It also, however, presented us with the id (the unconscious, a potentially explosive mixture of instincts and repressed memories). This aspect of the self is, by definition, resistant to investigation but, because of the forces which are contained within it, continually influences every aspect of human thought, feeling and behaviour. It is obviously difficult to accommodate within a view of the self which emphasizes socialization, continuity, and conformity rather than individuality, conflict, and change.

Yet the 'I' is an inescapable part of education. Books such as those by Jersild (1952) remind us that the encounter between teachers and learners is an emotional experience. Richardson (1967; 1973) and Salzberger-Wittenberg *et al.* (1983) used an explicitly Freudian perspective to explore the actions and reactions of student teachers and teachers in relation to their pupils and colleagues.

Abercrombie carried her work on the unconscious nature of perception into higher education, increasing the autonomy and responsibility of medical and architecture students by helping 'each participant to understand his own behaviour and acquire better control over it' (Abercrombie 1981: 52). Her work with teachers, guided by the same insights, is reported in Abercrombie and Terry (1979) and Lintott (1986). There is, then, growing evidence that teachers' attitudes, actions and responses are influenced by their unconscious as well as their conscious selves, by the parts of themselves which they have rejected or 'split off' (Holland 1977) as well as by those which they accept.

Self-psychology

However, not all psychoanalysts adopt a view of the 'I' which involves the denial and repression of parts of it. Rather, self-psychology (Kohut 1971) stresses the continuation into adulthood of self-love or narcissism, seeing it as the means by which many admirable human qualities are developed. Kohut presents a view of the self which, drawing upon infants' apparent inability to distinguish in early life between self and others, argues that nurturant figures in their environments become what he calls 'selfobjects' (Kohut 1971: 27). Since young children are inescapably self-regarding, these extensions of self mirror back to them their own sense of 'narcissistic grandiosity' (Kohut 1971: 25). Infants also expect to be able to control these 'selfobjects' as if they were themselves. With the passage of time, they learn to differentiate self and environment and they realize the limits of both the care provided by their nurturant figures and their own controlling powers. As this happens, Kohut argues, the qualities detected as missing from their nurturing 'selfobjects' are incorporated into their own egos and adopted as their own ideals (so, each generation aspires to what it feels it did not have in its own formative years). At the same time, the self-love and self-importance of the growing child become less extreme and unrealistic and are integrated into the ego as socially acceptable aims and forms of ambition. In other words, early care-providers fulfil both a mirroring and an idealizing function for young children. As these functions are gradually internalized, individuals develop a stable capacity for self-regard and self-regulation and a mature ability to love people and things that exist independently of themselves.

As adults they also retain their early tendency to relate to the world and people in it as if these were part of themselves. Kohut does not, however, see this as deplorable or regressive for, he argues, self-love and self-esteem can develop into culturally valuable attributes such as creativity (self-expression) and the ability to see situations from others' perspectives as well as our own. This development is accompanied by and, in some senses, is enabled by the fact that we do not lose our need (especially in periods of intellectual, biological, or social change) for relationships which mirror or affirm our sense of self-esteem and present us with an idealized picture of strength and concern for others. The fact that we are able to revert at times of stress and confusion to infantile levels of self-regard enables us to perceive particular others as 'selfobjects' who will be at our beck and call, ready to protect and cherish us while our need for them persists. The existence of these relationships ensures that there will be transitional periods during which we can reshape or rebuild our 'selves' in a realistic manner, more in tune than previously with the external circumstances that caused our distress.

This account of the ego differs from that of classical psychoanalytic theory, in positing in individuals a separate development of the capacities to relate both to their environments as part of themselves and as independent of them (as opposed to the Freudian view that the normal individual develops beyond narcissism — relating to the environment as part of ourselves — and that the persistence of the latter is a sign of regression or dysfunctional dependence on a mother figure). Now, widespread acceptance of Freudian notions has resulted in a socially defined view of the ego, and thus of the individual teacher, from which not only negative emotions but also self-love are largely banished. Yet the persistent self-referentialism of teachers, their apparent tendency to treat their pupils as 'selfobjects' (i.e. to identify with them, to seek simultaneously to control them and to look to them for reinforcement of their self-esteem) suggests that Pajak (1981) may be right in pressing for a fuller understanding of Kohut's views among educationalists. It may well be that a continuing capacity for self-love underpins the development of many adult aspirations and qualities. Certainly, any view of the 'I' which discounts it, is as incomplete as one which ignores the controlling super-ego and the instinctual drives of the id.

Conclusion

There are many factors, then, inviting individual primary teachers to be self-referential in the ways in which they conceptualize and carry out their jobs. The historical, financial and philosophical traditions of primary teaching, the culture and physical context of schools, all create a situation in which who and what people perceive themselves to be are seen by those inside and outside the profession to matter as much as what they can do. As a result, teachers expect the job to make extensive calls upon the personality, experience, preferences, talents, skills, ideas, attitudes, values and beliefs of each individual. Equally, they expect the freedom to ensure that the ways in which, and still to some extent what, they teach are consistent with the values which are most salient to them. Primary teaching as an occupation makes heavy demands upon the self.

However, this leaves us with the problem of how to conceptualize the 'self'. Symbolic interactionism offers several fruitful insights into this slippery notion, particularly that the self as 'me' is socially constructed by 'significant' and 'generalized' others, and that, although much of what constitutes our 'selves' is situational, varying with context, we also have a well-defended, relatively inflexible substantial self into which we incorporate the most highly prized aspects of our self-concept and the attitudes and values which are most salient to it. Symbolic interactionism is however less helpful in delineating and defining the self as 'I', that is, the 'ego' which does not depend for its existence upon social conditioning. In particular, symbolic interactionists have been reluctant to come to terms with the powerful, instinctual drives which, since Freud, have been accepted as part of the human psyche. Nor have they made room for alternative views of the ego such as that provided by Kohut. Yet if we accept the salience to primary teachers of their 'selves', we must take account of the 'I' as well as the 'me', and acknowledge in teachers, as people, the urge at times to be impulsive, angry, rebellious, creative, and, if we follow the lines suggested by self-psychology, to be self-regarding, demanding of others and ready to see them as extensions of ourselves.

In the next three chapters I am concerned mainly with the teacher's self as 'me', in both situational and substantial forms, returning in Part 2 to the affective components of the self as 'I'. Yet we should try not to lose sight of the fact that the two co-exist, that under the ordered analysis of teachers' self-image to which I next turn, lie the elusive and often disorderly identities of individual men and women.

Chapter two

The nature of the teacher's 'self'

The purposes of this chapter are to suggest that despite their differences, primary teachers see themselves in similar ways, to indicate what these are and to point out their significance to an understanding of teaching as work. It is, however, based on material obtained indirectly from those with whom I talked. I did not, during either set of interviews, ask them any direct questions about how they saw themselves. The reasons for this are twofold. First, it was only after the first interviews were completed that I gradually realized that almost every response contained some self-referential comment. This realization in turn directed my attention to the central importance of self-image. Secondly, when, 10 years later, I conducted the second interviews, I felt that little would be achieved by direct questions — few people can easily articulate their view of their substantial selves, especially at short notice. Instead, I listened carefully as we discussed other matters for comments which would throw new light on the topic. In addition, I asked all my second interviewees if they thought they had changed in the last decade. In the event, neither I nor they could detect much change in self-perception except in terms of becoming more relaxed or self-confident, so the material in this chapter is drawn mainly from teachers' reflections on their first decade of work.

Of course, it seems contradictory to argue that our understanding of an individualistic profession can be advanced by presenting what appears to be the corporate self-image of a hundred teachers. Nevertheless, unique though each of these teachers was in terms of personality and experience, they shared common views of themselves, especially in terms of motivation, values and ideals. Patterns emerged; it is these which are reported here.

Unfortunately, there is little existing work against which to compare these patterns. There are several studies (most of them summarized and reviewed in Thomas 1980; Burns 1982; Wragg 1982) of aspects of teachers' self-concern and self-esteem (though the majority were carried out with students and we should therefore be cautious about applying their results to experienced teachers). These studies are generally concerned either with measuring the extent of individual self-esteem or with the relationship between measures of self-concept and aspects of teaching behaviour. They do not give much insight into the nature of the 'self' which is being measured nor its potential for change, and even less into its roots or origins. Yet a few trends emerge. Bown *et al.* (1967) claimed that American student teachers see themselves as warm and caring towards children, a point confirmed by Lortie (1975). In a British study, Morgan and Dunn (1978: 47) concluded that 'students choose to be primary teachers for soft-centred or, perhaps, idealistic reasons'. Ashley *et al.* (1969), examining students' reasons for becoming teachers, suggested that the only self-perceptions shared by younger diploma women, graduate women and graduate men were fondness for or an interest in children. Other reasons they gave for their career choice were 'intellectual involvement in, and social commitment to, the education of children', 'doing good', 'freedom and an absence of boredom' (Ashley *et al.* 1969: 67). The authors go on to suggest that different patterns of loading by the four groups may 'relate respectively to stereotyped self-images of the "aspiring professional", "the interested and concerned mother", "the charitably inclined middle class lady" and "the student"'. Cohen *et al.* (1973), studying achievement-need in student teachers, reported self-images of 'ambitious', 'hardworking', 'individualistic' and 'sure', but in the context of their study this is not surprising.

A second group of studies based mainly on interviews with and self-reports by individuals (Ebbutt 1982; Ingvarson and Greenway 1984; Spencer 1986; Smith *et al.* 1986) suggest generalizations about the particular influences, incidents and experiences which have proved especially powerful in shaping their sense of identity. These studies differ from the first group not only in the method of data collection but also in allowing the concerns and values of primary and secondary teachers to emerge through reported speech and action. Yet here, too, few generalizations are possible. Ebbutt's men and women (school co-ordinators of a teacher research project) seem to have a fairly enduring view of themselves as hardworking and idealistic but, in the context of the research project, also as shrewd managers. In the study by Smith *et al.*, the 'innovators' are committed throughout their varied careers to a particular set of educational values that the authors describe as 'true belief' (1986: 25). The women studied by Spencer are torn between their desire to fulfil domestic commitments and their wish to feel successful professionals.

Although Pollard (1980) and Woods (1981) had both drawn attention to the importance for teachers of their self-image, the latter study broke new ground by combining a theoretical examination of the concept of 'identity' with the use of life histories (see also Woods 1984; Pollard 1985). Applying to the biographies of two male secondary teachers, Cohen's (1976: 9) notion of identity as 'sets of claims' that an individual makes about himself in order to establish himself as 'somebody special, sufficiently different from his fellows to save him from anonymity and different in ways that command some admiration, respect or affection' and using Ball's (1972) distinction between the substantial and situational selves (see Chapter 1), Woods convincingly argues that both teachers acted so as to preserve the values and ideals which formed the core of their selves. Sikes *et al.* (1985) also found, in their life-history studies of twenty-four secondary teachers, that the maintenance of a stable self-concept was a continuing preoccupation for these teachers throughout their careers. Yet, although these studies come closest in orientation to my own, none of them analyses teachers' self-concepts in detail.

So, there is very little previous writing to guide my attempt at sketching the main lineaments of primary teachers' corporate self-image. To make the task more difficult, not all teachers identified with their work, (i.e. they did not see themselves as 'teachers'). Although a few had so identified (usually in childhood or early adolescence), most did not incorporate their work into their self-concept until they had been engaged in it for some years. In other words, I found (as Sikes *et al.* 1985, did of secondary teachers) that most of these teachers initially saw themselves as having made a short-term commitment to the profession. They spoke of themselves as people who had chosen, for an undefined period, to teach rather than as 'teachers'.

'Commitment'

There is one further complicating fact. The notion of 'commitment' was obviously central to how these teachers saw themselves and others (though they used it in both a positive and a negative sense). Over and over again in their interviews they used the term (synonymously with 'involvement', 'dedication' and a number of colloquialisms such as 'the faithful few', 'the stay-behind mob' and the 'out-by-fourers', 'the beer-at-lunchtime crowd and those of us who take the job seriously', 'the keenies and the not-so-keenies') to distinguish categories of teacher, to suggest degrees of motivation, to explain polarities. Yet it was plain that they were using it with different meanings, a confusion which has been compounded by educational writers who have, at various times, employed it to suggest motivation, to indicate outcomes and to describe career stability. Lacey (1977: 89), for example, distinguishes 'professional commitment' (an intention to make a career in teaching) from 'commitment to education' ('liberals' with strong ideals for education and society who 'if blocked from realising their ideals through teaching are prepared to explore other means of bringing them about'). Lortie (1975: 189) makes the word synonymous with 'involvement', indicating 'a readiness to allocate scarce personal resources' (e.g. time, money, energy) to work. Becker (1960) defines it as the process of placing 'side-bets' by which an individual increases the investment which he has in a particular career or institution, thus decreasing the likelihood that he will change to another and Woods (1979), similarly, sees it as entrenchment within an occupational structure (he speaks of secondary teachers who stay in the job because 'they are not trained for any other [work]', p. 144.)

Yet although teachers recognize in themselves, and in one another, different reasons for remaining within the profession, they do not use 'commitment' in discussion of them. Rather, they normally employ the term to describe the amount and quality of thought and energy with which individuals address their work. To be sure, I found a minority who used the term to imply a sense of being trapped by domestic obligations within their initial choice of occupation. In the first interviews I talked to three teachers, and in the second to one, who were disillusioned with teaching, but could not afford to leave it. In addition, in the first interviews there were four and in the second interviews two who, though depressed by their conditions of employment, had made so much progress up the promotion ladder that they could not, for the moment, see much point in moving to other jobs. Yet the number of such teachers was very small compared to those in whose vocabulary 'commitment' meant, in Lortie's terms, a willingness to dedicate scarce personal resources to the day-to-day performance of the job.

To understand that primary teachers generally attach this meaning to 'commitment' enables one to make sense of the fact that they commonly use the term when highlighting significant divisions between individuals, within staffrooms, or within the profession at large. 'Commitment' is seen as the quality which separates the 'caring' or 'dedicated' from those 'who are not concerned about the children', who 'put their own comfort first'. It is also the characteristic which divides those 'who take the job seriously' from those who 'don't care how low their standards sink', and those who 'feel a loyalty to the whole school' from the teachers 'who only care about their own classes'. Further, it distinguishes those who see themselves as 'real teachers' from those whose main occupational interests lie outside the school. It appears to be far more significant as a descriptor than allegiance to any particular philosophy or espousal of any specific teaching style or form of classroom organization. Yet this important fact receives no mention in any published study of teacher perspectives.

Now, almost by definition, there are never enough human resources to meet all the personality and learning needs of pupils in infant, junior and middle schools. If we accept that those who entertain a long-held vision of themselves as teachers, who are committed to their ideals for education and society or who want to teach well, are likely to be willing to devote personal resources to that work, then we can easily understand why this distinction should have grown up. Within the profession, it makes relatively little difference to the lives of individuals or groups whether or not their colleagues intend to take up alternative careers. But the presence in school of one or more teachers who give freely of their own resources may fundamentally affect the whole life of that institution. Moreover, those who are willing to 'give to the job' are likely to turn for mutual support and reinforcement to others with the same willingness, whatever the nature of their individual motives for doing so. In other words, provided that the end result of commitment is, as Kanter (1968) claims, that 'actors' (teachers) are willing 'to give their energy and loyalty to social systems' (schools), teachers have no incentive to disentangle one another's precise meanings and the implicit motivations which underlie them.

Indeed, the ability of primary and middle schools to accommo-date teachers with different priorities and thereby to allow many of them opportunities for 'involvement' on their own terms may be one of their strengths as institutions. As Barnard (1938) pointed out many years ago, personal and institutional goals are seldom co-terminous; the skill of management lies in ensuring that there is sufficient correspondence between the two for the achievement of crucial institutional goals. It is often to the benefit of the school as well as the individual that, provided 'commitment' results in hard work, generosity of spirit and self-expenditure, it should remain relatively undefined except in circumstances where the persistence of ambiguity makes it difficult for individuals to attain their own ends. What 'commitment' means to individuals perhaps matters only when a precise understanding of their perspectives can lead to the provision of greater incentives for them to invest in the work of their schools. The need for this understanding has been increased by the pay scales introduced into schools in 1987. Given the lack of external recognition, in the form of salary differentials, now available to primary teachers, other means will have to be found of providing status for those to whom this is an incentive.

This is not to say that a distinction cannot be made between types of commitment. Indeed, in Nias (1981) I suggested that teachers see themselves as 'committed' to one or more of four things: to 'caring' for children, to the attainment of high occupational standards, to seeing themselves as teachers or to a career they cannot afford to leave. But because these forms of 'commitment' overlap and co-exist, I have not used them to structure the sections which follow. Instead, I have looked at the personal and professional self-image of these teachers, stressing that individuals can be 'committed' in the first of these two senses without feeling that their career choice is either long-term or binding. However, 'commitment' and its occupational synonyms continually recur in the rest of this chapter. No understanding of primary teachers is complete which does not take the centrality of this concept into account.

Self as 'person' in teaching

Many of these teachers saw themselves as people with a strong concern for the welfare of others; they wanted (sometimes passionately) to improve the lives or life-chances of children. A minority had been drawn into teaching by the desire to propagate or sustain deeply-held religious, social and humanitarian ideals. 'If you care about your religion, you have to do something about it', said one of them, while a head teacher, praising the 'dedication' of a woman staff member claimed, 'She really had a calling to teach. . . . Her church attachment was very important to her'. 'I'm a Christian first', said another, 'but that is why I feel committed to teaching'.

The language used by the larger number of secular idealists was very similar: 'I see myself as a crusader'; 'I can only go on if I feel I am a missionary'; 'The teachers in my school lack any commitment to anything, to any views which they feel are worth defending'. One woman contrasted herself with a colleague: 'She put the children before everything else, even herself . . . I'm not so committed to teaching that I'm prepared to risk my health for it. There are limits to how much I'm prepared to give'. A man said, 'I've always felt, I suppose, that I ought to do something for the ones who haven't got . . . it's the children who obviously come off worst, so often, so I chose teaching rather than anything else', while his head teacher commented, 'He's totally committed to teaching, thinks first and foremost of the children all the time'. Several other teachers expressed similar views e.g. 'When I was at university, I was told that a child's life chances depended on what happened in the early years. So I thought, that's it, that's what I'll do to help change things'; 'I suppose I'm an idealist; I want to change society, make it fairer, and school seems a good place to start'; 'I shall leave fairly soon. I'm discouraged by the gap between my ideals and what is practically possible to achieve. I'm politically committed in the broadest sense, and so few other teachers seem to care'. Lortie (1975) argues that in America few of those who enter teaching with service motives wish to change the status quo. By contrast, the studies by Lacey (1977), Woods (1981), Ebbutt (1982), and Sikes *et al.* (1985) confirm my view that in Britain this is not the case; about an eighth of the teachers whom I interviewed were actively concerned to create, through their teaching, a more humane, socially just and constructively self-critical world. The tradition of the teachers who see themselves as 'crusader' and 'missionary' is a long-standing one in this country (Floud 1962); it should not surprise us that it still exists. Indeed, there is evidence that the work itself is capable of inducing this frame of mind. Three teachers described how they had embarked on their first posts without any great sense of involvement and had then been 'motivated by the job into wanting to work hard for something'. One explained, 'For the first time in my life I was doing something useful . . . Now I couldn't contemplate giving up'.

In addition, almost all my interviewees expressed a deep concern for the welfare and interests of children. This they normally described as 'caring', though sometimes their emotions were more strongly expressed. It is not fashionable for teachers to speak of 'loving' their pupils, but one man put his feelings very plainly in a letter:

> It is now the day after the end of term and I am deeply
> depressed . . . It must be indescribable for those with classes
> consisting entirely of fourth years, who lose them all every
> year. It's amazing how much one comes to love a class in a
> year.

Sometimes 'caring' was expressed in terms of what individuals felt was lacking from other teachers' attitudes. Typical comments were: 'Everything in this school is geared to making things easy for the teachers. It's their comfort that counts, not the children'; 'One of the things I don't like about teaching is teachers who put their own interests first. There's no social feeling in some schools, no commitment'; 'I went into remedial teaching in a secondary school because I found that the teachers cared about the children far more than the ones in my junior school did; most of them didn't even seem to like the children'. An urgent, clamouring desire to work in an atmosphere 'where the children are not treated with contempt' shone through nearly a quarter of my early interviews and most of the later ones. One man said, 'Closing the classroom door is escapism. If you care about children, you have to be committed to doing something about the way the whole school works', and a head teacher's perspective was, 'He is so committed to the school, so ready to give to adults as well as children . . .'. As another man complained:

> Teachers only seem to be interested in what goes on inside the classroom. They don't seem to think about their aims or the consequences of what they're doing . . . but if I shut the door, I feel it's a confession of failure. I suppose I'm committed to doing something about the whole system.

It is not always easy to distinguish this kind of dedication to personal and social ideals from the client-oriented concern of teachers who view themselves as 'professionals'. However, there are differences between the two types of self-identification. 'Caring' in a social sense tends to be associated with high 'inclusion' (see Chapter 1), whereas when 'caring' occurs as part of a general concern for 'good teaching' it is usually accompanied by reference to the need for high 'professional standards'. These, in turn, are often equated, as one teacher put it, with 'the pursuit of principle'. Teachers confidently claimed: 'The key to the way I try to do my job is my inner conviction about what's right'; 'Whatever the other staff do, I'm not going to let my principles go'; 'I live in my own world, make my own standards'; 'It comes down to what satisfies you as an individual'. Moreover, the principles to which they referred often appeared to be deeply internalized. When I asked people what the origins of them were a few referred to their PGCE course but most said they owed them to their own upbringing, in particular to their parents.

The standards they expected of themselves were expressed in several ways. The most obvious was 'taking the job seriously and making it work'. Precisely what this involved varied with the teacher and the school, but it always seemed to include working hard. Although some heads and teachers saw the dangers of over-involvement, many of the group apparently used hours of work and energy expended as a measure by which to judge themselves and others (e.g. 'One of the things I don't like about teaching is the nine-to-four teachers. When some of us are working really hard, it's frustrating to feel that some are having it easy, doing nothing'; 'I'm not really committed to teaching. For one thing, I'm not prepared to work that hard for so many years'; 'I work harder than the other staff, even my friends. I think that's because they're more easily pleased than I am. I have to do a certain amount or I wouldn't be satisfied'.)

'Work' was also seen to extend beyond the classroom (e.g. 'To get the best out of teaching you have got to be willing to go beyond the mere job'; 'You have got to be committed to it, spend the time on clubs and so on, be part of the "stay-behind" mob. Otherwise you don't do it as well as you should and it soon stops being satisfying'.)

Teachers who were committed to achieving high professional standards constantly sought to increase their own knowledge and expertise, often referring to acknowledged experts for help and advice. For example: 'I was shocked to find that most of the other teachers at this school don't have their own libraries. I may not know everything, but at least I know where to look if I don't . . . I really do want to do the job well'; 'I keep looking for the right way to challenge [this class]. I even rang up the adviser and asked his advice. The head didn't like that'; 'I'm always looking for ways to improve what I do. I'm hardly ever satisfied'.

To aspire to high professional standards also meant being concerned about reliability, punctuality, efficiency and classroom competence. So in some situations teachers felt: 'I've got to do the job as well as I can for the children's sake — if I ever lose that, I'll give up'; and 'I used to wonder in my last school how people could reconcile what they did with their professional consciences'. One teacher put it this way:

> If I felt I would sink to their level and do some of the things the others do I'd pack it in . . . of course you make compromises, and do some things you thought you wouldn't, but I'd leave teaching tomorrow if I thought that I'd ever give children a Banda outline of an Eskimo and tell them to colour it in while I sat down and filled in the pools.

Two women made comments which summed up the viewpoint expressed in one way or another by two thirds of the group:

> I'm not committed to spending all my time on education, but I am committed to making as good a job of what I'm doing as I possibly can.

I can only do this job for a few years, because doing it well takes so much out of you. To enjoy it, I have to put everything I've got into it. I can't do that for ever.

Of course, not all of my interviewees saw themselves as concerned to achieve high levels of occupational competence. But most clearly felt that they should be (e.g. 'How much easier life would be if I could stop feeling guilty every time I fall short of the standards I know I ought to achieve'). They saw such 'falls from grace' (as one called it) as deriving either from their own uncertainties (e.g. 'Unless you're totally sure about what you believe, it's easy to lower your standards') or from membership group pressures (e.g. 'In the first two years, I took other people's standards and then in my third year I began to think for myself'; 'The only way of coping [in that school] didn't seem idealistically right, but I needed to survive so I fell in line'; 'The teacher role in this school is inconsistent with how I think children should be treated, but I don't have any alternative, unless I can get out'). Either way, self-styled 'backsliders' measured themselves against internalized standards and felt 'guilty', 'inferior' and 'ashamed'. The idea that teaching is a 'total' occupation in a quasi-religious sense, reminiscent of the nineteenth century ideal held up by the first training colleges in England (Rich 1933), appears still to be deeply embedded in teachers' thinking.

That this may be a culturally determined characteristic is suggested by a comparative study of English and French primary teachers (Broadfoot 1985; Osborn 1985; Broadfoot & Osborn 1986) which demonstrates that the latter feel their professional responsibilities to be both more clear-cut and more bounded than the former. Whereas English teachers feel morally accountable to their head teachers, parents, colleagues and society in general (as well as to their own consciences and to pupils), French teachers feel their main responsibilities are only towards their consciences and their pupils. Further, English teachers expect more of themselves in their work and impose far more ambitious goals upon themselves, with the result that they take responsibility, in relation to their teaching, for a much broader range of outcomes than their French counterparts. In the USA, the situation appears to resemble the English rather than the French situation. Biklen (1985; 1986b) describes many of the women teachers whom she studied as outstanding practitioners who brought a high level of idealism to their work and argues that 'their major frustrations came when they were forced to make compromises which they felt endangered their educational vision' (Biklen 1985: 226). She and Smith *et al.* (1986) also identify teachers who take upon themselves a broad range of moral responsibilities. Cultural differences clearly deserve further exploration.

A different kind of self-expectation also kept many of my interviewees in teaching despite the self-doubt, strain, fatigue and ill-health of their first encounters with it. Some of them suffered for 2, 3 or 4 years the kinds of self-expenditure, exhaustion, disappointment and despair also documented by Hannam *et al.* (1971), Taylor and Dale (1971), and Hanson and Herrington (1976). Why, I asked them, did they not give up? The answer was always the same. They were not used to failing and could not believe that, in time, they would not succeed. They saw themselves as 'stubborn', 'obstinate', 'liking a fight', 'not used to being beaten'. Like Poppleton *et al.*'s (1987) inner-city secondary teachers, survival against the odds was a matter of pride. One woman, in her fourth year of teaching, and her second job, said 'It's hell, but I don't want to give up. In fact, if I discovered I was pregnant, I'd be miserable — I'd feel that I'd failed!'.

Idealism, conscientiousness and tenacity were not, however, the only self-defining characteristics that these teachers shared. As a result of their own educational experiences, most also valued ideas, and were willing to disagree publicly about them. They described themselves as 'intellectually curious' and 'keen on ideas', distinguishing themselves from colleagues who 'never talk about anything except football and the price of detergent', or who 'won't ever get involved in discussion of educational ideas'. In view of the widespread notion that primary teachers are interested mainly in the practical implications of ideas, it is worth noting that this group claimed to retain, even after a decade in the profession, a keen appetite for the intellectual side of their work, and that they valued discussion highly. It is also clear, however, that they found it hard to sustain this aspect of their self-image in school. The relatively trivial nature of 'staffroom chat' has often been noted (see, e.g., Pollard 1987). Although such 'chat' serves an important function in maintaining the culture of the school (Nias *et al.* 1989), it does little to reassure the increasing number of newly qualified primary teachers with intellectual interests and qualifications that they have chosen the right milieu in which to work.

Finally, about half my interviewees also saw themselves as individualists, giving as one reason for their career choice the fact that primary teaching appeared to offer scope for initiative, the chance to use varied talents, and the opportunity to 'be myself in the classroom'. They defended the right of themselves and their colleagues to 'teach as you feel happy'; 'to do it as I feel most comfortable', arguing, for example, 'I'm unique. I've developed my own format and style'. As Noad (1979) reports of Australian students, these people tended to see teaching as a means of self-actualizing (e.g. 'I get a sense of achievement when it's something I've devised myself'; 'I keep trying new things and I'm curious to see how far I can go'; 'I felt the need to assert *my* ideas'). By the same token they were ready to leave teaching when they felt that they were no longer being personally extended, that they had no time or energy to 'be themselves' outside the classroom or that their uniqueness was under threat (e.g. 'Before I started I used to think I could set my own standards as a teacher . . . now I'm becoming a "professional teacher". I'm becoming compromised, falling back on what I know works, not on what is really me . . . I'll probably give up'). Constraints implicit in the 1988 Education Act may have a damaging effect upon the commitment and self-expenditure of teachers such as these.

In addition there were a handful of people whose individualism took the form of returning to their roots. Three men chose to return to the area in which they grew up and then waived the chance of promotion in order to stay there. Each explained this decision in similar words: 'I feel at home here'; 'It's where my roots are'; 'I was brought up here and I wouldn't be happy anywhere else'. Smith *et al.*, in their longitudinal study in America found a similar but more pervasive phenomenon; 15 years after their teachers' pioneering work in Kensington School most of them had returned to their home-town or state. The authors explain this tendency to 'go home again' in terms of coming to terms with 'childhood demons' (Smith *et al.* 1986: 220), a hypothesis, based on life-history interviews, which reminds us that, in making career and other decisions, teachers are influenced by their turbulent unconscious drives as well as their capacity for objective, rational thought (Chapter 1).

Self as 'teacher'

Many of my interviewees had well-defined views of themselves, established before they entered the profession, as people with particular standards, principles, personalities, and needs. However, this did not mean that all of them also saw themselves as teachers. Even though nearly all of them had made a deliberate career choice (only two said they had 'drifted into teaching', and six were using teaching as a means of entry into educational psychology), and although several had overcome resistance from parents, spouses or university tutors in making the decision to train for primary teaching, more than four-fifths, when interviewed in their first decade of work, did not feel themselves to be 'real teachers'. A particularly high proportion of these had taught for between approximately 2 and 4 years. Typically, they said: 'I'm still not convinced this is for me'; 'I don't yet see myself as a teacher, though I'm beginning to see my way to becoming one'; 'On a bad day, I ask myself, "Am I really a teacher?" ' Some of those with longer experience also found identification difficult, often because they could not measure up to their own standards for an 'ideal teacher' (a phrase they often used). For example, they said: 'I think of myself as an idealized teacher, not as the teachers I know'; 'Yes, I do feel like a teacher, but at the same time, I feel different from most of the teachers I've worked with. I still have an idea of what I'd like to be like'.

Another reason why many people were reluctant to identify as teachers was because, as one said, 'It is so easy to let teaching take over your life'. It was fear of this that led some women, in particular (as Spencer (1986) also found to be true of teachers in the USA), to contemplate other careers (e.g. 'You feel more and more involved, sometimes I think too much'; 'Teaching's a bit too absorbing. It seems to eat up all my life, all my interests'; 'There's so many other things I want to do, so much I want to try'). Some indeed had made the decision to look for less 'inclusive' jobs, saying: 'I'm giving up, because this takes up too much of my life'; 'I'm not so committed to it that I want to think, eat and breathe school. I'd like a job where I can stop at 5 o'clock and be a different person'; 'My personal life is important too and I had no time for myself'.

However, a few teachers (both men and women), even in their early professional years, had learnt how to 'safeguard my own life'. As Elliott (1976) also found, when he encouraged teachers to undertake self-study on the Ford Teaching Project, some could teach with interest and conviction but retain a sense of their other lives: 'I've learnt when to stop, when to have my own life'; 'My other interests enrich me; I'm not 100 per cent a teacher'; 'Teaching fits in as part of my whole life — I can be myself through all of [my activities]'. Further, several men and a few women welcomed the high 'inclusion' of primary school life: 'What other job could I do which would use so many of my talents?'; 'I really enjoy the extra-curricular activities. It almost isn't work'; 'With this job [in a village school] I don't have to leave myself at the door, and become a teacher. When I was in industry, I had two lives, at work and outside. This is the closest I suppose I can come to bringing both together'. A handful of men and women also spoke of encouraging children to visit them at home, and liked 'the fact you don't have to separate school from real life'.

At the time of their first interview, five men and twenty-nine women had decided to reject identification as teachers (a point which is explored in further detail in Chapter 4). Typical of the comments made were:

> If that's what being a teacher is, I'm certainly not one. I couldn't ever feel I was that sort of person.

> I don't think I've ever managed to think of myself as a teacher. I'm not personally committed to it in the way that I am to educational psychology . . . well, my degree was in psychology, and everyone expected me to go on with it, I suppose you come to have an image of yourself as something specific.

> Teaching adults means much less role-playing than teaching children. I can't feel committed to being a primary teacher as long as I can't feel that I'm myself while I'm doing it.

Whatever the motivation of those who were still teaching at the time of their first interviews only fifteen were unequivocally 'committed' to teaching in the sense that they accepted 'teacher' as part of their self-image. This identification was typically expressed as:

> I don't want to do anything but teach. I wasn't sure at first, but I know now, I've committed myself to it.

> There's a lot of satisfaction in knowing you could do something else, but I want to do this.

> I think of myself as a teacher. I can't imagine doing anything else.

> I've always wanted to teach . . . I've never really thought of myself as anything else . . . I don't always like what I find in schools, and I certainly don't want to be like a lot of teachers I see, but I suppose you could say that I'm personally committed to the idea of being a teacher.

Two men and five women had wanted to teach for almost as long as they could remember; the remainder had made up their minds at many points between the ages of 14 or 15 and the end of their fourth year of teaching. Indeed, three persisted in 'feeling I'm a teacher' despite prolonged lack of positive reinforcement from colleagues. For example:

> I know I can teach; the fact that I won't do it the way [my head] wants me to doesn't mean I'm not a teacher. Inside *I know* I am.

From the beginning I felt as if I was a teacher but no one [in my first school] would admit it.

I always thought I was a teacher, and I still think I am, but it hasn't come out in this school . . . I'm still the same person inside but somehow it isn't finding its way out.

Conclusion

Six points emerge from this analysis which throw light on primary teachers' substantial selves. First, is the surprising one that men and women can teach, enjoy their work, and, in the eyes of their head teachers, teach very successfully without identifying with their chosen occupation, (i.e. without seeing themselves as, or 'feeling like', teachers). Moreover, these people often suspended professional self-identification for longer than the few years that Sikes *et al.* (1985) found to be characteristic of secondary teachers. Indeed, my second point is that identification as 'primary teacher' often appears to grow slowly. While for a minority it is rooted in childhood, for the rest it appears to come through repeated experience of the job itself.

Third, the personal values (or 'belief systems', Smith *et al.* 1986: 117) which are incorporated in individuals' substantial selves play an important part in the way they conceptualize and carry out their work. Fourth, these values seem to be of two general kinds: those which represent education as the translation of social, moral or religious ideals into action (especially by 'caring for' or 'loving' children), and those which determine the standards to which individuals try to carry out the job itself. Of course, these sets of values are not mutually exclusive. In particular, the educational conduct of the minority who described their commitment to teaching in crusading terms was also governed by high, though largely self-imposed, expectations: for example, relating to their hours of work, the definition and execution of their school and classroom responsibilities, and their obligation to undertake in-service education. In other words, to 'care for' children was to teach well and to accept the need for continuing self-improvement. Although their goals were often expressed in social or affective terms, they sought to attain them through the application of rigorous professional standards. It may be for this reason, too, that most of these teachers also saw themselves as interested in educational ideas as well as the practicalities of teaching. All in all, 'caring' was not a soft occupational option.

Fifth, primary teaching also appeals to those who are looking for work which will use a wide range of their talents and skills and which will allow them scope for self-expression. These people, one might speculate, are likely to be those most vulnerable to the threat of boredom later in their careers (see Chapter 8). On the other hand, it is possible that it is they who become the 'remarkable' older teachers identified by Smith *et al.* (1986: 37) for whom 'teaching demanded and pulled [out] the best of their creative talents . . . As they talked . . . one of the most striking aspects was their vigour, energy and creativity'. Without further longitudinal studies it is impossible to say whether teaching as an occupation enables or frustrates those who see themselves as needing and responding to opportunities for self-expression. Either way, however, such people are likely to respond protectively to perceived encroachments (e.g. through recent legislation) into their classroom autonomy. If, in the long run, the political developments of the late 1980s discourage creative, autonomous individuals from becoming or remaining teachers, pupils and schools will be the poorer.

Finally, because primary teaching allows for self-expression and the use of multiple talents, it has the potential to be highly 'inclusive'. This in turn encourages some people to fuse their personal and occupational self-image but has the opposite effect on others who choose instead to distance their 'selves' from their work. Yet the latter course is not easy to follow. While the substantial self is not, by definition, an ephemeral phenomenon, the nature of teaching makes it difficult for individuals to remain immune from situational influences, some of which bite deeply into their core of self-defining values. In the next chapter I explore teachers' response to this tension — looking, in particular, at how they defend the most central parts of their self-image.

Chapter three

Defending the self in teaching

It is reasonable to assume that people who are fortunate enough to be able to select their paid occupation will look for a sense of 'fit' between their self-image, their place of work and what the work itself involves. They are especially likely to seek for compatibility between self and context when they see themselves as idealistic, or, less powerfully, when they are aware of self-defining values in tune with which they wish to live and work. Yet the substantial self, and the values it incorporates, is itself socially conditioned, especially by early and powerful significant others and social groups (generalized others). The assumptions we learn to make about ourselves and our worlds become embedded in generalized perspectives and the correctness and accuracy of these are in turn confirmed by contact with people who have similar perspectives ('reference groups'). So, when we enter the world of work (or any similar new arena) we open ourselves to a potential conflict — between the beliefs and values built up in our early years and sustained by our significant and generalized others and those exemplified by the people with whom we now interact every day. Moreover, the more important we perceive work to be, both as a general cultural phenomenon and in terms of its likely place in our own lives, the greater the possible conflict. But, in terms of psychological comfort, the less of this kind of cognitive dissonance we are forced to experience the better; we generally prefer to work in environments in which our substantial selves are confirmed, both by the ways in which work requires us to speak and act, and by those with whom we interact. Where the latter implicitly or explicitly challenge our perspectives, we may try to avoid contact with them. However, if we cannot do this, we may find ourselves under pressure to change our own values and thus our view of ourselves, a painful process from which we protect ourselves whenever we can. Moreover, we are particularly likely to resist the discomfort arising from a change in self-definition when we are under pressure in other areas of our lives (e.g. from domestic circumstances, fatigue, or the necessity to learn new skills). Yet these conditions occur with especial frequency when we take up a first, or a new job.

For all these reasons, it is likely that teachers starting work for the first time will cling to their existing identities and, therefore, to established significant others and 'reference groups'. Indeed, unless they find in their initial encounters with their schools a harmony between their substantial selves and the social context of their work, they may try to cut themselves off from their colleagues, a course of action which almost inevitably leads to increasing isolation from the adult membership group of the school. Now few people are wholly indifferent to the potential support offered by a membership group, whether or not they also perceive it as a reference group. In particular, those who are insecure, anxious, afraid, or tired (states of mind and body with which new teachers are all too familiar), are likely to find group membership seductive. Friendliness, sympathy, the actual or symbolic cup of tea, knowing where to hang one's coat and when to pay one's coffee money greatly reduce the initial tensions of embarking on a new life. Few inexperienced teachers are so robust that they can afford for long to maintain total isolation from their staff group.

Moreover, schools develop what Pollard (1982: 26) describes as an 'institutional bias', (i.e. a set of understandings negotiated by staff members with different values and varying amounts of power which determine many of the routines and practices of the institution). Because they are rooted in power differentials, these understandings in turn affect and may constrain staff and pupils alike. In other words, routine and taken-for-granted ways of behaving within any school reflect the values of dominant staff members, among whom the head teacher is particularly significant. Newcomers, especially probationers who initially have very little institutional power, are therefore likely to be faced with two inter-related sets of tensions. They may find that their own values are inconsistent with the 'institutional bias' of their new school. At the same time, they may wish to protect their 'selves' from influence by dominant people within the staff group, but to do this without forfeiting friendly support from their colleagues.

In this chapter I examine the strategies which my interviewees adopted to counteract both sets of pressures. Each of these strategies enabled individuals to maintain situational selves which avoided open conflict with powerful colleagues (including the head) without sacrificing their most treasured ideas, beliefs and ways of behaving. I look first and in most detail at 'reference groups' —

though, when these were located outside the school,
did little to help individuals reduce the tension
'selves' and their need for social support within the st₎
Indeed, because membership of such groups reaffirmed indiv₎
own values and priorities, it often deepened their alienation fro₎
their colleagues. Reliance on external reference groups led to the
reconciliation of self-protection with affiliation only when it was
accompanied by other strategies, such as isolationism, impression
management or passive resistance. I look at these, therefore, in the
later part of this chapter. Nor was the adoption of an internal
reference group necessarily helpful as a means of securing the
support of the whole staff group, since the price of self-affirmation
was often to become embedded in a divisive clique or sub-group.
The most desirable situation, but one which teachers found it hard
to attain, was membership of a whole staff which shared the same
aims and worked co-operatively together towards their realization
(an idea which is further explored in Chapter 8).

Evidence for the strategies described in this chapter is taken
mainly from the first interviews, because the need for self-
protection features much more prominently in the thinking and
talking of teachers in their early years than is the case later on. By
mid-career, most of my interviewees had either found a self-
supporting context in which to work or had left the profession (see
Chapter 4).

Reference groups

The term 'reference group' has come to have three meanings. When
the American social psychologist, Hyman, first used it in 1942, he
intended it to indicate a group serving as a standard for comparison
in the self-appraisal of, for example, status or material rewards.
Within a decade it was also established, notably by the work of
Merton and Kitt (1950), as a phrase describing any group by whom
people wish to be accepted and treated as members of, and thus by
whose norms and values they evaluate themselves. Used in the sense
of a normative group, it was quickly accepted by some sociologists
as a very potent force (e.g. Strogdill, 1959, claims that reference
group identification may determine an individual's satisfaction
with a membership group, his or her support of its activities,
acceptance of its norms, perception of the legitimacy of its role
system, aspirations for status and chances for upward social
mobility within it).

The phrase has also been extensively used by social psychologists
interested in perception. Now it is perception, I argued in Chapter 1,

which lies at the heart both of the teaching process and of the teacher's self-image. Accordingly, reference groups in this sense are part of the process of 'ego-anchoring' (Sherif and Wilson 1953): that is, they are groups whose norms are used by individuals to help them create a stable perceptual field which is then employed as an organizing device with which to order new experiences, perceptions and ideas, especially those relating to the self. Shibutani (1955: 63) takes this argument further, claiming that the 'ordered view of one's world' or 'perspective' so created is 'an outline scheme which, running ahead of experience, defines and guides it'. So, once one has internalized the perspective of a particular group, it becomes a 'frame of reference' which is brought to bear on all new situations. Most powerfully, it determines what is accepted as information about reality. However, since we all participate simultaneously in a variety of social worlds, we are all likely to be confronted from time to time with the need to choose between two or more conflicting frames of reference. It is in such situations, where alternative definitions of reality are possible, that problems of interpretation and thus of loyalty arise. According to Shibutani, in order to understand people's behaviour when they face these kinds of conflict we need to be able to ascertain:

> how a person defines the situation, which perspective he uses in arriving at such a definition, and who constitutes the audience whose responses provide the necessary confirmation and support for his position . . . [The use of 'reference group' allows us to focus] attention upon the expectations the actor imputes to others, the communication channels in which he participates, and his relations with those with whom he identifies himself.
>
> (Shibutani 1955: 171)

Understood as a perceptual device, a reference group may therefore be seen as a filter, determining what information individuals receive and the interpretations which they place upon it, and as a conduit, shaping the nature of the responses such information evokes and the audiences to whom they are directed. Reference groups are then an important means of self-protection, for individuals supported by them can easily ignore or misinterpret messages sent from outside the group. People's reality becomes and remains that which is confirmed through interaction with other group members, whether or not the latter are also part of a salient membership group.

Out-of-school reference groups

Since individual teachers' views of themselves as persons are necessarily earlier than their self-concepts as teachers, it is not surprising that many of the people in this study were supported to a greater or lesser extent, and for varying periods, by reference groups outside their schools. Such groups were particularly important in relation to social, moral and political issues. One in eight of my interviewees remarked on the legacy of a religious (Christian or Hebrew) upbringing, of their own schooling, or of the continuing influence of parents who were socially or politically active. Others spoke of the current effect of church membership (e.g. 'I'm a Christian first and everything else is shaped by that') or of political affiliations (e.g. 'I couldn't keep going in teaching if I wasn't politically involved').

The power of such early reference groups is encapsulated in the career of one socially-concerned, talented and hard-working young woman, a convent-educated Roman Catholic, who had been actively involved in student protests at her university. She entered teaching with genuine affection for her pupils and believing strongly in the importance of cultivating creativity and individuality in them. Her first teaching post, by her own choice, was in a self-styled 'progressive' school in a large city. There she was inescapably confronted by the dissonance between her frames of reference. All of the rest of the staff were committed to encouraging autonomy and creativity in their multi-ethnic, inner-city pupils. When she decided, at the end of her first year, to give up teaching, she explained:

> The real problem for me was not being able to decide how much was up to the teacher. I'd spend the weekend making reading materials for [a seven-year-old] because he needed to learn his phonics, and give them to him on Monday morning. When he turned round and said "Piss off, Miss, I want to make a monster", I honestly didn't know whether he'd learn more about reading if I insisted he do the cards, or if I let him make a monster and then write about it. The rest of the staff were quite happy — they believed in the monster — but I could never completely see it that way. I felt I had a responsibility to teach him what he needed to know.

As this episode also reveals, it is not always easy to distinguish individuals' moral or social beliefs and values from their educational ones: to 'care', as this teacher did, meant both loving children and making educational demands upon them. Certainly many of my interviewees expressed a need for referential support on specifically educational issues, not just on moral ones. Unfortunately, at some point in their careers, the majority of them found themselves in a school in which there was no person or group other than pupils to whom they could turn for self-confirmation in relation to their educational goals. Lacking a reference group in their own schools, they therefore actively sought for one elsewhere. They went on courses, claiming that they did so 'for reassurance/to listen to people agreeing with me/to find someone like-minded to talk to'. As one put it: 'I don't care whether or not the rest of the staff approves of what I'm doing, but I do wish I had someone to discuss my ideas with. I'm so desperate I've signed up for a course at the Polytechnic'. Others returned to their training institutions or the friends they made there (e.g. 'I don't see all that much of them, but I'd hate to lose touch with them because they're there to talk to if I need them'; 'I draw a lot on the PGCE course. It's there in my mind and bits come back . . . I suppose that's why I keep in touch with [my tutor]. It keeps me from losing all my ideals which I would if I just listened to the teachers [here]'. The research on which this book is based really started when an ex-student from my PGCE course came back three years later from 300 miles away to talk about her work and said, 'I do wish you could come and see what I'm doing now. No one at my school seems to care and I'm losing heart!'. Many others telephoned, wrote, dropped in at half-terms or in the holidays. 'No', said one, 'I didn't really want your advice. I just wanted someone to tell me I was right'.

Teachers who were hoping soon to take on responsibilities at a different hierarchical level also tended to have reference groups outside their schools but within the profession. As individuals began seriously to aspire to management posts, they invoked the real or imagined standards of, for example, their local Deputy Heads Association or of head teachers generally. Such groups helped individuals move from one career stage to another, but they do not seem to have been especially influential in determining subsequent educational policy or practice. Teachers who shaped their behaviour by normative reference to a specific occupational group (e.g. deputy heads) still needed, once they had attained their new status, to seek or maintain a 'frame of reference' which would help them translate their beliefs into action. The later interviews suggest that newly appointed deputies and head teachers tended initially to look, for this kind of support, towards groups or individuals outside their schools, but that they did not begin to feel themselves fully effective in their new posts until they had developed a reference group within them. This suggestion is confirmed by the Primary

School Staff Relationships Project (Nias *et al.* 1989) which found that new head teachers identified strongly with the staff whom they had themselves appointed and looked to them for help in installing, as the keystone of school policies, the values which they jointly espoused.

Similarly, although many of these teachers initially tried to find, within their schools, colleagues who would support them in their view of themselves as people who valued ideas and intellectual debate, they felt that they seldom met with a sympathetic response. The cumulative effect of repeated rebuffs (as they saw the failure of their efforts to stimulate staffroom discussion to be) was to force them back into contact with established reference groups outside their schools and eventually to alienate some of them from teaching. One of my interviewees put it this way, 'I'm intellectually lonely at school, I'm the only one who reads the *Guardian*, the only one interested in politics or literature and there is only one other who's ready to talk about art and music'. Similar comments were: 'My educational reference group is certainly not in school — it's a few intimate friends from university and scientists generally'; 'I don't identify with [my colleagues] as people like me. I'm more aware of other things outside school than [they are]'; (from a man teaching in an infant school) 'I love the children and the work, but I have no contact with any adults with whom I have any ideas in common. I feel intellectually starved'.

This felt-need to maintain contact with the world of ideas and of passionate debate led people down several different roads. Ebbutt (1982) has suggested that teachers can be sustained in an intellectual view of themselves by an academic reference group which they initially find through advanced courses and research projects. Within a decade, several of these teachers had embarked upon advanced courses in search of such a group. Four others were actively involved in politics or related organizations (such as the Child Poverty Action Group). Two had begun to write for educational journals, four said they read voraciously, three were actively seeking posts as college lecturers or advisers. Two of the six who within five years had left primary school work for posts in further education or as specialists in secondary schools spoke of 'miss[ing] the stimulation of my subject'. Overall, in the early interviews about two-thirds talked of wanting to leave the classroom eventually, because, as one woman put it, 'My mind feels starved'. Yet the later interviews show that those who chose to make a career within primary teaching found their own ways of making it intellectually satisfying (see Chapter 5).

Failure to find satisfactory confirmation of important aspects of the self in teaching led many people at some point to contemplate a move into another career (see also Kremer and Hofman 1985). Although the point at which this happened varied with individuals and their circumstances, in general people seemed to know after about five years whether or not they wished to identify as teachers; if they did not, they began to look for an alternative. However, even those who made a positive choice to 'become' teachers sometimes experienced periods of self-doubt or disillusion. At all such moments, out-of-school reference groups were important. Moves into other careers were always supported by reference to long-established significant others, particularly parents, spouses and friends, and the possibility of such moves was also thoroughly discussed in the family, the church group or with trusted friends.

Moreover, it was groups of this kind which reassured the minority into whose self-concept 'teacher' had long been incorporated. Sometimes the main support for this early identification came from family (e.g. 'My family used to say, "You'll be a marvellous teacher one day", so I can't go back to them and say I've failed, can I?'), at other times from ex-teachers or tutors (e.g. 'Whenever I have doubts about whether it's for me, I go and see my old primary school head, he's retired now and he says, "I've always seen you as a teacher — how's it going?", and I sit down and tell him').

Extra-school reference groups also played an important part in confirming the self-image of those who saw themselves as competent professionals but not necessarily as 'teachers'. Family, friends, ex-tutors helped to sustain those who made heavy weather of their first encounters with the job in a positive view of themselves (e.g. 'All my family teach and I didn't want to be the only failure — I had to keep on trying'). Nor did they subsequently cease to be valued (e.g. 'My father [a retired HMI] — I ring him a lot'; 'My mother still teaches and I talk to her a good deal'). Even more frequently cited as time went on were parents-in-law (e.g. 'Richard's mother kept me going. We used to go and see her in the holidays and she used to support me in what I was trying to do'; 'Frank's father is a headmaster of a junior school [in another part of the country] and I rely a lot on his reassurance. He rings every week.' Siblings (especially sisters) were occasionally mentioned, and five referred to their own children (e.g. 'I think — would I want that to happen to them?'). By 1977, eleven of the men were married to primary school teachers and eleven of the women to secondary school teachers (none to primary school teachers). Despite the relatively small number of spouses in like employment, most (but not all) cited their spouse as someone with whom they discussed their educational problems and ideas 'all the time'. One said, 'He's never been inside the school and I don't think he'd want to, but he really helps me sort my ideas out. He's a sort of touchstone, I suppose. If he thinks it's OK then it usually works'.

Individuals also looked for confirmation of their professional self-images to teachers outside their families. Ten had kept in touch with a particular teacher or head teacher from a previous school at which they had taught, either before or after training, and regarded them as a 'very influential person in my development'. Four referred to people who had taught them at school (e.g. 'I still keep in touch with her, I'm always interested in what she has to say about education'). Most had teacher friends from other schools whom they perceived as very important (e.g. 'If you're isolated you begin to question whether you're right'; 'I've got one friend from another school and we meet in a pub once a week . . . it helps reinforce your belief that you are right').

In-school reference groups

No matter how strong their affiliation to external groups, none of my interviewees enjoyed working in a school in which they felt they had no referential support. As they said, they needed people on the spot who 'felt the same way as I did'; 'had the same philosophy'; 'saw things the way I did'. It was often too long to wait till 'the Thursday night gathering at the pub', even till the phone call that evening, for confirmation that 'I was right in what I was trying to do'. Accordingly, once assured of a capacity to survive as classroom practitioners, they tended to move from school to school, looking for a context in which 'I can be the sort of teacher that I want to be'.

In-school reference groups did not have to be large in order to provide this kind of reassurance. The existence of 'just one other', as these teachers repeatedly put it, confirmed the goals and aspirations of otherwise isolated individuals, kept them from leaving their schools, supported them in innovation or retrenchment, deepened their satisfaction, and fuelled their discontents. As one teacher said of such a reference person, 'We fed each other'. Some people initially expected their head teachers to be the one to 'set a standard' or 'help with my ideas' and were disappointed if they did not live up to this expectation. In default of their heads, they turned to a colleague, particularly a more senior one, or, occasionally, to an adviser. Whoever it was, the support afforded by such a person was out of all proportion to either the size of the 'group' or to the time spent in communication.

In a few instances, individuals were able to point to a group of like-minded colleagues. When such a group existed, it tended also to have a social dimension which strengthened its referential impact (i.e. it became a membership group; see also Sherif and Sherif 1964). Members could identify one another and indicate where they usually interacted (e.g. 'We have a pub lunch once a week'; 'We stay behind after school'; 'We don't talk in the staffroom, but we often meet in [the year leader's] classroom'; 'We're the mob in the corner — you'll see us there at lunchtime most days'). Riseborough (1986) and Poppleton (1988) show how damaging conflicting reference groups can be in secondary schools, in restricting curricular and other forms of whole-school development. This theme is further explored in Chapter 8, in relation to primary schools.

Members of in-school reference groups may readily adopt strategies, such as those described by Pollard (1985) and Sikes *et al.* (1985), to secure their educational interests. At Ashton First School, in Pollard's study, a group of junior staff who were also friends 'sought to influence and change the values and priorities of the institutional bias' of the school, using the strategy of 'subversion'. Their leader did not openly challenge the norms of the school or the authority of the head. Instead he 'used his autonomy, competence and energy . . . [and] managed to undermine the sense of what was possible and what should be done at Ashton so that in the end even the head teacher began to be influenced by him' (see Pollard 1985: 138, 140). A similar strategy, 'strategic compromise', is labelled by Sikes *et al.*, who describe groups which 'find ways of adapting to the situation that allow room for their interests, while accepting some kind of modification of those interests' (Sikes *et al.* 1985: 238). In both these strategies, like-minded individuals change an existing situation in the direction that they desire, by the use of influence rather than by confrontation and at the cost of partially modifying their own goals.

On the rare occasions when a whole staff was perceived as being concurrently a membership and reference group, it had a powerful effect upon its members. Five teachers spoke of being at schools where 'we accept that we all have common beliefs and that gives us a common basis for discussion', or 'there's lots of lively talk in the staffroom'. By contrast, I was given three examples of staffs which were so tightly knit, philosophically and socially, that other teachers felt 'driven out — they had to leave if they wanted to survive'. In all of these cases, shared goals and standards were reinforced by joint social activities (e.g. staff parties, theatre visits) and by a good deal of open discussion.

When a reference pair or group developed an affective (as distinct from a social) dimension it could become an even more potent force. Three examples make this point very clearly. In one case, a value difference brought to the surface by a new head teacher led to the formation of a forceful staffroom group: 'There's four of us — all women. We share the same political views, we do a lot socially together and two of us live together. He'll find it hard to break us up'. In another, a married couple who taught together in a double unit, each independently said to me, 'I don't listen to what anyone else on the staff says. They all think differently to me, and now I'm working with [my spouse] I can just talk to [him/her] and we support each other'. Thirdly, two teachers working as a team — each married to teachers in other schools — began to live together. They explained:

> To make the team work we had to talk a lot, and that meant we spent a lot of time together and we began to realize how many ideas we had in common and how much we liked each other . . . well, team-teaching, especially in a shared unit, has to be a bit like a marriage. If it's going to work, you have to want the same things, have the same values, and if one of you is male and the other female and you obviously get on well together, the kids begin to treat you like mum and dad.

Whether such a relationship then became divisive within a school depended on the extent to which it was perceived by members and others as exclusive (for an example of a powerful, non-exclusive pairing see Nias 1987b).

Important though in-school reference groups were, teachers joining a staff for the first time usually found it easier to confirm their own professional commitment by seeing other teachers as negative reference groups (i.e. as groups of which they would not want to become members) than to locate people with similar perspectives to their own (Newcomb 1943). As they said, 'It's easier to find teachers you wouldn't want to be like than ones you would . . . You don't meet many teachers who make you feel "That's the sort of person I'd like to be", do you? Usually it's the other way round'. Negative reference groups were often treated emotively, especially when they were perceived to exist within an individual's own school. In this case they were often described as 'the opposition' or 'the enemy'. 'Emotions run high', said one man, 'when it comes to teaching maths. There's a right way to teach subtraction and if you don't believe in it, you don't belong. It can even be quite difficult sometimes to go into the staffroom'. It is possible that treating some or all of the rest of a school staff as a negative reference group precedes the strategy of 'challenge' that

Pollard (1985) saw adopted by some teachers who wished to resist the dominant values of their schools.

Of course, school-based reference groups were not always perceived as working in the direction of greater professional commitment as Riseborough (1986) shows in relation to secondary schools. A few teachers, candidly describing themselves as 'feeling less worried by my own conscience', 'learning to grow a skin when things aren't perfect', 'learning to compromise', felt, 'We make each other lazy'; 'It's difficult to work hard if no one else does. The norm here is about putting teachers' interests first'; 'I know I'm a worse teacher than I was three years ago. It's difficult to do what you think you should do when you know you're on an island'. Siegel and Siegel (1957) argue that individuals seem to be particularly strongly influenced by membership groups which become reference groups. Such comments may reflect realignments of this kind for some teachers.

A few teachers, disillusioned by teaching but bound to it by financial commitments and similar 'side-bets' (Becker 1960) used in-school reference groups to support their rejection of a 'teacher' self-image. Such pairs or groups reinforced one another's psychological separation from their work. One man put it this way: 'It's a job — nothing more. I need the money, but I don't put more into it than I have to. My real life is with the band. That means I often come in exhausted in the morning — my main aim is to keep the kids quiet — off my back . . . If society doesn't put itself out for us, why should we bother for them?' 'I'm not the only one [here] who sees it that way'.

One last point needs to be made in relation to in- and out-of-school reference groups. Separation of them is artificial. Woods (1981) described an experienced secondary school art teacher who maintained his morale and sense of purpose by creating 'bridging devices' which enabled him to move between his external groups (e.g. the adult education classes which he taught, his community interests, the friendly adviser whom he occasionally met for a drink) and the groups within school which shared his educational perspectives. One of Pollard's (1985) teachers derived many of his views on teaching from past and present contact with groups outside the school but also had the backing of a reference group within it. Similar examples exist in Sikes *et al.* (1985) and Smith *et al.* (1986). The teachers whom I studied also tended, especially in mid-career, to draw on groups both outside and inside their schools. Sometimes these complemented one another; at others they allowed individuals to manage the pressures bearing upon their substantial selves by juggling or balancing their professional and other interests (see also Pollard 1980).

Pupils as reference groups

So far I have not mentioned pupils, even though their opinions and reactions (as Broadfoot and Osborn 1986 noted) matter much more to English than they do to French primary teachers. Indeed, in this study they were the reference group most frequently invoked by teachers of both sexes and all lengths of service. Typical claims were, 'I didn't much mind about anyone else, I had to make it work for them'; 'It doesn't matter that I don't agree with the rest of the staff, I can cut myself off from them by working with kids'; 'Blow the other [teachers] — I keep going because the kids enjoy what I'm doing and that tells me I'm right'.

Of course teachers spend most of each working day in the company of children who are therefore better placed than anyone else to confirm or deny the views that the former hold of themselves. In particular, pupils can validate their teachers' professional competence or make them feel technically inadequate. When I asked these teachers, 'How did you know whether you were being successful?' the invariable answer was 'the children's response' (though the less experienced also sometimes admitted their need for recognition by an adult sanctioning figure). Failures were determined in the same way: 'It only needs one child not to learn . . .'; 'If the children don't like it, it doesn't matter how good anyone else thinks it is'; 'I used to judge by whether or not I'd had to send Kevin to the head . . .' Moreover when things went wrong my interviewees habitually blamed themselves rather than their pupils (e.g. 'I blame myself'; 'You always ask yourself "What did I do?" '). One summed it up: 'If you haven't taught, you don't have any idea how much it matters when you have a bad day. You can't go home and forget it, it nags away all evening, all night if you're really low. It hurts — in a way you can't explain to people who aren't teachers'.

Indeed, so great is children's capacity to affirm or destroy a teacher's self-image and self-esteem that they emerge again and again from the interviews as the critical 'reality-definers' (Riseborough 1985) for all members of the profession, not just for the probationers (see also Sikes *et al.* 1985). In a study of the relationship between one child and an experienced primary teacher, Riseborough has vividly described the power of career definition which individual pupils have for particular teachers. As learners, they can engender in teachers feelings of guilt and worthlessness and cast doubt upon the soundness of the latter's career choice. By contrast, they can confirm them in their own eyes, making them feel loved, needed and successful. All in all, their capacity to shape, confirm and destroy individuals' future careers, by moulding the latter's view of their own characteristics, capabilities and aspirations, has probably so far been underestimated. Small wonder that the teachers whom Pollard (1985) observed negotiated within their classrooms a 'working consensus' with their pupils which enabled children and adults to emerge from most of their encounters in a relatively stress-free fashion, with self-image and dignity intact.

The existence of this working consensus can, however, make it quite difficult to judge the nature or quality of the educational values and practices in which pupils and teachers are jointly participating. Since many teachers work in physical isolation from each other and are often protected even in open-plan schools by the 'norm of disregard' (Hitchcock 1982), it is difficult for anyone to challenge their claims about client-satisfaction. As long as classroom processes remain largely hidden from all except participants, pupils may be invoked as a reference group to justify many different decisions and types of behaviour. They are the joker in the hand of every teacher, capable of being used to confirm any number of beliefs and practices.

Self-isolation, passive resistance and impression management

Teachers cannot avoid, even if they should want to, the company of pupils. They do, by contrast, have some control over the extent and nature of their contact with the other adults in their schools. The greater the reliance of my interviewees upon their extra-school reference groups, the more they appeared to isolate themselves from their colleagues, working long hours in their classrooms, running lunchtime clubs, absenting themselves from the staffroom in breaks. They described their behaviour in these kinds of ways: 'It was my fault really, I wasn't prepared to spend any time with any of them, because we didn't see eye to eye about the way things should be done in the school. So I spent all the time with the kids or in my classroom'; 'I never made any attempt to make any relationship with them'; 'I shut myself up and got on with the job; getting to know them wasn't important to me'. One man said, 'You've got to be prepared for conflicting pressures from the staff . . . you've got to be prepared not to be liked', and a woman who left teaching after three years summed it up: 'I never had a personal relationship with any of the teachers I worked with. It takes time and effort to create a common language, especially when all my previous experience was so different from theirs. I wasn't ready to give that amount of effort to it'. This strategy (self-isolation) is similar to that described by Pollard (1985: 137) as 'bypassing' — 'a withdrawal from the institutional bias behind the defence of either autonomy or expertise, or both'. As he points out, however, 'bypassing' depends upon the capacity of the individual or group to sidestep the conventions, attitudes and routine practices of the school and, because probationers generally lack appropriate autonomy and experience, 'it is not a strategy readily open to [them]'.

I found, however, that even probationers would reject the practices of their colleagues when they felt the psychological costs of adopting them were too high. No matter how kindly the intention behind the proffered assistance, if it did not fit an individual's beliefs, it was, as I further describe in Chapter 7, countered with passive resistance. People told me, for example: 'She offered to "deal with" my worst children herself, but I knew what that meant and I couldn't have gone on teaching if I'd felt I was treating children like that'; 'He gave me some of his worksheets, but they went against everything I believed in and I couldn't bring myself to use them'.

Not everyone was as 'confident in my own decisions' or 'relaxed about what other people think' as these speakers appeared to be. Further, many people, when faced with the demands of the classroom, found that they wanted their colleagues' approbation and comradeship. So, almost every teacher fell back at some time upon a set of strategies similar to those described by Shipman (1967) as impression management and by Lacey (1977) as strategic compliance. Membership groups always impose a certain level of behavioural conformity. Schools, in particular, require their members to show (e.g. through dress, language, and appearance) many signs of social orthodoxy; primary schools are sometimes markedly restrictive in these respects. For example, I was told stories of female teachers who had been sent home by their head teachers to change from their trousers into skirts, of a woman teacher who had been asked by the male deputy to clean her car because the children had been putting their initials in the mud which habitually clothed it, of men and women who had been reproved by their heads for using the local vernacular in the hearing of the children or for publicly admitting that they watched particular TV programmes. So, my interviewees wore suitable clothes ('my school uniform'), adopted appropriate school behaviour (e.g. in assembly, on playground duty), fell in with staff-room conversational norms (e.g. 'I don't disagree for the sake of peace'; 'They're my mates, so I try to behave as they want me to'), used 'teacher language' when speaking to children in front of colleagues. In short, they bought social approval by consciously maintaining a double standard. As one said, 'You do the visible, conforming things . . . not because you believe in them but because that's what you see everyone doing. But in your classroom, you do what you think is best'. Studies which show that probationers move in their opinions towards those of their established colleagues (e.g. Finlayson and Cohen 1967; Morrison and McIntyre 1969) ignore the possibility of impression management. My evidence suggests that it is widespread among teachers in primary schools, especially in the early years of teaching.

Importance of talk

Throughout this chapter, I have repeatedly drawn attention to the importance of communication, especially of talk, as the critical element in the formation of reference groups. Staffrooms in which probationers 'found it difficult to get to talk to people' tacitly encouraged them to seek extra-school reference groups with whom they kept regularly in contact. I also became aware of the importance which my interviewees attached to their telephones and of the amount of communication which went on, across the country, through this medium. It enabled the maintenance of many far-flung referential networks.

Similarly, it was talk which enabled newcomers to establish reference groups among the staff of their schools. They placed a high value upon their colleagues' willingness to discuss aims, priorities and practices. Many of the experienced teachers whom they cited as 'important influences' were physically accessible to them, in school or because they travelled together, and were prepared to spend time talking (Chapter 7). As one woman said, 'The staff [in my first school] included several exceptional people, people who were prepared to talk about what they were doing and listen to me'. Another said of a colleague, 'He was particularly influential in shaping the way I work now. We used to chat after school and compare notes'. By contrast, others complained, 'It's been hard to get teachers in this school to talk about their philosophy; I always wanted to talk and they wouldn't', and 'I left soon after she did — I couldn't cope without somebody to talk to — I lost sight of what I was trying to achieve'. Indeed, the absence of opportunity or appetite for discussion with their colleagues emerged as a major source of dissatisfaction among these teachers, especially in their early years (Chapter 6).

The phenomenological view, that it is through talk that participants create and make sense of a shared social order, offers a means of understanding this need for discussion. Working in isolation from other adults, many of these primary school teachers failed to find in their schools the means of forging negotiated understandings or the incentive to do so. A vicious circle existed. Needing referential support for their values, they turned to those who would readily provide it. Often such groups already existed outside their schools, so they talked to them. The more they interacted with the latter, the fewer understandings they shared with their colleagues and the less desire they had to talk to them, particularly when they spent the bulk of their working day with their pupils. Thus the reality which sustained their substantial selves came to exist anywhere rather than in the adult life of the school. In Chapter 1 I drew attention to the lack of a common technical culture among teachers. I would suggest that the individualistic nature of the profession, particularly in the primary sector, goes deeper than this, that teachers' reference groups result in and reinforce multiple realities which give individuals a false sense of having achieved agreement over ends and means within their schools. In short, lack of opportunity is not the only reason why teachers do not talk to one another. In addition, they neither can, nor do they wish to. They cannot talk to each other because, outside their reference groups, they lack a shared language by which to attach meanings to their common experience. They do not want to because the process of creating such a language would threaten the social context which sustains and defends their substantial selves.

Conclusion

To sum up, in this chapter I have described the most common ways in which teachers seek to preserve their sense of self when they are working in schools in which the majority of teachers have different values and priorities to their own. Chief amongst these are reference groups, used as a perception-confirming device. Individuals defined reality through, communicated with and directed their actions towards selected audiences, many of whom (e.g. family, church, friends) had existed long before they made the decision to teach. Interaction, usually talk, with members of these groups served the inter-related functions of defending the substantial self and defining the reality to which that self had to react. However, the more frequently people interacted with extra-school groups, the less convincing they found their contacts with their colleagues to be and the less incentive they therefore had to make contact with them, particularly when they spent most of their time in school with their pupils. In consequence they became increasingly impervious to any communication they had with adults inside the school and more anxious to look for support outside it. Often this cycle was broken only by the decision to leave the school, or in some cases, the profession.

Reference groups outside the school, often of long duration, were particularly powerful in relation to those aspects of the self-image which were shaped before entry into the profession. These included social, moral, religious and political values, respect for the power of ideas and debate about them, concern to achieve high standards of occupational competence and, for a minority, a long-standing identification as 'teacher'. Over time, existing groups were supplemented by others which confirmed individuals in more specifically educational beliefs. Often these later reference groups developed from teachers' urgent, sometimes desperate, attempts to find support for their practice from like-minded people in other schools or parts of the educational system. Like longer-established groups these, too, sometimes had the effect of insulating individuals (or sub-groups) from their colleagues or of encouraging them in the decision to change careers. In addition, individuals frequently defended their own beliefs and practices by using other teachers in their schools as negative reference groups.

No matter how strong confirmation was outside the school for the substantial self who worked within it, teachers preferred to be in schools in which they received referential support from their head teachers and colleagues. Such support did not have to be numerous, however — the presence of one other like-minded person was often powerfully self-confirming.

Referential relationships with groups or individuals were particularly potent when they were also social or affective. Under these circumstances, in particular, they sometimes served to depress rather than raise levels of occupational commitment and performance.

Pupils were also a crucial reference group at all stages of teachers' careers. They had a particularly strong influence on individuals' views of their own professional competence and moral worth. However, the traditional privacy and autonomy of class-room practice means that pupils' support can be invoked to justify a wide range of educational priorities and policies.

Although reference groups helped many teachers to sustain a stable self-image, some people found that they could not withstand the influence of their colleagues without isolating themselves from contact with them or without being selective to the point of resistance in their dealings with them. Others who wanted, or needed, the friendly support of an in-school membership group, but who did not perceive their heads or colleagues as reference persons, dealt with the resulting tension by impression management. The account given in this chapter of the power of the self-image and the strength of the individual's will to preserve it from situational influences, however well-intentioned, may have presented a picture of teachers as impervious to personal or professional change or development. Yet, as the following chapter shows, this is not the case. It is to this apparent contradiction that I next turn.

Chapter four

The development of personal concerns

This chapter is concerned with the ways in which teachers develop and with some of the reasons why they do. Central to the argument which it presents is the notion that development is not the same as change; the latter term implies a break with the present more fundamental than the former. Much of the recent writing, which has attested to the glacial slowness with which educational practice alters, overlooks this fact (an admirable summary and commentary is to be found in Fullan 1982). Explanations for teachers' well-documented resistance to change have only gradually expanded to include the latter's own perspective. Modifications in professional practice often require individuals to alter deeply-rooted, self-defining attitudes, values and beliefs; the personal redefinition which this involves is likely to be slow, stressful and sometimes traumatic (Marris 1968; 1974).

This is not to argue that teachers, as people, are incapable of changing their 'basic assumptions' (Abercrombie 1969) about the nature of teaching and learning and of their part in both. Examples of personal change in members of the profession make it clear that radical redefinition of the self can occur, whether through a 'road to Damascus' experience (Razzell 1968) or by slow, painful accommodation to the views of trusted participants in a professional group (Nias 1987a). To press home the claim that the substantial self of the teacher is stable and well-defended is not to argue that its practitioners are static or moribund or that the educational system is incapable of growth.

Nor is it to suggest that teachers cannot develop or modify their behaviour over time and in response to circumstances. In the first place, they are human beings and such a claim would therefore be manifestly untrue, given what we know of adults' physical and mental changes during maturation and ageing (e.g. Kimmel 1973). Similarly, there are a number of theories of human development which presumably apply to teachers as much as they do to any other adult and so suggest the possibility of personal development within the professional role.

Theories of adult development

One such approach sees the teacher as an adult learner. It derives from theories and concepts which assume that human development results from changes in cognitive structures and draws upon studies by Piaget (cognitive development), Kohlberg (moral decision-making), Loevinger (ego development) and Hunt (conceptual development), (see Johnson-Laird and Wason 1977; Kuhn 1979; Bee and Mitchell 1984). All of these writers posit a sequence of cognitive structures, or stages, which are organized in an invariant, hierarchical sequence from less complex to more complex. Qualitative changes are held to occur at each stage, resulting from the learner's need to accommodate to environmental dissonance. It is claimed that, as individuals progress through the stages, they become more and more adequately fitted for life in a complex society, since at the higher stages they will function more comprehensively and empathetically than at the lower. Viewed in this light, teachers at higher cognitive developmental levels are likely to be more flexible, stress tolerant, and adaptive than their colleagues at lower developmental levels. They may also be better able to decentre (i.e. to assume multiple perspectives), to cope with complexity in dealing with the fluctuating demands of classroom life, and to use a greater variety of teaching strategies.

There have been attempts (notably in the USA) to apply these notions to teacher-education programmes. Glassberg (1980) — summarized in Veenman (1984), Oja (1981), Sprinthall and Thies-Sprinthall (1983) — have reported some experiments designed to promote the ego, moral, and conceptual development of student teachers and teachers; Lieberman and Miller (1984) and Veenman (1984) comment on others. Although Alexander (1988) does not explicitly draw on this tradition, his account of the professional thinking of a number of experienced teachers in English primary schools suggests that their perceptions of classroom events and of individual learning difficulties may indeed vary with developmental levels and that the latter may be affected by involvement in in-service programmes. Similar conclusions are implied in the study in the USA by Bussis *et al.* (1976) of elementary teachers' understanding of curriculum.

Life-stage theorists (e.g. Erikson 1950; Havinghurst 1953; Huberman 1974) also take a developmental view of human behaviour but focus on psycho-social rather than cognitive growth.

Like other developmentalists, they argue that development is through an invariant sequence of hierarchical steps, that it is interactional and that each stage is qualitatively better than previous ones. However, movement from one stage to another is seen to result not from accommodation to the physical or intellectual environment, but from successful resolution of the successive tasks or crises faced by individuals in the normal course of their lives.

A somewhat different view is taken by life-age theorists (e.g. Sheehy 1976; Levinson *et al.* 1978); see also Peterson (1964) on adult development in middle class careers generally) who examine the roles and coping behaviours faced or adopted by the majority of adults (although in existing studies these are almost exclusively white, middle class, and male) at particular ages. Like the life-cycle theorists, these writers argue that changes in adults are evoked by environmental concerns, but they do not take an evaluative stance towards them nor claim that they signal or result from qualitative psycho-social alterations in the individual.

There has, however, been no critical examination of either theory from a feminist perspective and few attempts have been made to apply them to teachers. Life-stage theories have been particularly neglected, although Smith *et al.* (1986) use an implicitly Freudian perspective (that of Gould 1978) to interpret some of the later career decisions made by their educational innovators. Within the life-age framework, Sikes *et al.* (1985) structure their exploratory model of the life cycle of English secondary teachers (of both sexes) on *The Seasons of a Man's Life* (Levinson *et al.* 1978), while, in the USA, Fessler *et al.* (1983) have developed a tentative and hypothetical 'career cycle model' from an extensive review by Christensen *et al.* (1983) of studies of teachers' concerns, ambitions, perceptions and capabilities at different points in their careers. Many of these studies were initiated by Ryan (1979) and most, though they speak of 'stages', derive from the life-age tradition. Moreover, they are generally of student teachers or of teachers with up to five years' experience. Only two (Peterson 1979; Newman *et al.* 1980) focus on retired teachers or on those nearing the end of their careers. Each uses different criteria to characterize development; further, some do not make their criteria explicit. Thus, though the labels attached to different 'stages of career development' are often similar, it is hard to judge what distinguishes one 'stage' from another, to make comparisons between them or to see what causes movement between 'stages'. Evidence for the later career development of teachers is particularly lacking in differentiation and is often presented in terms which are open to subjective interpretation. In general, therefore, the usefulness of either life-stage or life-age theories in providing a fuller understanding of teacher development awaits further enquiry.

Such theories have, however, drawn attention to the ways in which individuals' personal and occupational lives interact. Similarly, there is a sociological interpretation of professional socialization which points up the interplay between individuals' needs, capabilities, purposes on the one hand, and the institutional constraints upon them on the other. Lacey (1977) and Zeichner and Tabachnick (1983) challenge Coulter and Taft's (1973) argument that teachers' 'social assimilation' into their schools proceeds passively — from compliance and identification to internalization. In studies of new teachers in England and the USA, they show how individual teachers take an active part in their own socialization, strategically redefining their institutional settings and causing others to 'change their interpretation of what is happening in the situation' (Lacey 1977: 73). Gehrke (1981) and Sikes *et al.* (1985) have elaborated this pro-active view of becoming a teacher by stressing its developmental aspects; Gehrke focusing on the way in which new secondary teachers progressively adapt their work to meet their needs, Sikes *et al.* upon secondary teachers' shifting perspectives and adaptations during their life cycles.

In some respects these studies resemble the work of Fuller (1969) and Fuller and Bown (1975). (See also Hall and Loucks 1979, who used Fuller's work to look at teachers' concerns in relation to innovation.) Fuller was an educationalist in the USA who, over time, related research on teachers' perceived problems to that on changes in their expressed concerns. Reflecting on the patterns which emerged, she posited a three-stage development of teacher concerns. The first is one of survival, and is characterized by anxiety about *self*, in particular about one's adequacy as a teacher, about class control, and the evaluative opinions of both pupils and supervisors. The second stage is one of mastery; teachers want to perform well. It is marked by concern with *task*; in other words, with features of the teaching situation (e.g. numbers of pupils, time pressures, and resources). In the third stage, teachers may either become resistant to change in their routines or become concerned about the *impact* of their actions upon pupils. Impact concerns relate to the social and learning needs of individuals, discipline methods and classroom climate, the choice and teaching of particular curricula. According to Veenman (1984), unpublished studies in the USA since 1975 broadly support Fuller's theory (as does Taylor 1975, in the UK), though concerns over discipline and the impact of teaching on pupils are seen to emerge at all levels of experience.

Despite their differences, these theoretical formulations have two things in common. First, they focus upon changes, in teachers as people or in their life-circumstances, which are likely to affect their practice. Second, they do not conceptualize teacher development simply as skill development. In suggesting that the person who is the teacher may change and that this change may affect their teaching practice, they are tacitly making room for a view of professional development in which the practitioner and the person interact.

However, only the cognitive developmentalists and Fuller are closely concerned with changes in teachers' classroom practice. While the former take a view of pedagogic skill which does little justice to its strong, affective component (see Chapter 1), Fuller, by contrast, takes a more holistic view of teaching as work. In the rest of this chapter, therefore, I use her theory of the development of personal concerns as a model round which to structure an account of teachers' career and professional development, arguing that, throughout, the latter have one overriding 'personal concern' — the preservation of self-image — but that this concern is directed in turn and under different circumstances to self, task, and impact. I go on to suggest that the ways in which teachers experience their work alter in certain respects over time. I do not, however, present evidence which relates these shifts in personal concern to other aspects of their development as adults. In other words, I have not attempted the potentially fruitful task of drawing inferences from other branches of adult developmental theory that might suggest which age- or stage-related factors in teachers' personal lives affect particular aspects of their occupational ones (such as inter-personal relationships or readiness to innovate) at different times, or that might indicate how teachers experience, and react to, the inter-action between different aspects of their 'selves'.

My evidence is drawn from both sets of interviews, since development does not stop after any given length of service. For obvious reasons, descriptions of early concerns are drawn mainly from the first interviews and later ones more from the second. The fact that patterns of development suggested by the first interviews were repeated in the second (particularly in relation to task and impact concerns) confirms my confidence in the potential offered by Fuller's work for an understanding of long-term development in teachers.

Survival concerns

Despite the fact that most of my interviewees had chosen to become primary school teachers they all found their first experience of the work very hard. They recalled, for periods varying between 3 months and 2 years, being 'permanently tired', 'lurching from one infection to another', 'never feeling well after the first 2 weeks of term'. Often exhausted or even ill, working 80 or more hours a week, they found it hard to sustain a social life 'apart from the weekly moan in the pub with [other teachers]'. Locked into a cycle of sleep and work, they felt they were becoming boring, narrow-minded, and petty. They told familiar stories of large classes, children with acute learning difficulties and behaviour problems, unattractive buildings, colleagues lacking interest or even sympathy, and heads who gave no support. Allowing for a natural tendency to overstate difficulties in retrospect, and for the felt-need to experience an occupational *rite de passage*, their recollection of their early years in teaching made consistent and depressing listening.

In addition, almost all of them had massive doubts about their personal adequacy in the job. They mentioned as characteristic of those early months or years the same preoccupations which had filled their minds on teaching practice and which are, almost to the word, those cited by Fuller (1969) as typical of 'early concerns'. Could they cope with class control? Would the head or the inspector judge them fit to pass their probationary year? How could they teach all the subjects on the curriculum in an appropriate and interesting manner? In short, were they up to the job?

Nevertheless, all but 6 of the 99 teachers initially contacted worked for at least 1 year, 82 for more than 2 years. Some of them endured 3 or 4 years when 'most days I didn't want to go to work . . . yes, of course, there were the good bits, but if you'd asked me then if I was enjoying it, I'd have said "No — I hate it"'. Yet, as most of these teachers were graduates, they could have obtained alternative employment in another occupation. That they did not seek at that stage to leave teaching, despite the costs to them of persistence in it, is a reflection of what they felt to be at stake for them as people. For a few there was a deep-rooted sense of identification as a teacher; for all there was a self-concept as a 'non-quitter', 'a survivor', 'a success'. Moreover, as Lewis argues, in our culture, failure:

> threatens our self-esteem by causing us to doubt our
> character, our competence, or quite possibly both. To the
> extent . . . that our aspirations go unrealised (whatever the
> reason) we are threatened or troubled by personal guilt.
> Fearing that we have done less than we should, we are all too
> frequently haunted by the sense that we have done ill.
>
> (Lewis 1979: 17)

To have given up teaching while the going was rough would have been to admit not so much a mistaken choice of career as an inability to cope and, in consequence, to incur a sense of moral inadequacy.

Identification: a period of search for self

This overwhelming preoccupation with survival did not last for long, however. By the start of their second year (though often sooner and sometimes later) my interviewees generally seemed confident that they could fulfil the occupational obligations of 'being a teacher', since pupils and colleagues or superiors with a validating capability had confirmed their capacity to survive in the classroom. However, although a handful were certain that they wanted to 'be' teachers, the rest did not necessarily wish to 'see themselves' as teachers or did not know 'what sort of teacher I want to be'. So, for a period which often lasted a further 2–4 years they proceeded to test their career choice against their experience of the profession.

A test of this kind was particularly necessary because, despite their growing feelings of competence, most of them were not at all sure how they saw their occupational futures. Despite the fact that many had already begun to earn the golden opinion of their head teachers and that they did not feel unskilled, they were not yet ready to 'become' teachers. Some were unwilling to foreclose on a particular occupational identity (e.g. 'It isn't that I don't like teaching — I do, especially in this school. It's just that there are other things I'd like to do'; 'I'd like to have a go before it's too late at some of the other things I'm good at'; and 'I like teaching but I don't want to have to think of myself just as a teacher. That would be too limiting'). Others simply said, as two women did, 'I love children but I hate schools' or 'You don't meet many teachers you'd like to be like, do you?'.

Once individuals felt technically confident, their willingness to identify as 'teachers' depended in large measure on their ability to find a school or sector of education which 'felt right for me', which would enable them to 'be myself'. They began to change jobs, 'looking for a school where I'd feel I fitted in' — several moved three or four times in as many years. All of them trained for work in primary or middle schools, yet within their first decade of work, one or another of them had taught in fifteen different types of school, other than mainstream state schools for children of 5–13 years. Between them they found 'the right place for me': in further education; remedial and subject departments in secondary schools;

private, denominational, nursery, hospital, and special schools (of five different sorts); and home teaching. They also tried working in schools with large numbers of Asian, Caribbean, Italian or 'traveller' children, and in inner-city, suburban, and rural areas. So, the teacher (one of seven to move to special schools) who applied for a job in a hospital school said, 'As a teacher in an ordinary job, I cannot give children the attention I feel they need. With smaller numbers I can care more, and that's what I want to do'; and the infant teacher who moved to the remedial department of a secondary school explained, 'I knew that in that department, children came first, as I believe they should'. Similarly, two teachers had deliberately changed from schools on re-settlement estates to suburban areas, because, as one said, 'I don't believe that teachers should be social workers, I want to *teach*'. Others moved for similar reasons, one commenting that they could not 'use [their] art in that school', another that 'there was no scope for [their] sort of English teaching'. In short, most of my interviewees were reluctant to give up teaching until they had satisfied themselves, through a careful search, that they could not 'be themselves' anywhere in the profession.

Identification also appeared to depend upon finding an in-school reference group. One woman argued, 'I need to move . . . I don't believe you can behave for very long in a particular way without becoming that sort of person . . . and I don't want to be like that', while another said, 'It's so difficult trying to act one way if everyone else behaves in another. You begin to wonder what sort of teacher you really are'. I interviewed thirteen teachers in their fourth or fifth year of service who were very positive about the ways in which they did or did not like to teach and about their short- and long-term aims. All were actively seeking a change of schools and all gave reasons which suggested a felt-need for school-based referential support. All located their main reference groups outside their work but deplored this fact. 'I want', as one said, 'a school where other people share the same goals I do'. The following comment is typical of the feelings they expressed:

> You begin to feel it must be you who's wrong — I knew I
> wasn't but I needed somebody else to tell me. . . . My father-
> in-law was marvellously supportive but we only saw him in
> the holidays and I'd got to the point of giving up when [a new
> head arrived]. . . . You do need someone on the spot,
> someone who knows the same kids you do and is interested in
> what you're doing. Otherwise you begin to lose confidence in
> yourself, not just in what you're doing, but in your aims, in
> why you're doing something this way rather than that.

Ashton *et al.* (1975) found that older and more experienced teachers, who held more 'child-centred' views than their colleagues, tended to move schools more often. There are many possible reasons why this might have been the case; one is that they changed jobs in order to preserve their beliefs, as many of the teachers whom I studied did — as one of them said, 'You tend to go to a school where there are people who think the same as you do'. However, since the early interviews took place, it has become virtually impossible for a primary teacher to make rapid sideways moves between schools. It seems likely, therefore, that many more teachers will learn to preserve their ideals in what they perceive as a hostile professional environment, by using the strategies described in Chapter 3. They will not, in the process, become happier or more ready to learn.

Consolidation and extension within teaching: task concerns

At the end of this phase of search, both men and women appeared to reach a decision about their immediate careers. Those who had found a school or type of teaching in which they felt they could 'be themselves', (i.e. who had achieved a match between their substantial and situational selves) settled into a period of consolidation. Their concerns, as Fuller found, were not with task as such, but with their performance of that task. Secure in the knowledge that they were in the right job, they turned their energies to doing it as well as they could. Two pieces of evidence from the USA offer tangential support for this notion. Levinson *et al.* (1978) argue that it is between the ages of 30 and 40 that adult males are uniquely equipped, through a conjunction of experience and physical energy, to succeed in their careers, while McDonald (1982: 5) found that, after about 7 years of work, individual teachers 'create if they choose their own ecologies' and that these ecologies largely determine whether or not they continue to grow professionally. In other words, those who decide to 'be' teachers appear to want to become 'good teachers'. In my study, such people sought out courses of a practical nature, experimented with different types of classroom organization and teaching method, worried about the quality of resource provision and the size of their classes. They expressed relatively high levels of job-satisfaction, and talked of feeling 'competent', 'extended', 'purposeful', 'fulfilled'. Their discontents were generally caused more by the features of school life which appeared to reduce their effectiveness (e.g. inefficient administration, lack of whole-school aims) than by teaching itself. They wanted to teach well and resented it when apparent thoughtlessness or weakness on the part of the head prevented them from doing so (Nias 1980). Having decided that they were teachers, they pursued the highest professional standards of which they were capable and expected others to do the same.

At the same time they took on such professional responsibilities beyond the classroom as they found personally extending. They learnt extra skills, undertook curriculum development or administrative tasks, began to specialize in curriculum areas or aspects of learning difficulty. Men, in particular, became very involved with extra-curricular activities. Indeed, it is possible to identify in both interviews a sub-group of eight men who thoroughly enjoyed working with children, especially in the context of games, environmental studies, field trips and the like, and who admitted to finding classroom work rather boring, but who carried on teaching because it offered them the chance to do more of the things they enjoyed than any other job would apparently do.

Many people also sought confirmation that, as teachers, they could continue to be intelligent adults with a lively interest in ideas. They began to express a desire for more intellectual challenge in their work, applied for advanced courses, began reading once more and enthusiastically discussed educational ideas whenever they could. They expressed dissatisfaction at the level of staffroom debate, deplored the 'pettiness' of many aspects of school life and the 'unthinking' quality of much classroom work and drew heavily upon intellectually-oriented reference groups, usually outside school.

Yet, though many of them maintained contact with a reference group which confirmed that they were not 'merely' teachers, their significant others at school were those with whom they worked most closely: pupils and like-minded colleagues (occasionally, therefore, the whole staff). Indeed, spouses to whom I spoke during or after individual interviews would say things like: 'It's a good job I feel that way about my work too, otherwise I'd be feeling left out'; 'I never go to school but I must know as much about her class as she does. She's always talking about them'; 'Sometimes I get fed up with the amount she puts into school but she wouldn't be happy if she didn't, I suppose'.

It is difficult to relate this phase of task-concerned fulfilment and extension to particular ages or lengths of service. If an individual, (whether a late or normal entrant to teaching) had a strong sense of personal identity, and easily found a congruent context and favourable working conditions, then they were likely to pass rapidly through earlier phases and be confidently established by the start of the second year. On the other hand, as both the first and second interviews revealed, half of those who had been teaching for 8 or more years were still exhibiting these kinds of concern with task performance. One said, 'I was a late starter — I hated my first 4 years and it's only since I came here that I've been able to teach at all properly'. Another claimed, 'You can always go on getting better at this job. I'm nowhere near the end of it yet — anyway, I've been lucky, I've had promotion within the school, and new responsibilities almost every year. I always feel stretched. . . . I suppose I might start looking soon for a deputy's job, but I don't really want to. . . . I'm happy just teaching.' By contrast, Poppleton (1988) suggests that in secondary schools there is a marked difference between the 'motivational investment' of teachers with less than 5 years' service and that of their more experienced colleagues.

Increased influence: impact concerns

In the first interviews, 5 people with between 7 and 9 years' experience and three who were older but had not been so long in teaching, and in the second interviews a further twenty, expressed concerns which went beyond their classroom practice. They wanted wider responsibilities within the educational service, to fulfil their view of themselves as persons of leadership potential and/or educational vision. Sikes (1986) reports similar changes in the concerns of English secondary teachers, and Riseborough (1986) argues that unfulfilled ambitions of this kind account for much of the frustration which he found among 'veteran' teachers in secondary schools. Several of my group were applying for headships or deputy headships, four were active in their professional associations, sixteen were teacher-governors or were closely involved in parent associations. In each case they expressed a desire to influence or change other people in the direction of their own ideas. They spoke of their educational ideals and of their frustration in 'not being able to get anything done because I'm not at the top'. One woman said, 'I used to think I didn't want promotion, but recently I've begun to realize my ideas are better than most other people's that I meet. Why shouldn't I try to do something about them? Other people do'. Those who had turned to union affairs expressed similar views, but argued for the power of direct action rather than the influence of bureaucratic position. All of them showed what Fuller has described as 'impact concerns' but aspired to have a direct effect not just, as she suggests, upon pupils' learning but also upon other aspects of the educational system.

This change towards a wider view of education was accompanied by a broadening of reference groups. Teachers with impact concerns were likely not only to air their own educational philosophies and ideas, but also to quote the opinions of educationalists as widely disparate as A. S. Neill, Chris Searle and Rhodes Boyson. Several harked back, in interview, to one particularly inspiring teacher or head teacher whom they had known or read about, according this person almost the status of a personal guru. To be sure, they were not indifferent to the financial gains of promotion, but their main aim in seeking it seems to have been to acquire a base from which to put their own ideas into action. Like the head teachers in the Primary School Staff Relationships Project (Nias *et al.* 1989) they had a 'mission' which they wanted to accomplish in their schools (see also Hoyle 1986).

At the same time, teachers with specific career aspirations took note of the opinions of their head teachers, of advisers, of colleagues with influence in the system — in short, of those with validating capabilities at the next hierarchical level. Promotion, after all, depends on the recommendation of one's superiors. Teachers who want to leave their footprints on the sands of time cannot afford to ignore those who act as gatekeepers to the beach.

The fact that individuals were seeking promotion did not mean that they lost sight of pupils. The latter remained important but their significance was different from that which it had been in teachers' early careers. Whereas they used to gain a keen satisfaction from meeting children's classroom needs and organizing their learning effectively, they now appeared also to enjoy nurturing them in a broader sense. One deputy claimed, 'I love these children', another argued, 'If I leave teaching at this point, I shall feel I have let the children down. I know enough now to help them — I must go on and try'. One man put it this way:

> I've always liked children . . . but as you go further up the ladder, you begin to think about all of them, not just your class. It may sound trite, but I have always felt I have a responsibility beyond my own teaching. Now I feel ready to try.

In addition, as Chapter 5 makes clear, the second interviews revealed a significant shift of perspective on teaching among both those who were absorbed in task concerns and those who were looking for promotion. In mid-career many more teachers were concerned, as Fuller suggests, to make a lasting impact upon children than was the case in their earlier years. Indeed, one of the major satisfactions that they reported was feeling that they had, for example, 'taught them something they'll never forget' or 'started an interest they'll have for the rest of their lives'. Impact concerns can, it seems, relate both to classrooms and to the wider educational scene.

Consolidation and extension outside teaching: sequential careers

At the time of the first interviews, twenty-six people had left the profession and a further eight were planning to go very soon. All of those who had left, at the time of either interview, gave similar reasons for their decision. Some (including the four men who had always intended to become educational psychologists at the earliest opportunity) did not see themselves as teachers. As one woman said, 'It's no good; I've tried and I'm not a teacher'. A much larger group (all women except for one man who had exchanged roles with his wife) had chosen an alternative career in parenthood. Of this group, some had changed careers because they had felt unable to identify as teachers, some still wanted to teach but had been unsuccessful in finding a congruent setting, some had come to the end of the personal growth which seemed possible in particular schools. Whatever their reasons they saw parenthood as a positive step in another, but related direction. They liked children, they and their husbands wanted a family at some time; at the point when they had made this decision, sooner had seemed more personally satisfying than later. At the time of the first interviews, few wanted to go back to being primary teachers, though most spoke of an eventual return to the profession in another sector or capacity. 'Yes', said one, 'I'd like to go back to teaching eventually — but I didn't want to become the sort of person primary schools were making me be'.

I also interviewed three women who were hoping very soon to become pregnant, or, in one case, to adopt a baby. In each case, they admitted to 'having lost interest in the job'; 'I feel I'm getting in a rut, I need something new. . . . My centre of interest seems increasingly to be at home'. Their significant others were clearly pressing them, or colluding with them in their desire to take on another occupation. By contrast, I spoke to one woman who said 'I want to go on teaching, I'm not bored yet, in fact I love it, but I'm under so much pressure at home . . . my parents, my husband, my mother-in-law. They all want me to have a family . . . I feel trapped'.

In the first interviews I met six women who were still in the profession after 3 or 4 years, but were actively searching for a more congenial career. By the second interviews, none of these was still in teaching, and I met at that time only one man and one woman who were looking for alternative careers. One man and two women also went to jobs abroad at the end of 4–6 years' teaching, two men and two women moved at the end of 6 years to jobs in secondary schools or further education (to be joined by a further three women in the next decade). In each case, individuals made the decision to move for reasons which closely resemble those taken by would-be parents. They were looking for 'new challenges', 'something fresh to tackle', 'a job which was a bit different'. As several said, 'I had started to find [my last job] too easy'. Like their peers who stayed in primary teaching, their goal was personal extension and to achieve it they were prepared to pursue sequential careers. As Bethell (1980) points out, one of the limiting features of teaching as a lifetime occupation is the difficulties it presents to anyone who wants to opt in and out at different points, in accordance with the dictates of felt-needs for personal growth or refreshment.

Redefining 'career': the example of women

However, those for whom teaching brings a second and sometimes subsidiary income into the home (i.e. in Western society, normally married women with children) have in some instances managed to turn the single-line vertical career structure of teaching to their advantage. Or, to put it another way, though disadvantaged by the multiple roles they carried, by the prejudices which existed against their promotion to senior posts in schools and by the mobility sometimes enforced upon them by their husbands' jobs, some married women with families had managed to make a virtue out of necessity (see also Ball and Goodson 1985; Acker 1987). This they had done in two ways. Some, as Biklen (1985; 1986b) points out, had redefined the meaning of 'career' and had turned their energy, talent and enthusiasm into a kind of lateral extension similar to that described earlier in this chapter, but different in that it also involved the capacity to exert a good deal of influence. One in eight of my second interviewees named as the person (other than their head teachers) who had most influenced their professional development 'a [married] woman in her 40s'. All of the latter turned out to be either late entrants to teaching or 'returners' after child-raising. A similar woman in one of the schools in the Primary Schools Staff Relationships Project exerted a tremendous amount of school-wide influence. Reflecting on her failure to obtain a headship, she said that she had eventually realized that she could fulfil her aims by staying where she was, that there was little that she wanted to achieve educationally that she could not bring about by influencing others as a deputy (Nias 1987b). It appears to be possible for older women teachers to create a satisfying role for themselves in primary schools which enables them to exercise a profound influence on their colleagues without becoming head teachers. Poppleton (1988) indicates that this also occurs in secondary schools.

Other women found outlets for their creativity by choosing to return to teaching in roles which were peripheral to conventional schooling and which therefore gave them a good deal of freedom. In Chapter 6, I describe the plight of those who step off the career ladder (normally to raise a family) but then want to return. By contrast, a few of those who had resumed paid employment after a break (and one single woman) enjoyed the flexibility afforded by part-time, temporary or supply teaching and the personal extension offered by moves into work with, for example, children with special needs, English as a second language, or theatre workshops. Lyons and McCleary (1980) and Smith *et al.* (1986: 110) found the same trend: 'Beyond the self-contained classroom . . . there exists a huge array of other options for teachers. Our [women] teachers found and created a number of those'. One of my interviewees, once again in a full-time job, said, 'Being able to go part-time saved my sanity. I was beginning to hate everything about teaching, even the kids, but having had a break from the full-time grind for two terms I'm now really loving it again'. Three others had used their period of full-time parenthood to think again about the sort of professional they wished to be, and, in their second decade, were happily pursuing lateral careers in adult education of various kinds.

This is not to argue for the perpetuation of career norms which, notoriously, handicap women (especially those with families). Rather it is to highlight the advantages to be gained from a flexible definition of 'careers' and to urge that these benefits be available to main bread-winners (usually men) whose morale and enthusiasm might also be revived by the opportunity sometimes to move sideways (or out) as well as up.

Privatized workers: parallel careers

Among my interviewees, there was also a small group of people (in 1976 three women and in 1985 two men) who had, at the time of each interview, exhausted the possibilities, in terms of personal satisfaction and extension, which teaching appeared to offer them. All but one were described by their heads as competent teachers, yet all wanted to give the job up. Each had domestic circumstances which made this difficult. During the preceding years, two had tried other schools in an attempt to find one in which they felt that they 'fitted'. One had succeeded but confessed to 'stagnating' after four years there. All talked in negative terms about their lack of involvement with the job and their dissatisfaction with it. They saw their discontent as resulting in part from their own lack of commitment and felt that this was due partly to their domestic responsibilities, partly to lack of enthusiasm. They all saw themselves as 'being rather 9-to-4, I'm afraid', or 'getting very lazy', a stance for which they had found referential support in their schools. The important part of their lives appeared to go on at home; it was in the lateral roles of parent or child that they found significance. They had, in short, become 'privatized workers' (Goldthorpe *et al.* 1968).

Another, more positive way of viewing this development is to talk in terms of 'parallel careers'. Certainly all but a few of my interviewees remained very involved in their jobs for as long as they found them personally satisfying and/or extending or could realize their values through them. It was only when this was no longer the case that they tended to look for other career outlets, or, where this was not possible, to invest heavily in their lateral roles. In other words, they still had much to give to teaching which their schools were failing to tap. This suggestion echoes that of the Rand study in the USA (Berman and McLaughlin 1977; McLaughlin and Marsh 1978) which found strong evidence of a plateau in professional development after 5–7 years; teachers tended to become less effective after this time — less capable of change, less enthusiastic about innovation and teaching. The study attributed these changes to unsatisfactory staff development policies, not to the intrinsic character of teachers or of teaching roles. A similar conclusion is embedded in the studies of art teachers by Bennet (1983), Woods (1984), and Sikes *et al.* (1985), while Riseborough (1986) and Poppleton (1988) blame the frustration and disillusion of older secondary teachers upon shifts in national policy.

A slightly different reason for pursuing a parallel career is suggested by the people who, because of competing pressures in their personal lives, wanted to be able to transfer their attention temporarily away from classroom and school, but without leaving teaching, or who, by contrast, sought refuge in school from their domestic circumstances. First, there was the man who had previously been an enthusiastic teacher, but whose attention, at the time of interview, was focused on his home life. Having not long before married a widow with three children, he said:

I know I'm not teaching as well as I could at the moment

but the important thing for me just now is to make a success of being a step-father. . . . Everything else is second to that. . . . I find it immensely satisfying. What I need to do is find a balance between the two.

Second was a group of three women and one man who had turned to work after marital breakdown because as one said, 'I needed to find something I was good at again'. The man explained: 'I coped by just working. For months I didn't do anything else. Like a lot of people, I suppose, it was work that kept me going', while a woman recalled: 'I felt rejected . . . I turned to something I knew I could succeed in and that was my job. Through that, my confidence improved'. All of these people had brought or were hoping to bring their 'two lives' (as one put it) into balance again.

We should not find this switch of attention between home and school surprising. Work, after all, has to take its place alongside other life-age commitments. Subjectively viewed, career development is not likely to proceed in a straight line. Rather, one can predict that, over a life-span, the involvement of individuals with teaching will fluctuate as a factor of their satisfaction with it (however caused), and of the satisfactions and obligations attached to other roles. Whatever their reasons, people's success in following parallel careers will depend upon their capacity to 'juggle' their competing interests (Pollard 1980; Sikes *et al.* 1985; Spencer 1986) or to build 'bridging' devices between them (Woods 1981).

Conclusion

These teachers appeared to move through career phases which were dominated and determined by personal concerns. These were, in turn, as Fuller suggested, for self, task, and impact. However, on closer examination, changes in personal concern appear to be the expression by individuals of their need to preserve their sense of self. The decision to teach, and the consequent need to survive their first experiences of the classroom, raised urgent questions about personal adequacy and career identification for a group of people unused to failing. Survival assured, many then set about establishing whether or not they wished to identify fully as teachers. For most of them this was dependent upon finding a school or sector of education in which they could find a reference group and so experience a reinforcing match between their situational and substantial selves. Those who succeeded took on the next challenge — that of consolidating and extending their identities as teachers through their mastery over the task. Those who did not, moved on to other careers (notably parenthood) in which they believed they would find it easier to live consistently with their values and/or to encounter opportunities for personal growth. Emerging from full-time child raising, some women came back to teaching but with a redefined view of 'career', as a type of task concern which included a desire to influence others, or as an opportunity to exploit the freedom and flexibility offered by marginal roles. Meanwhile, a few men and women who did not wish to see themselves as teachers but who were trapped by personal circumstances into the job, located their substantial selves mainly in their lateral roles, often seeking to pursue parallel rather than sequential careers. Finally, a number of the longest-serving teachers, assured by their job satisfaction and proven competence of the match between self and occupation, turned for further self-development to impact concerns; in particular they sought both to influence pupils deeply and to achieve hierarchical positions which would enable them to spread their ideas to others.

It seems, therefore, that the personal concerns of teachers do develop but that in a fundamental sense, they remain the same. The heart of this paradox is the notion that the substantial self is the core of both person and teacher. In other words, although teachers can and do develop, they will not change professionally unless they also change as people. It is, inexorably, the person who takes up and carries out the job — and people, as I have argued in Part I, are characterized by a stable sense of self, imbued with values and beliefs which are powerfully self-defining. In Part II, I carry this idea further, examining the lived experience of teaching as work, first through teachers' job satisfactions and dissatisfactions and then in relation to their changing relationships with their colleagues.

Part two

Chapter five

Job satisfaction among primary teachers

In this attempt, in Part two, to capture and present to others the lived experience of primary teachers' work, I turn first to the aspects of it that they enjoy. There is one main reason why this is an appropriate place at which to start. Many of my interviewees claimed that in making their choice of profession they had consciously looked for one in which job satisfaction was said to be high, even if monetary recompense was low. Primary teaching, they reported, had that reputation. As a result, they tended to embark on their work expecting to find much of it rewarding. It therefore seems logical to examine whether or not their expectations were met, and for what reasons.

I encountered several difficulties in the process. The first was a conceptual one. As a topic for enquiry, teachers' job satisfaction has been largely ignored. Partly in consequence, it lacks clarity of definition. Only Poppleton (1988) offers an incisive analysis: distinguishing satisfaction with secondary teaching as an occupation and as a professional career; and differentiating between the rewards of classroom teaching, those of the job presently held, those of the school in which respondents were currently teaching, and those of likely career advancement. Studies of satisfaction among primary teachers (e.g. Jackson 1968; Lortie 1975, in the USA; Galloway et al. 1982, in New Zealand; Primary Schools Research and Developmental Group (PSRDG) 1986, in England) do not make these distinctions. Nor is discussion of the causes of job satisfaction convincing when the latter derive, as they often do from questionnaire items which have not been generated by teachers themselves. Accordingly, I have joined Lortie (1975: 89) in accepting that 'the level of satisfaction is thought of as summarising the person's assessment of his total rewards in teaching' and have, for example, taken primary teachers' self-reports of 'the most personally rewarding aspects of their work' (PSRDG 1986) to be synonymous with their chief sources of job satisfaction.

The questions that I used in both sets of interviews were consistent with this loose definition. In the first I simply enquired: what do you like about your job? What plans do you have for the future, and why? In the second, I used these questions, but also asked those who said they liked their jobs to tell me half a dozen things they enjoyed doing and to give their reasons. On both occasions interviewees were encouraged to talk for as long as they liked and I often asked further questions. This may have provided some protection against the difficulty raised by Klein (1976) who found when interviewing mechanics that they gave different causes of job satisfaction as the interviews went on. I have also made use of other relevant material in both sets of interviews.

A second major problem remains unsolved. It has been very difficult to draw valid or reliable comparisons between the two sets of interviews. In the first place, the numbers had halved in the decade between the two occasions, though the gender balance within each group remained about the same. More seriously, the composition of the second group was different in one important respect from that of the first. Many of the latter felt they had made only a short-term commitment to teaching, whereas almost all the second group had identified as teachers and most were making progress, in career terms. In other words, my second interviewees were very much more clearly self-selected than the first and may therefore have presented an unrepresentative picture of job satisfaction within the profession. During 1975–77 I was in direct or indirect touch, for other reasons, with many of those whom I interviewed. It is therefore possible that they agreed to my request for information out of courtesy or deference. By contrast, in 1985, only those who were quite happy to be re-interviewed needed to reply to my postal overture. It may well be that the four people who received my letter but did not respond to it, but whom I knew still to be primary teachers, were unhappy with their choice of career and therefore did not want to talk about their work. Nor do I know why I was unsuccessful in eliciting a response from forty-one others: did my letter not reach them or were they so disenchanted with their careers that they chose not to reply? In addition, on this occasion I spoke only to three of the twenty-two people whom I knew had moved to other careers outside teaching (including full-time parenthood). So I do not know whether the ten married women who sent back questionnaires indicating an intention to return eventually to teaching had made those plans out of financial necessity or a genuine interest in the work that they had left.

Comparison between the responses is also difficult because of the very different political climate surrounding education on the two occasions. The first interviews took place soon after teachers had received a substantial pay rise and at a time when morale within the profession was relatively high. The second occurred when salaries were very low and when the industrial action of 1984–6, in which almost all my interviewees were involved in one way or another, was well under way. It has proved impossible to estimate accurately the effect of these factors upon the high level of dissatisfaction with the status of teaching as a profession and its conditions as a career which many of them expressed (see also Riseborough 1986; Poppleton 1988).

So, although towards the end of this and the next chapter, I have drawn some broad conclusions about teachers' job satisfaction and dissatisfaction, it should be remembered that, especially when these involve comparisons over time, they stand in need of further refinement and testing.

Next, in Chapters 5 and 6, I have occasionally illustrated my argument with numbers as well as quotations. Generally, these represent teachers naming a source of job satisfaction (in Chapter 6, of dissatisfaction) but sometimes I have also indicated how many times (in a given number of interviews) a topic was mentioned, believing that this crude quantification is one way of conveying intensity of feeling as well as its cause. It should be remembered, however, that this is a qualitative and not a quantitative study and that numbers are used only, as 'quasi-statistics' (Becker 1976), to indicate ratios or trends. They are not intended to point up fine distinctions between types of job satisfaction nor to establish truth-claims. They should not, therefore, be viewed as an easy way of making comparisons between patterns of response in the two sets of interviews, especially since there were twice as many interviewees in 1975–7 as there were ten years later.

Another difficulty which I encountered when I started to analyse my interviewees' responses was the absence of a theoretical framework which would help to make sense of the patterns which emerged. In particular, there appeared to be no existing educational work which treated job satisfaction separately from job dissatisfaction. Rather, the two were seen as interdependent and both tended to be related to motivation. Teacher job satisfaction has generally been seen as important only in so far as it bears upon morale and commitment within the profession or the school. One reason for this may be that, in all areas of school organization and management, there has been a tendency to rely fairly heavily upon theory generated in studies of business or industry. In line with this tradition, considerable use has been made, on educational management courses, of Herzberg's (1966) 'two-factor' hypothesis. In an empirical study of engineers and accountants in Pittsburgh, Herzberg found that the causes of their job satisfaction appeared to be substantially independent of those of their job dissatisfaction. Job satisfaction appeared to be intrinsic to the nature of the work and was expressed in terms of achievement, recognition, responsibility, advancement and the work itself ('satisfiers'). By contrast, job dissatisfaction apparently derived mainly from the context in which the job was done (i.e. policy and administration, supervision, interpersonal relations, working conditions, and salary). Thus, the removal of a 'dissatisfier' (e.g. by a rise in salary) was a 'hygiene' factor because it prevented dissatisfaction but it did not thereby represent a 'satisfier'. Conversely, when a job was made more satisfying (e.g. by the provision of more responsibility) the level of dissatisfaction was unaffected. Herzberg argues that to achieve mental well-being at work, and thereby to increase motivation, attention should be paid to both 'satisfiers' and 'dissatisfiers'.

Although much of the existing work on teacher satisfaction and dissatisfaction tacitly accepts this hypothesis and the possibility of its fruitful application to life in schools, neither the hypothesis itself nor its transferability from industrial management to teaching has been subjected to much rigorous examination by educationalists. Yet, since Herzberg appears to be making claims about the ways in which work is experienced which, if true, would have far-reaching implications for the management of education, it is important that this should be done. Accordingly, in this chapter and the next, I have used his hypothesis as a framework for analysis, with a view to establishing whether or not it helps us further to understand life in classrooms and schools. I have identified and commented upon 'satisfiers' in the first and then the second decade, taking this term to refer to those aspects of teachers' work which led them to like or feel satisfaction with it. I have then attempted to draw tentative comparisons between the 'satisfiers' and commented upon the hypothesis.

'Satisfiers': the first decade

All my interviewees found it easy to say what they liked, or had liked, about their jobs. In addition, their replies came so swiftly and were given so confidently that I felt I was being given honest answers, especially since they all elaborated their replies and gave illustrative detail to substantiate them.

Overwhelmingly, they liked children. Some aspect of 'liking children' was mentioned 146 times, and by 80 people, a finding which is consistent with all the research cited earlier. However, replies can be further divided into the affective and those which suggest an interest in teaching competence. For forty-one teachers, simply 'being with children' provided its own satisfactions (these are, perhaps, the 'psychic rewards' identified by Lortie 1975: 104). Moreover, the number of men and women giving this reply was in proportion to the gender composition of the total sample. Ten more (mostly men) added that they particularly liked being with children out of school (e.g. football, camping, and field trips). As one man said, 'I wanted to work with children, and in our culture there aren't many jobs open to a man who wants to do that, especially if he's a graduate'. Twelve people liked 'knowing the children', claiming that children were 'nicer', 'more interesting', 'better company', 'more honest', 'more spontaneous', 'more enthusiastic' than adults, and two men added that they felt more at ease with children than they did with adults. In addition, one man and one woman specifically said that they liked being with children because they were amusing ('Every day something happens to make me laugh') and two women said, 'They're so beautiful' ('I look at them sometimes when they're doing PE and think, "How perfect their bodies are" '). The 'happy atmosphere' in the classroom was a source of satisfaction to a further ten teachers, and five mentioned the gratitude and support of parents as rewards.

Some teachers were also quite open about the way in which teaching met a felt-need to love and be loved. Several mentioned 'giving' as one of their rewards. A few were more explicit. One woman, who had earlier been a laboratory technician, said, 'You get so much physical contact when you work with young children. You're not cut off from people in the way you are in some jobs'. An infant teacher told me, 'Don't think I'm the one who's doing all the giving . . . I know that by the end of the day several people will have shown that they love me'. Three men spoke of their deep affection and concern for their pupils. One said, 'I honestly think I can love every child. It's not done in a lot of jobs to talk about loving the people you work with, but you can in this one', and another older teacher plainly stated:

> We can't have any children, so I suppose you could say this is my family, and I really get to love most of them during the year. I miss them terribly when I'm away from them. I actually look forward to Monday mornings.

Sixty-three teachers also indicated that their work made them feel occupationally competent. To be sure, it is difficult to disentangle affective involvement with pupils from interest in their learning. For example, were the twenty-one teachers who mentioned the 'responsiveness' of children as their main job satisfaction, reflecting an affective or a competence need? Probing suggested that, for the majority, it was the latter; they had chosen to teach in part because they wanted to help children learn and one sign that they were being successful in this was that their pupils were lively and enthusiastic. Less ambiguously, forty-eight specifically mentioned 'seeing the children make progress' as their biggest satisfaction. Typical replies were: 'When one suddenly says "Oh, I see!", well, that can keep you warm for a fortnight'; 'You look back at their books with them and you can both see how much they've improved since September, and that's really marvellous'; 'I can look back on every day and feel I've achieved something. Bob [who works in industry] can't do that. He often feels a week's gone and he hasn't achieved anything at all'. Two referred to falling rolls (e.g. 'Now that I've got a small class, I can get down to some real teaching and it's fantastic how much progress they make. I'd be quite happy to stay in this school').

Two-thirds of my interviewees also liked teaching because it provided opportunities for personal growth. Nineteen enjoyed the fact that every day there were 'difficulties to overcome', or 'problems to solve'. They found teaching 'taxing', 'stimulating', 'creative'. Twelve were conscious of 'always learning something new', four felt the job gave them 'scope' or 'responsibility', four found it intellectually demanding (especially the curriculum planning which went on outside the classroom), and eight enjoyed their autonomy and 'freedom to set my own standards'. Thirteen mentioned 'variety' (even though one of these put his point negatively: 'It isn't that I like all the things I have to do, but there's big variety during the week and in teaching I get less of what I don't like than I would in any other job') and three said, in the words of one, 'I chose to be a junior school teacher because I didn't want to specialize. I like the fact that as a class teacher I can do lots of things that I enjoy doing, but didn't have time for at university'.

Teaching met other personal needs too. Seven people spoke of the satisfaction they received from being praised or appreciated by colleagues or superiors (e.g. 'I like being told I've done something well. On the whole I do this job well, so I get plenty of praise. Maybe I wouldn't like teaching so much if people didn't tell me I was good at it'). Twelve admitted that they liked the power it gave them. Comments ranged from: 'I like talking, and where else would you get a captive audience for so many hours each week?' to 'I enjoy moulding children' or 'I like being able to influence other people'.

So far, everything I have said is consistent with Herzberg's notion that the 'satisfiers' in a job have to do with the work itself, and in particular with the opportunities that it offers for personal achievement, recognition and growth, findings which are confirmed by Poppleton's (1988) survey of 700 secondary teachers. However, nearly a quarter of these teachers also derived satisfaction from extrinsic factors. Ten liked the hours and holidays, two thought they did not have to work very hard, one enjoyed the physical setting provided by his new open-plan building. Twelve (all women) enjoyed the comradeship they found in staffrooms.

'Satisfiers': the second decade

Despite deep and widespread unrest in the profession in 1985, my interviewees expressed very high levels of satisfaction with teaching as an occupation. Most, when invited to name things they did not enjoy doing, found it hard to go beyond mundane chores such as playground duty on a cold day and clearing up after sick children or routine activities such as marking. Many spontaneously made comments such as, 'It must be rare in a job to look forward to Monday mornings, but I do'; 'I love every moment of it'; 'I can't think of anything about it that I don't like'; 'There can't be many people that get up and look forward to going to work each day, but most days I do. There's the sense of satisfaction you get from a lesson or a day or a week, or whatever it is'. They spoke of feeling 'confident', 'professional' and 'fulfilled'. Several women told me their non-teaching husbands envied them their job satisfaction. One recalled, 'My husband used to say it was a pity that I was the one who had to give up work and have the baby. He felt that I had more satisfaction from my work than he got out of his'.

Moreover, with the exception of the two privatized workers (see Chapter 4), no one expressed unmitigated job dissatisfaction. I suggested to all of them, no matter how enthusiastic they sounded, that 'no job is perfect' and asked them to talk about the things with which they were not content. With very few exceptions, they finished these reflections with comments such as, 'Even that I can't really say I don't like, because it's part and parcel of the whole experience. You take it on as a package . . . To be truthful, there's not a great deal that I don't like'; 'There's really very little that I dislike about it — the basic irritations of the job, but they're always there', and 'There isn't anything that I really dislike about it, I truthfully do love my job. The things I've just talked about, they're the superficial irritations that you'd get anywhere. Even the getting tired, that's part of it. You can't love teaching and not get worn out doing it'. Other studies (e.g. Otto 1982; Lieberman and Miller

1984; Primary Schools Research and Developmental Group 1986; Poppleton 1988) which allow teachers to speak for themselves instead of pre-structuring their responses have also found that reports of dissatisfaction are qualified by expressions of deep satisfaction.

Self-esteem

Many of these teachers were still in the job because, as one said, 'It fits and feels right'. A woman explained:

> When I was in the classroom . . . that was the only time that I'd ever felt — you know when people talk about 'finding themselves' — I was myself in the classroom. I was doing something in my own right that I was good at and it was the only time I felt it, I never felt it at university.

Another woman, describing her feelings on returning to part-time teaching, said 'I thought, "I've been out of teaching nine years. How on earth is this going to go?" I walked into the classroom and within two minutes it was all back. I was really thrilled . . . I thought, "This is something I know how to do" '. A man told me, 'I feel at one with my career . . . education is something in which I'm interested, involved, active, from my own point of view successful . . . I don't feel as if I ought to be anything else'. Many people said they talked a great deal about school and pupils when they were away from them, particularly if they were married to other teachers. One man recalled how he had abandoned his first career to take up teaching largely because in his local pub he regularly used to meet several teachers who had amusing or interesting tales to tell: 'I used to think it must be marvellous to have a job you wanted to talk about in the evenings. I couldn't forget mine quick enough'. Sometimes, especially when school also provided a vigorous and interesting social life or the work was deemed particularly fulfilling, the blurring of the distinction between the personal and the professional became one of the pleasures of teaching. Several people, married to teachers, chose to tell me that 'work makes an extra bond between us'. A typical comment was: 'Jean and I have exactly the same job and the discussion of the job and the doing of the work is part of our relationship at home because it started that way — we worked together before we did anything else'.

In short, as one man said, 'The main thing I get out of teaching is a recognition of me as someone valuable'. For some, especially married women returners who had experienced the low status accorded culturally to full-time mothers, it was a question of social regard: 'Coming back to school provides the feeling of being a professional, even if it is a very low status, low grade, part-time professional. It provides something that home life doesn't, because people just don't value that'. For others, self-esteem was part of the job itself, an experience summed up by the woman, who, talking about what she liked doing in the classroom, suddenly stopped and exclaimed, 'It's all the feedback things, isn't it — all the things that make you feel good about yourself'.

Affective rewards

As was the case in the early interviews, it was to children that all the teachers most often owed this sensation of personal worth. As before, positive feedback from children can be broadly divided into two categories: those considered 'affective'; and those relating to 'competence', though once again it is hard to distinguish between them. For example, two-thirds of my interviewees referred to children's 'responsiveness' or 'openness': 'I like to see the children laughing when I'm reading a story and really enjoying themselves. When they say "Read it again", I love that'; 'Children let you know if they're fed up and equally you will know if they're excited — that's good'; '99 per cent of them would always be willing to put themselves out and try, no matter what you asked them to try and have a bash at'. Yet it is not clear — nor do I feel teachers themselves could make the distinction — whether pupils' responsiveness is most valued because it gives teachers a sense of emotional well-being or an awareness of professional success.

Certainly, over half the group (men and women being represented in a proportion which reflected that of the total) were open about the pleasure it gave them to feel loved; children's affection was very important to them. Typically: 'In what other job would you know that when you came to school, 150 people would throw their arms round you and show that they love you? And they're so forgiving — the ones you hammered last week or last year, come up smiling and affectionate the next time you see them'; 'There are unpopular teachers, but most children love their own class teachers — I like that'; 'The relaxed atmosphere that you can enjoy once they know who you are and they respect you, to be part of that kind of atmosphere is great, it's very warming and comfortable'.

Similarly, one in six mentioned humour and 'being able to have a joke together'. Seven people (five of them men) drew attention to extra-curricular activities which provided opportunities to 'do things with the children that we both enjoy', and several also found this kind of satisfaction in the classroom (e.g. 'Enjoying a book together and discussing it'; 'When they get excited about literature, maths, exploring their environment and you can do it together'). References to 'enjoyment' and 'fun', to classes and schools with a 'happy atmosphere', or 'happy attitude' occur in just over half of the interviews.

It was also hard to distinguish 'being loved' or 'happiness' from the satisfaction which came from feeling needed. Over half the group made statements such as: 'When I took those children on, I found I had something to give and I really enjoyed it'; 'I get an enormous amount of pleasure out of working with the younger children . . . You're a very important person to them. They rely on you so much. I enjoy the relationship with them — the give and take — I give a lot as well, but they give so much'; 'When I was doing the DES course . . . it was nice to go back the next morning and they were glad to see me back, even if it was only after a day with somebody else'.

The conviction that they were making a valuable contribution to children's lives was particularly evident among those who worked or had worked in inner cities or the less affluent New Towns (see also Poppleton *et al.* 1987). For example: 'You were the only regular person in their lives, you were there every day and children came in knowing that you were there and however distraught they were outside, at least there was somebody that did care'; 'I feel I am doing more for them than their home is'; 'We really met people's needs there. We could see the changes in families and in children . . . There was no way we felt we were spare, or a luxury, or not really necessary to the children's lives'.

One in four teachers now felt that parents, too, made them feel needed. They mentioned, for example, 'the pleasure which parents show when a child makes more progress than they had expected', 'parents who were very concerned about their children and would do a lot to help you if you needed it', or 'parents who gave you plenty of support, with their own children, but also for school things too'. A man summed it up:

> The most enjoyable time of the year for me has always been the end of a school year because it gave me a tremendous sense of satisfaction to speak to parents at an open evening or afternoon, when they'd spoken to their children beforehand, and looked at the way they had developed — to know I'd done a good year's work and to have seen that the children were satisfied with what they'd done. And also the opposite of that, that I felt able to say to some parents that I felt I'd

failed, because I don't believe any class teacher can succeed
with 100 per cent.

A sense of competence

All in all, the capacity of teaching to provide individuals with
affective satisfactions appeared to increase over time; every teacher
made some mention of it, several of them many. But so too did its
power to make them feel skilled and competent (95 per cent
alluding to this at some point). However, though the nature of the
affective rewards of teaching remained very similar across the two
decades, the way in which occupational competence was expressed
changed in two ways. First, three-fifths of the teachers enjoyed not
merely helping children learn but also 'moulding' them, 'teaching
them things they'll know for the rest of their lives', 'sowing seeds
which may not develop till they're adults', 'sparking off interests
they'll always keep'.

Second, they knew much more precisely than they had a decade
earlier what they felt they were good at and how they knew this.
The pleasure they mentioned most frequently and the one they
described most vividly was realising that a child had learnt something: 'I love it when a child says, "Something went ping in my
head and I got it" '. One teacher said:

It's what I call the three cherries syndrome: where you can
work with a child for weeks and weeks and weeks and you
feel you're achieving nothing. And then one morning there's a
look in their eye which just tells you 'I understand now!' and
it's as if the three cherries have arrived on the slot machine.

Another remarked:

I enjoy a time when you've worked very hard with the child
for maybe two or three weeks and they haven't understood a
word of what you've been saying and suddenly the penny
drops. You see that lovely smile and their whole face lights up
and they say 'Oh yes! I've got it now!'.

Gradual progress could, however, be as gratifying as the sudden
breakthrough. One in ten spoke of the pleasure of 'just watching
the children grow, being able to do it slowly, which you can as a
classteacher', of 'seeing them change, mature, gain more insight
into themselves and their surroundings during the year', or of
similar satisfactions accruing from long service in one school.

Whether sudden or gradual, such progress gave teachers a sense
of personal achievement (e.g. 'You're making it happen at first

hand, that's what's happening, actually teaching the children to do it'; '[with infants] they make such dramatic progress and you feel "Gosh! I had a hand in this" '). Children's written work contributed to this sense of achievement: 'You put a lot of effort in and get little back in rewards, but the one reward is the satisfaction of what they produce. It's one of the reasons why I like classroom teaching because at least you have that'; 'A child will hand in a piece of work . . . I get excited about it. I say "Look what so and so's done for me". Because that's what I'm there for . . .' But teachers were conscious of their pupils' development in other areas too, such as music and drama. One in four also mentioned teaching specific skills, 'like using compasses. At the beginning of the session they didn't know and at the end they did — and they knew that they had learned and I knew that I had taught something' or, 'I like to see the children using a new skill that I've just been responsible for teaching them'.

Although direct teaching of this sort brought rewards, the sense of being in partnership with pupils was even more frequently mentioned as a source of satisfaction. Typically: 'I used to get a great kick out of starting them off with an idea or a story and watching where they took it'; 'It's enjoyable when you have talked about something and children come back to you the next day with some totally new, fresh ideas that surprise you'; 'I enjoy the discussion, when they've got things to say — and when they've done some writing and come and say "I'm not keen on that", when they've got some critical judgement of their own work'; 'I love trying to show them new things, encourage them to explore, to become more independent, to find out things for themselves and begin to express themselves'.

Whether or not teachers seek to foster in their pupils the capacity for independent learning, they have to learn to see success in little things. For example, half this group spoke of 'going home knowing somebody has finished his reading book and I thought he never would', 'realising that Gary really does know now that twenty means the same as two tens', 'If I see one child sharing something instead of grabbing — something like that — then I feel we're getting somewhere'.

However, a few also reflected on the difficulty of charting 'success' with any accuracy: 'You just get a feeling, don't you, of what things are going well'; 'It's not always obvious to outsiders what the children have achieved from the beginning to the end of the year or perhaps just on one particular occasion in the year. It's a difficult thing to put your finger on'. It remains to be seen whether the introduction of national attainment targets and assessment will increase teachers' satisfaction by giving them clearer yardsticks by which to judge their efficacy or whether it will make them feel de-skilled, by reducing the value accruing from their intuition and experience.

When I told one of these teachers that they all seemed to derive greater satisfaction from teaching in mid-career than they had earlier on, he replied, 'Surely, that's not surprising. We've spent 15 years developing the skill of relating to children. It would be odd if we didn't enjoy feeling good at it'. Yet only one person specifically referred to feeling she possessed a generalized skill in teaching ('which after all is an art form'). By contrast, nearly a quarter commented on their growing ability in specialist areas such as English as a second language or special educational needs and another quarter enjoyed some element of specialist teaching (e.g. French, mathematics, history) because they felt they taught those subjects well. However, successful specialist teaching was felt to be more closely related to personal liking and involvement than to formal qualifications (e.g. 'I love teaching music because it's an important part of my life'; 'Literature, especially poetry, is so important to me personally that I love sharing it with children, even though I've got no special qualifications in it').

Working with colleagues

Three-quarters of the group also found a blend of affective and occupational satisfactions in their relationship with their colleagues. They spoke enthusiastically of being part of a group or team, or of supporting, guiding, or organizing other adults. Since these aspects of teachers' work are discussed in full in Chapters 7 and 8, they are simply mentioned here. However, they are important for two reasons: they signal a broadening of teachers' focus of attention from classroom alone to classroom and school; and they suggest the existence of alternative sources of professional satisfaction, derived from influencing and relating to adults rather than (or, as well as) children.

Personal extension

Although mid-career teachers enjoyed being with children and helping them learn, pupils were important for another reason too. Many of my interviewees confessed to living in dread of professional stagnation; they valued children because, as one woman said, 'They make sure you stay alive'. A third repeatedly spoke of specific classes or pupils in terms such as 'buzz', 'drive', 'inspiration', 'feedback', 'vibrancy', 'keenness', 'enthusiasm', 'surprise'. One man said, 'I find children fascinating and stimulating', and a woman warmly recalled her first 'work with computers — that was fantastic. It was me and the children discovering things together, I mean children aren't empty vessels, we learn an awful lot from them'.

As a result, for some people teaching was 'exciting'. One man likened it to walking a tightrope, another one said, 'I hope I'm always close to the edge. There's that little tingle if you're not quite sure it'll work out . . . I like an edge to what I'm doing'. Teaching, said someone else, 'ought to be something that's an inspiration to you', as it clearly was to him.

Similarly, the unpredictability and variety of the job were often seen to be one of its assets. One in six spoke in terms such as 'There's something different cropping up all the time'; 'I like the stimulation of teaching every subject'; 'It appeals to me that I can be doing art one minute, science the next and English the next'. One man spoke of 'the challenge that comes from getting a fresh class every 12 months when there are thirty new personalities to learn all about'. Another felt that:

> No two days are ever going to be the same — that must be one of the biggest pluses for this job. You can call teaching a lot of things, but it is never boring. When you've got a class of thirty children, all of whom are demanding personal . attention and with their own ideas and their own ways of expressing themselves, their own strengths and weaknesses, and you're catering for all this, at times it's frustrating and tiring and all sorts of other things, but it's never boring.

Moreover, people who took this view of teaching sometimes suggested that others had only themselves to blame if they found the work dull. Typically, 'Many teachers don't take the trouble to be innovative enough — that's why they get bored'.

Some potential sources of stimulation (e.g. taking on new roles, curricular or administrative responsibilities, or a change of school) were less under teachers' control, however, than their classroom work. Some people enjoyed a measure of specialist teaching because it meant they regularly had to adapt to different classes and subject areas (e.g. 'There are lots of new things for me to find out all the time'; 'I like the bits where I'm trying something new and breaking fresh ground . . . It's an outlet for my creative abilities'). Extra-curricular activities sometimes served a similar purpose, once again especially for men. One head reflected that, as a class teacher, he had 'enjoyed the experience of finding that I was good at things that I didn't know I was going to be good at, like producing a play. Then when it was a success thinking, "Ah, that's another thing I can add to my list of accomplishments and be able to do in the future" '. Working with parents and other non-teaching adults could also be satisfying because, as one woman said, 'It gives you a change of perspective and of company, too'.

Intellectual satisfaction

Remembering that, in their early years, one in five of my interviewees had not found teaching sufficiently stimulating intellectually, I asked them on the second occasion whether they experienced adequate intellectual satisfaction in the job, and if so, from what. Nine-tenths gave positive responses, though some distinguished between 'actually teaching children' (which was not usually seen as intellectually demanding) and 'thinking about teaching children' (which often was). Four felt 'stretched' or 'extended' by the most able children, especially the older ones, with whom 'you could have serious discussions about all sorts of things'. Several claimed that 'there's an intellectual challenge in explaining things simply'. As one man put it:

Older children especially can ask some quite tricky questions
. . . The intellectual task is not giving an answer (there are
plenty of those and plenty of philosophy books full of them),
it's giving an answer that they'll understand. How do you
explain the whole universe to an 11-year-old?

But many more said it was their work outside the classroom which 'keeps me on my toes mentally'. The most frequently mentioned activity was planning (also described as 'preparation'), a broad category which involved several aspects of the job, the most often cited of which were coping with children's learning difficulties and acquiring new knowledge (e.g. 'I got really interested in the Norsemen, the Icelandic sagas. Then somebody showed me the new translation of *Beowulf*, so I want to get that when I'm in town. I would like to do that with them next term, that's partly because I will learn by reading it myself'; 'I like doing local history with the children and I spend a lot of time researching that'; 'When I started teaching again, I found it very invigorating to spend my evening working and researching instead of watching telly and ironing and things like that . . . it woke my mind up, I started using my brain again'). One in eight mentioned wider planning undertaken as part of their formal curricular responsibilities (e.g. 'Thinking out how the environmental studies might be taught and teasing apart the different kinds of skill that might be involved has been an intellectual task which I've enjoyed, one of the very first I've had to do since I left university'; 'All the time you're learning as well, especially from the planning and organization').

Most spoke of the way in which they constantly puzzled over teaching methods (e.g. 'I ask myself why didn't so-and-so go well, and that keeps me thinking'; 'It was one of those schools where you were expected to keep good notes and records, so you had to keep writing each week what you were going to do and how it had gone and that kept me on my toes'). Other activities mentioned as 'requiring thought' were discussions with head teachers and colleagues (e.g. 'When my head saw something he disapproved of, he asked you why you were doing it. At the beginning it was very off-putting but . . . it made me sit back and think'), supervising students, reading and writing (one man and one woman were preparing textbooks).

Just under a tenth saw teaching as 'quasi-intellectual, in that it involves a lot of practical problem-solving', or 'problem solving with people'. One said, 'I do find it challenging, I suppose because of the great breadth and depth of the problems it throws up. Your solutions to them are a huge mixture of common sense, the highly technical, the purely academic, all mixed together in a package that works. It all exercises the brain wonderfully . . . you find that there's an awful lot of thinking to do'. By contrast, three argued that the job was not intellectually satisfying, but did not mind that because, as one man suggested, 'I've got my own interests, I enjoy reading and music and such like. I don't feel that you've got to be intellectually stretched all the time. Yes, you try to improve your job, and that stretches your imagination maybe . . . but I've never been a person who particularly bothers about intellectual exercise'.

Yet despite the high proportion who found intellectual stimulation in one aspect or another of the job, one in eight had also undertaken (or were engaged in) courses of advanced study in order, as they said, 'to talk about ideas', 'to be with a group of intelligent adults who will discuss things', 'to go back to my subject again to learn more about it, even though I only teach it to 9-year-olds'. Some indeed spoke of these courses in fervent tones as, for example, 'an oasis', 'my sanity', 'what kept me going in that job'. Although advanced courses may only appeal to a minority of mid-career teachers they evidently fulfil an important need for those who choose to pursue them.

Control and freedom

Whereas in the early interviews fewer than one in ten mentioned the 'freedom of class teaching' as a satisfier, in mid-career well over half made reference to the pleasure of 'feeling in control'. Men and women spoke of the gratification of knowing that 'it's all revolving round you, you are controlling things', that 'you're the one who is making it happen at first hand', or 'it's you who's instigating things in the classroom'. Four (all men) were even more direct: 'I think the relationship's concerned with control. I'm very egocentric and I need to feel, as a person, that I have some control, and it's easy with children, because they're open and they respond'; 'I suppose when it comes to the bottom line what I really want is the ability to know I'm in control'; 'I think control is a personal thing for me. I don't like the idea of having a situation that I can't control. I think I could teach myself to tolerate it but I don't think it comes naturally. I don't like things to be out of hand, I think that's why I like teaching the 9-year-olds because they are easier to control than the older children'. Other men and women liked being 'in charge', 'your own boss', 'queen in my own classroom', 'making decisions about how you're going to spend your time' and feeling that 'there is no job at all where you would have the freedom you've got in the classroom, unless you're working from home'.

It is still too early to tell whether the introduction of contractual hours of work, of a national curriculum and of national assessment will seriously reduce the job satisfaction and thus the motivation of teachers like these or whether they will be able to find enough scope within the new constraints to feel that they still have a satisfying level of control over the central part of their working lives.

Working conditions

No teachers in the second interviews mentioned as a 'satisfier' any aspect of their working conditions.

Conclusion

Direct comparison between the satisfactions of teaching in early and mid-career is difficult for all the reasons stated at the start of the chapter. Notwithstanding, a few tentative generalizations may be made. To help this process, some crude quantifications are set out in Table 5.1, but the reader should remember that these figures indicate trends not 'proofs'.

The affective rewards of being with children — giving and receiving affection, talking and laughing together, sharing common

Table 5.1 Sources of job satisfaction: first and second decades

	First decade		Second decade	
	Numbers % (n = 99)	'Mentions'	Numbers % (n = 50)	'Mentions'
Affective rewards from children's company	69	87	100	63
Sense of occupational competence through helping pupils learn	63	69	95	57
Extension of personal skills and qualities				
— through teaching	65	72	67	34
— through other responsibilities mainly involving colleagues	16	26	75	42
Working conditions	13	13	0	0
Company of other teachers	12	12	20	11
Feeling autonomous	8	8	59	31

interests, enjoying shared activities — are high at all times. Indeed, if these figures are typical, teachers become increasingly conscious of them as they become more experienced. 'Committed' teachers evidently like children more rather than less as time goes on. By the same token, they become more aware of children's dependence on them, especially in areas of high social need, and many find it gratifying to be unmistakably important in their pupil's lives.

Also high are the rewards associated with 'helping children learn' (i.e. the satisfactions associated with feeling competent and skilled in one's daily work). These, too, seem to increase over time, but become much more clearly associated with making a long-lasting impact on one's pupils. With greater experience teachers also become more capable of describing children's responses in detail and of reflecting analytically upon their part in their pupil's achievements. They are increasingly aware of children's development over the long term, and of their own pedagogic skills.

Another major cause of satisfaction in both decades is feeling one's skills or qualities extended — by solving problems, taking on fresh challenges, assuming new responsibilities and so on. Yet here too, satisfaction appears both to increase with experience and to alter slightly in kind. The proportion of people who find the 'variety' of primary teaching rewarding does not change significantly over time, remaining at just over one in ten, but a larger number (one in three) now explicitly find their pupils stimulating. In addition, many teachers have turned for additional challenge to the staff group or the wider educational scene and find fresh rewards in extending their sphere of influence from their pupils to their colleagues. By contrast, the proportion looking to their colleagues for friendship or a social life remains about the same.

Most of the mid-career teachers had also learnt how to find adequate intellectual stimulation in their work (I have no comparable evidence for the early years). The majority did this by undertaking extensive work out of school — planning, preparation, puzzling over individual children's learning difficulties and their own teaching methods. However, an increased number had also turned to advanced in-service courses and spoke warmly of the stimulus they received from these and of the contribution these made to their professional thinking.

Over the two decades, satisfactions derived from feeling autonomous or in control of one's professional life increased sharply, from 8 per cent to 54 per cent. The emphasis which is given in mid-career to the importance of a sense of autonomy may reflect a growth in self-confidence, itself due to increasing identification with the teacher's role and to a successful search for pedagogic and curricular competence (i.e. with 'task' concerns, see Chapter 4). It may also indicate that individuals have developed 'impact' concerns (see Chapter 4), and are aware of having more personal and professional influence over colleagues than they felt they did in their early years (see Chapter 8).

In general, then, the sources of primary teachers' job satisfaction did not change a great deal from early to mid-career, though there was a clear tendency for more experienced practitioners to become increasingly concerned with their impact upon both pupils and colleagues. I did not find, as Poppleton (1988) did, that job satisfaction was greater in women than in men. Indeed, although teachers' reasons for liking their jobs remained very similar across two decades, the intensity of satisfaction for both men and women increased on every dimension that they named. Successful and committed mid-career teachers appear to find their work extremely satisfying, deriving from it a strong sense of fit between self and occupation, and a good deal of self-esteem. These findings are confirmed, though much less clearly, for secondary teachers by Poppleton (1988).

All this is in marked contrast to the drop — from 13 per cent to none — in the number of people mentioning aspects of their working conditions as a cause of job satisfaction (see also Poppleton 1988). This decline is consistent with Herzberg's hypothesis, that job satisfaction derives primarily from work itself and is not dependent upon the context in which the latter is set. Indeed, Table 5.1 seems to offer unqualified support for his hypothesis, the figures for the first decade showing 237 satisfactions deriving from the nature of teaching against 25 relating to its social and material context, and those for the second 309 and 11 respectively.

However, two alternative explanations for these figures are possible. One is that these teachers were the slaves of occupational rhetoric and gave 'received' answers, stressing the 'child-centred' nature of their task and therefore attributing their satisfactions to contact with their pupils (i.e. to work itself). Another is that they did not stress the context of their work as satisfying because there was little in the conditions under which they worked to bring them any satisfaction. To consider these interpretations further and to continue examination of Herzberg's hypothesis, I turn in the next chapter to an analysis of job dissatisfaction and its causes.

Chapter six

Job dissatisfaction among primary teachers

If Herzberg's hypothesis holds for primary teaching we should expect to find that the job dissatisfactions of which its practitioners are aware derive from the context in which 'work itself' (i.e. teaching) is set, and not from involvement with pupils in classrooms; or, to put it another way, that the intrinsic pleasures of teaching are offset by conditions in schools and events in the wider educational system, and not by aspects of the job itself. However, the evidence presented in this chapter suggests that this separation of 'satisfiers' from 'dissatisfiers' is over-simplistic. First, the absence of satisfaction is in itself an active component in job dissatisfaction, since many teachers enter the job expecting that a high level of job satisfaction will offset low material benefits. Second, and more powerfully, there appear to be aspects of the work which regularly cause unhappiness or frustration but which, once remedied, allow job satisfaction to develop (a finding strongly confirmed by the survey undertaken by the Primary Schools Research and Developmental Group (PSRDG) 1986). I call the latter 'non-satisfiers' to distinguish them from more obviously contextual 'dissatisfiers', such as pay.

In this chapter, I identify and compare the 'non-satisfiers' and 'dissatisfiers' of teachers in early and mid-career. I conclude that a further weakness in Herzberg's hypothesis, when applied to teaching, is that practitioners themselves find it virtually impossible to distinguish between the job itself and the context in which it takes place. Little of a teacher's work in the classroom can be fully isolated from what happens in the school, and events in the wider educational scene have such a strong impact on the self-esteem and potential for self-realization (or as Maslow 1954, calls it, 'self-actualization') of individuals that they can change the way in which the latter perceive and define even 'work itself'.

Two other points need to be made by way of introduction, both relating to the difficulty of conceptualizing job dissatisfaction among teachers. First, there has been a tendency among some researchers to equate it with stress (e.g. studies of secondary and primary teachers by: Kyriacou and Sutcliffe 1977, 1978, 1979; Otto 1982; Galloway *et al.* 1982; Dunham 1984). Other studies in the UK and USA such as those by Kearney and Sinclair (1978), Blase (1986), PSRDG (1986), and Poppleton (1988) accept that there is a close empirical relationship between stress and job dissatisfaction but see the two conditions as logically distinct. I have tended towards the latter interpretation, following teachers themselves in seeing stress as a phenomenon which often renders their work unpalatable but which is not the sole cause of their discontents. Second, most of these studies use questionnaires and it is not always clear whether or not the items in them arise from the researchers' or the teachers' concerns. Although some studies of primary teachers (e.g. Otto 1982; PSRDG 1986) make plentiful use of written self-reports, only Dunham (1984) appears to use oral material and he does not make it clear under what conditions it was collected. So there is a dearth of spoken testimony from these teachers about those aspects of their jobs which contribute to their dissatisfaction with them.

The material in this chapter is drawn from replies to two loosely framed questions which I asked in both sets of interviews: what do you dislike about the job and why?; what plans do you have for the future? In addition, I asked the mid-career teachers to name half-a-dozen things in their jobs that they disliked doing and to give their reasons. I have also made use of relevant remarks which were made spontaneously in other parts of the interviews.

The lengthy material contained in this chapter is addressed in chronological order. Within each decade, I have looked first at 'non-satisfiers' and then at 'dissatisfiers'. In each of these categories, I have examined topics according to the order of frequency with which they were named and wherever possible have, for the sake of clarity, used the same or similar sub-headings to describe them in each decade. At the end of the section on 'dissatisfiers' in mid-career I have used the testimony of part-time, supply, and temporary teachers to illustrate the importance to teachers of self-esteem and of opportunities for self-extension. I have then considered the usefulness of Herzberg's hypothesis to an understanding of teachers' work and, finally, using 'quasi-statistics' (Becker 1976) have attempted some broad comparisons between causes of job dissatisfaction in the two decades.

The first decade: 'non-satisfiers'

The most frequently mentioned and deeply felt dissatisfactions in teachers' early years derived from the job itself, or rather from their sense that they were not doing it as well as they wanted. Their complaints were therefore directed simultaneously at their work and at those whom they felt to be responsible for making it as it was. Nearly half mentioned the distress they experienced when their pupils were disruptive, unresponsive or failed to make progress, and when class sizes prevented them from giving adequate attention to every child. Some found unresponsive parents a similar source of job dissatisfaction. At the same time they and others referred to conditions within schools which they considered were responsible for their lack of pedagogical success. Most of these they laid at the door of their head teachers because they believed it to be the latter's responsibility to create a context which would enable them to give of their best in the classrooms.

Administration and communication

Their main complaints in this respect were inefficient administration and poor communication, absence of clear goals and of the structure necessary to attain them, and inadequate supervision of their work. Most frequently mentioned, sometimes indeed cited as a major reason for leaving the profession, was 'the inefficiency — that's the worst thing'. Nearly half my sample named 'disorganization' or 'inefficiency' as one of the most frustrating aspects of their jobs. Examples given included the following: broken, but unreported television sets or equipment; messages not passed on; incoming information (e.g. on courses) not circulated; lessons interrupted by children with notes; coaches or films not ordered as requested; inadequate advance warning given of timetable changes, or of visitors to the classroom; mislaid equipment; sudden shortages of stock; expenditure which resulted in over-generous provision of resources in some subjects ('All those AV aids gathering dust in the cupboard') and too little in others ('I even have to bring my own dictionary for the children to use — but you should see the PE equipment').

These and similar examples contributed to teacher dissatisfaction because they were seen as preventing teachers from doing their jobs efficiently and effectively: 'I'm fed up with organizing everything at the last minute, I like to plan ahead, and prepare my mind in advance, but we're never told anything until the last minute, so it's almost impossible to be organized yourself'; 'I've almost given up planning anything in advance, I used to plan and prepare properly, but because of the constant chopping and changing, I found I could seldom do anything I'd planned. So now I don't plan — I don't do the job so well, as a result, and I find that very discouraging'. Commenting on a local induction scheme for probationers, one teacher said, 'I think it's an abdication of responsibility on the part of the heads. There's no substitute for a well-organized school. If we had that, probationers wouldn't need special help in settling in'.

Remarks such as these reflect the anger which teachers feel when they believe that the effectiveness of their own teaching is obstructed by other people not fulfilling their responsibilities. To be sure, they do not cite a well-organized school as one of the things they like about teaching, but they comment with discouragement, bitterness, and disillusion upon the effects of working in a disorganized one. In this sense, poor administration and communication are seen as a form of bad manners because, in the eyes of those who perceive themselves as carrying the burdens of the job, they show lack of consideration for teachers and for the problems they face.

Lack of coherence

A lack of whole-school aims and policies was mentioned almost as frequently as inefficiency, because, in schools which do not have them, teachers' individual efforts often seem to be wasted. Twenty-five people complained about the absence of 'common goals' or 'common standards', of a lack of 'continuity', 'consistency', or 'direction' in school policy, or of a 'coherent philosophy'. Twenty-three more named other dissatisfactions deriving from a lack of whole-school planning, and five claimed that the frustration thus induced was a major reason for their leaving their jobs or even the profession. Typically, 'There must be priorities in a school, even if the priorities are wrong. You must be able to see coherent responses, agreed by the staff and parents. A school must be a unit, not just a collection of good groups', and 'I decided to move because I had to get somewhere where I could feel that the school was achieving something purposeful . . . A teacher must not only be good, but part of a coherent whole'. Put positively, this urge for coherence emerges as, 'What I do is worth it, because the next teacher is going to make use of it. It's worth the extra effort because you have something to build for. You see the standards of the children in the fourth year, and you know that you're setting them off along that path'. When this knowledge is lacking, teachers question the value of their own contribution and, in consequence, their self-confidence and self-esteem decline. As one said: 'How can I feel that what I am doing is worthwhile when the whole school is in a mess?'.

Lack of direction

Nor were teachers satisfied with 'too much freedom', feeling discontented when, as one said, 'the head let the staff get away with murder. I could have taught them Arabic all day and no one would have minded'. Statements like this one may not, of course, be objectively true, but what matters to classroom teachers is not the head's perspective but their own. Nearly a quarter of those interviewed indicated that they wanted to be kept up to standard by informed supervision. Their comments ranged from the vividly general ('In a system where you aren't supervised, the bad eggs run riot') to the self-critically specific ('After three years I decided to leave. The head never appeared in the classroom, never kept a check on anything we did. I was getting too good at papering over things, and he didn't notice', or 'By Christmas I needed to be told to put things right, and wasn't strong enough to do it on my own. I'd got into very bad habits and really would have appreciated it if the head had come in and told me so'). It seems that many inexperienced teachers, even those described in glowing terms by their heads, do not always want as much professional freedom as some heads offer them. On the other hand, there was no mention among factors contributing to job satisfaction of the obverse of this. Like inefficient administration, the absence of monitoring is a 'dissatisfier', but its existence does not serve as a 'satisfier'.

Lack of supervision was often associated with another cause of dissatisfaction — heads who were felt themselves to have low professional standards (e.g. with regard to punctuality or assembly presentation) and to set a poor example of commitment to, or involvement with, the school.

> In this school, you feel as if all your efforts are wasted because the head is so uninterested, and it rubs off on the staff. She really couldn't care less any more about teaching. We never see her in the classrooms; in fact we don't see much of her in the school. She often comes late, gets her hair done in school time, and when she is in, sits in her office learning her part for her amateur dramatics. She can't be doing requisitions all the time . . . If I can't move, I think I'll leave and have a baby. It gets so disheartening when you work hard yourself and there's no backup.

I got on well with the caretaker and cleaners who cared more about the school than the head did. They seemed to be more worried than he was by the low standards in the school . . . He was away by one minute past four every day, and since we never saw him while he was in school, there was no leadership . . . I was glad to leave that school. Here it's quite different. The head gives a lead and at least some of the staff follow.

Perceived absenteeism was as disheartening as perceived indifference:

We never saw the head when he was in school . . . but mostly he was out anyway . . . He was a key member of NAHT, I think, certainly he was always running off to meetings.

Nor were comments such as these an indication that the head was seen as unapproachable or unpleasant: 'She copes so badly, yet is so good with the children, it's impossible really to dislike her, although it's infuriating never getting a straight answer to questions merely because she doesn't know what's going on'; 'She's very nice, but a 9-to-4 head and never available to discuss anything. You have no incentive to improve when no one cares what you do'.

School-wide factors such as class size, perceived lack of supervision and of disciplinary and curricular policies, and administration which made it hard for individuals to meet their own standards of classroom performance were, then, the most frequently mentioned sources of dissatisfaction. Almost everyone referred at some point to at least one of them, most to several. All held their head teachers largely responsible for these and other aspects of institutional life which impinged on their central task, that of teaching (see Nias 1980 for further details of the relationship between teachers' job satisfaction and the ways in which they felt their heads behaved). Yet such factors cannot be construed as 'contextual' because their effect was to lower teachers' self-esteem and therefore to alter the ways in which they saw themselves as workers.

Conflict with individual principles

Teaching also conflicted more directly than this with some people's self-image. Forty-four teachers disliked an aspect of their work which was opposed to their principles (see also Biklen 1985). Fifteen found the dominant values of their schools ideologically offensive. 'The head is racially prejudiced and if I can't get another job, that will drive me out'; 'I'm expected to train children to obey authority, not to behave co-operatively or to think for themselves. It goes against everything I believe in'; 'Schools are so sexist, I hadn't realized how much, and it seems impossible to fight it'. An 'excessive stress on religion' was mentioned six times (in relation both to voluntary aided and to maintained schools). A further nine people disliked teaching 'because it forces one to be so unpleasant', or 'because you have to put on a show all the time. You can't be yourself'. As one woman who had left teaching said, 'I don't believe that you can behave in a certain way for very long without becoming that sort of person. I felt myself becoming bossy, bad-tempered, petty and I thought, "If I go on much longer those things will become part of me. So I started a baby" '. Ten also mentioned 'the low expectations which everyone seems to hold for children and teachers — I can't stand that'; or 'the chores, like cleaning paintpots, that I don't think a teacher should be doing'.

Perceived lack of autonomy in the classroom seemed rare but when it existed it was regarded as a 'non-satisfier': two teachers mentioned 'lack of freedom to do what I want', while a further two left the profession 'because I found I wasn't free to try and achieve my ideals'. Heads whose leadership was perceived as excessively directive were also strongly resented. Though few, their behaviour made a profound impression upon those who experienced it. Two teachers' views could be summed up by the comment of one of them: 'He was a bully . . . He caned the children and shouted at us all . . . I left the school as soon as I could'. A third I quote in some detail even though this account does not give the head's view of the incident and to that extent is only partial:

> One day the head called me in and accused me of defying him in ignoring his written orders [over the teaching of English]. I hadn't defied him, just hadn't realized they were orders, not guidelines, but he wouldn't believe me, and said he wouldn't give me a good reference when I asked for one, unless I learnt to fit his mould better. Next day the adviser turned up, and told me that if I were a shop-girl I'd do exactly what my boss told me, and my situation here was exactly the same. It was sheer stupidity, he said, for me to defy my head teacher in so calculated a fashion . . . I was too stunned to say much. Later on I was told that being a competent teacher wasn't enough, a teacher had to obey the head.

Lack of personal extension

A further twenty-three disliked teaching not so much because the activities or attitudes required of them conflicted with their self-image but because, as work, it seemed not to provide opportunities for personal growth (e.g. 'I don't like teaching subjects I don't find interesting'; 'I get bored with hearing Ladybird over and over again. I yearn for some sort of intellectual challenge'; 'It's so easy to get tired of doing Harvest Festival after the fifth time and then you start doing it badly and get bored with the whole thing'). Nine (mostly women) specifically mentioned as a dissatisfaction the lack of intellectual stimulation involved in working with children.

Lack of influence

Another fifth found the job uncongenial because it gave them little sense of power or influence over others. One woman candidly said, 'I don't like not having any power, except over the children'. Others spoke of 'being a nobody in the school, and it's not much better outside'. Two said, to quote one, 'The dinner ladies run the school. They're harpies and thoroughly unsettle the kids at dinner time, but we've no power over them'. Several deplored 'not being able to influence anyone or get anything done'. Interestingly, many more women than men expressed feelings of this sort, a fact which the later interviews suggest may reflect women's frustration with the social and career structure of primary schools.

Stress and fatigue

Numerically, stress features second only to institutional factors which impinge on the classroom, being mentioned by nearly two-thirds of the group as a source of job dissatisfaction. But I have left mention of it till this point because it did not have a single cause. It was clear from the ways in which my interviewees expressed themselves, verbally and non-verbally, as they reflected on their first decade as teachers that their dissatisfactions were frequently experienced as feelings — especially guilt, failure, frustration, anger, or regret at the absence of personal fulfilment. So, in part, stress had emotional roots. But it was also physical in origin. The work-load expected of and assumed by committed teachers left many men and women feeling 'drained', 'exhausted', 'shattered' at the end of every day. Together these led to cumulative fatigue or ill health.

Fourteen people found the level of 'stress' or 'worry' unacceptable, ten spoke of excessive fatigue, five (all women) had either left, or were contemplating leaving because of the effects upon their health, three 'were worn out by the constant theft, break-ins and vandalism'. For thirteen teachers, a corollary of these conditions, and of their own commitment, was 'lack of time to have any kind of private life'. This, too, was causing some of them seriously to consider whether they could continue to teach for much longer.

Now, it is clear that all these causes of job dissatisfaction derive either from individuals' expressed desire to do the job as they felt it should be done or from their expectation that their work would fulfil personal felt-needs for growth and influence over others. They are the obverse of the 'satisfiers' discussed in Chapter 5 and not 'dissatisfiers' deriving from the work environment.

The first decade: 'dissatisfiers'

It is possible, however, to identify three sources of dissatisfaction which were more clearly contextual, and which therefore meet Herzberg's criteria for 'dissatisfiers'. First, over half of the teachers found, or had found, schools to be uncongenial socially. Pettiness, boring or unfriendly colleagues, and the low intellectual level of staffroom discussion were most frequently mentioned. In addition, fourteen teachers spoke of isolation, lack of adult company or lack of male company (four men made this point). I take up all these points in Chapters 7 and 8.

Second, work conditions were often unsatisfactory. I visited schools where the rain dripped into a bucket on the classroom floor, where a teacher reported, 'We sweep the mouse droppings off the desks in the morning', where there were no staffrooms, or where toilet facilities were archaic and cramped. (In one school I was locked into the lavatory but was swiftly released by a child who said, 'It always does that so [the headmaster] says the person nearest the door in our classroom must listen hard and let the teachers out if they get stuck'.) Some schools were cold, or ill-ventilated, many were dirty or badly in need of decoration. To look out of the window in some schools was impossible; in others it was depressing. Altogether a fifth of my interviewees found their physical surroundings uncomfortable, unaesthetic, cramped or inconvenient.

In addition, seven (all women) complained of the lack of promotion or career prospects, and seven (five women, two men) of the poor regard in which teaching was generally held by those outside it. 'I've got a physics degree', said one woman, 'and many of my friends are involved in some sort of research. When I leave the pub saying, "I've got to go home and cut out some teddy bears", they look at me with pity'. 'I quite enjoy it,' said a man, 'but I'm leaving soon. Every time I go home all my friends say, "You're not still at that school, are you? Aren't you going to use your degree?'' '. Only two mentioned pay as a dissatisfier, but these interviews were conducted within two years of the Houghton pay award of 1975. Further, none of the teachers had at that time taught for more than nine years; the possibility of living or supporting a family on a low income in later years had perhaps not yet become a reality.

The school as 'work itself'

Many of the categories which I have so far used to analyse both 'non-satisfiers' and 'dissatisfiers' relate to the life that teachers lead inside the classroom (i.e. to the ways in which they experience teaching as work). Moreover, even those which at first glance appear to be a reflection of the context in which teaching takes place were important because of their effect upon classrooms rather than for their own sake. To be sure, all of the 'hygiene' factors which Herzberg lists as 'dissatisfiers' (i.e. policy and administration, supervision, interpersonal relations, working conditions, and salary) are to be found among teachers' negative concerns. Yet they discussed them as part of the job of teaching, not as something separate from it. In other words, factors which in other occupations may relate to job context appear in primary schools to be intimately bound up with the nature of the work itself. These teachers evidently felt that work in classrooms cannot be fully satisfying as long as there is a conflict between what they want to achieve with and for their pupils and the nature of their schools as organizations. The findings of Riseborough (1986) and Poppleton (1988) suggest that this may also be true in secondary schools. Certainly, a substantial minority of those interviewed were attempting, or had attempted, to cut themselves off from their colleagues and to concentrate their energies on teaching their classes (see Chapter 7). However, all children spend part of each working day outside their teaching areas and in the process come into contact with other adults. No matter how hard teachers try, they cannot ignore the effect upon their pupils of the overall school organization and ethos. Moreover, even in a school where teachers operate with the maximum of autonomy and the minimum of social interaction, decisions (for example, about resource allocation or disciplinary policies) taken by other members of staff, and especially the head, affect the individual's teaching, as do the actions of non-teaching staff such as caretakers, dinner supervisors and secretaries. It may well be that many of the frustrations which primary teachers suffer arise from the perpetuation of the false expectation that the job of teaching involves a relationship with children alone. They are not generally prepared by their training or by the conventional wisdom of the profession for the fact that participation in the life of the school is inseparable from teaching itself. Worse, because institutional demands prevent many teachers from working in ways which meet their own standards, they may be 'de-skilled' and, as a result, suffer frustration and dissatisfaction (see also Sarason 1982).

The second decade: 'non-satisfiers'

Any possible distinction between 'dissatisfiers' and job-related 'non-satisfiers' breaks down even further for teachers in mid-career. By the time of the second interviews there was little in the wider context of these teachers' jobs that they did not construe as part of their work, because environmental conditions were radically affecting the nature and standard of what they did and therefore of their professional self-image (see also Riseborough 1986; Poppleton 1988).

Furthermore although they named the same 'non-satisfiers' as they had a decade earlier, the weighting they gave to them altered, in some cases radically, giving further support to the suggestion made in Chapter 5 that the way in which teaching is experienced changes over time. This is consistent with Laughlin's (1984) suggestion, that Australian teachers are differently affected by four 'stressers' (pupil recalcitrance, curriculum demands, time and resource inadequacies, professional recognition) at different ages, with the last two becoming more prominent in mid-career.

Stress and fatigue

In mid-career, these teachers cited fatigue, tension and ill health as the aspects of their work that they most disliked; 84 per cent of the group mentioned one or another of them, particularly the first. These findings are repeated in the other studies of job dissatisfaction cited at the start of this chapter. As one woman said, 'No one who hasn't taught can have any idea how tired you get'. Typical comments from men and women were: 'By this stage in the term all you can think of is getting up at half past six, working all day, being exhausted at night and worrying about getting up in time'; 'What I find hardest about September is knowing how tired I'm going to get by Christmas'; 'I don't want to give up, but I do get so tired . . .'.

Even the most enthusiastic teachers talked of being 'incredibly tired', 'utterly exhausted', 'going home shattered but knowing

113

you'd got to prepare for tomorrow', 'getting run down and ill but still having to go on'. A head described how his teaching wife fell asleep as soon as she got home each day. A woman recalled meeting someone at a party who, unaware of her occupation, had said, 'They're funny people, teachers. They're always tired'. A late entrant, whose daughter had decided to teach, reported having said to her, 'You've seen me at weekends. Do you really want to finish every week feeling like that?'.

Chronic fatigue was partly a by-product of ageing (as one man said, 'I'm not as energetic as I was 10 years ago, but the work's no less'), partly of recurrent minor illnesses caught from the children. It was also due to the long hours which these teachers gave to the job, often because (in the words of one) 'If you're keen on the school you'll spend a lot of time there'. A teaching head claimed, 'My day at school is basically 7.30 am to 4.30 pm with an hour's stop and then I work at night at home — if we're busier I come in at 7.00 am'. While it was impossible to obtain any objective check on claims such as these, my interviewees constantly talked about the work which (notwithstanding industrial action) they felt impelled by their professional consciences to undertake outside teaching hours. Typically, one teacher comments:

> And there's an awful lot of work that we *have* to do in order
> to make our jobs successful — not just the marking and
> preparation for tomorrow but also the displays, the little jobs
> which take hours of time like sharpening pencils, washing
> paint pots, sorting out the collage materials, making sure the
> TV is working, booking the minibus. They're all little things,
> but they mount up.

Other commitments which were frequently mentioned were meetings with staff, parents, other schools, local authority officers, members of the educational support services, extra-curricular activities, in-service education, and supervision of students. What is not yet clear is whether the imposition in 1986/7, as part of teachers' Conditions of Service, of a contract requiring them to work 1,265 hours a year (roughly 6½ hours a day) will serve to limit the time worked by teachers like these. If it does, it may also increase their dissatisfaction with their jobs because they will not be able to do them as well as they want to. This, in turn, is likely to reduce their motivation and the effort which at present they put into their work (see Chapter 10).

Conflict with other lives

Even those who spent less time than the most conscientious on school work complained of the way in which (as one woman said), 'the children take up space in your head'. 'I didn't know when I started', one man complained, 'that I'd even think about the children in bed'. A married woman felt:

One is always the teacher, because it's always school which is the most important thing and looking at things for children. When we go out as a family and see things, I'm always thinking "could we use that in school?". My husband doesn't like it.

Another woman put it this way:

You don't actually go into teaching unless you're a caring person. And the thing about caring is that you care 24 hours a day, you don't just care from nine till half past three. So you take your worries, your thoughts, your enthusiasms home with you. I mean, when I leave here I'll go and walk round [the town] and I'll have half an eye open on what I might be doing on Monday.

Many of these teachers seemed to have accepted that work was, as one woman claimed, 'our life, not just a career'.

The corollary of this was often the curtailment of other interests and activities or a sense of tension between them (see also Spencer 1986). A man, whose wife was also a teacher, had this to say:

We used both to be involved in community activities. That has stopped, we can't keep it up. Many, many things. You mentioned gardening, the garden's gone to pot. When we have spare time we leave the town. We get in the car and we drive somewhere. Every weekend, on a Saturday we go away and we drive anywhere and wander the streets and look at the shops and drink a cup of coffee and sometimes go to a film and come back. Sometimes there's work on Sunday to do, so that's our relaxation. Apart from that, there isn't really anything else. Certainly nothing from Monday to Friday. We enter the week on Monday morning and come out of the tunnel on Friday night and we hardly see each other in between.

This kind of total involvement in work was reported by several teachers who commented that as a result they felt diminished as people. As one teacher put it:

I never do anything for me, to contribute to my own growth, not properly. These holidays, for example, I've done a lot of etching which I want to finish and it's been lovely just spending days doing it and I've got a book on landscape painters, I want to read that properly but I won't have time to do it and I know when I get back to work I'll be too involved in other things. I resent that — it makes me very unhappy and bad-tempered.

In extreme cases it led to an individual giving up teaching:

I think too much is expected of teachers very often. I would come home every night shattered at 4 o'clock with 2 or 3 hours work to do, if I was going to do my job properly. Who else has to do that? Weekends — I'd spend Saturdays sometimes rummaging round for materials, sometimes taking the kids out. I didn't have a life to myself, I really didn't. It was work, work, work . . . The long holidays just disintegrated into recovering from the terms . . . You can't just switch off at 4 o'clock, I couldn't. I think it's an awful job.

About half the group reported a specific conflict between work and family life. Five men spoke of the continuing tension between their domestic and professional commitments. One said, 'After [my son] was born, all I wanted to do at 3.45 p.m. was come home. The fact that most nights I didn't gave me a feeling of resentment'. Another told me:

It's been an ongoing dilemma. When I do things in the evenings, which I do quite often, connected with the school — things like PTA meetings, open nights, occasional kids' ice-skating –- and tell [my wife] that I'm going to be home very late, she accepts it but she doesn't like it. She still can't understand, because I go home and talk about certain teachers who give the minimum and she has said, in as many words, 'Why can't you be like them? . . . I do wonder, and I know she does, whether we would have had as many difficulties as we have had with our children, had I been there more of the time and had I devoted more of my energy to them, rather than school . . . it's been the cause of conflict several times.

Three married women with no children said (in the words of one): '[My husband] has never complained . . . but sometimes I think if he didn't have the telly to keep him in company . . . I feel the stress inside myself — you're pulling two ways'. Four women and one man reported that their enthusiasm for their jobs had contributed to the breakdown of their marriages (e.g. 'He said I was always talking about school'; 'I was working most evenings, or out at school — we saw less and less of each other') and four women said that they had regretfully decided to abandon their careers in favour of parenthood because, as one said, 'I asked other people, "How do you manage teaching and running a home?" and they all replied, "We don't!"'. One man claimed, '[Not to have children] was a conscious decision because I've always thought it would be unfair on them to be their father, because I would never have given the sort of job dedication to children that they'd deserve'.

Indeed, only three sets of circumstances seemed to leave married teachers with little or no conflict between their professional and domestic lives. The first, rarely encountered, was heavy joint investment in home-based child care. The second arose when individuals' partners were as involved in their own jobs as they were in theirs so that, as several people (mainly women) said, 'He doesn't resent the fact we hardly ever meet in the week because he's as involved in his work as I am in mine', or, 'It's alright because we know that we'll see each other in the holidays'. The third pattern was more traditional than the other two: one partner (in all but three cases the woman) treated her career as being of secondary importance. Yet even in these cases, tension between the demands of teaching and those of the home was always there in the background, 'waiting', as one woman said, 'to catch you unawares when you least need it'.

Conditions within schools

There were other causes of fatigue and tension too. An important one, as in the early interviews, was the existence of conditions within the schools which made it difficult for individuals to feel they were teaching well or which gave them a sense of teaching badly. However, the tendency now was to focus upon large classes, lack of appropriate resources, and the stress associated with controlling disruptive children rather than on factors such as inefficient administration and poor communication within the school as a whole.

Two-thirds of my interviewees disliked teaching when they had large classes with insufficient support from, for instance, ancillaries or special needs services, or had inadequate resources (e.g. books, mathematical or scientific equipment, transport facilities). Their usual complaint was that in these circumstances particular children made less progress than they seemed to be capable of. One in three deplored lack of time — 'to stand back and observe the

117

children', 'to work with parents as partners', 'to find out what children do in the rest of the school', 'to reflect', 'to cover the whole curriculum properly'. A quarter did not like teaching specific curriculum areas, most commonly because they did not feel they did it well. Three mentioned lack of parental backing.

These perceived constraints often contributed to problems with individual children who were seen as preventing their teachers from helping either them or other pupils to learn. Just under half my interviewees spoke of particular pupils who, from time to time or in specific classes, had undermined their confidence in their own professional abilities. One man confessed, 'I remember thinking, "If I have another year like this, I think I'll give up teaching, because I'm making such a poor job of it"'. Others recalled, 'I hated [that year] when I was spending more time policing and controlling than teaching, no matter which way I turned or how I tried to work it', and, 'There was that nucleus of boys who for most of the year managed to stop me doing much teaching'. Specific classes or, more often, children, stuck in their minds as 'awkward', 'disastrous', 'difficult' or, 'almost impossible to handle'. One woman said, 'All the teachers in that school got frustrated because we weren't doing the job we'd trained for; we were doing emergency social work — like working on a social fire brigade'. Three women also found encounters with unruly children to be particularly 'draining' or 'exhausting' because, in the words of one, 'It was your will against his will and you could either let him go and say "I don't care about him" — which I never could — or you could keep battling and end up a prison officer. Then you'd get angry because you'd let him make you into something you know you aren't and don't want to be'. As I argued in Chapter 4, pupils remain 'significant others' for teachers of all lengths of experience and retain the capacity to undermine their self-confidence and self-esteem.

Such channelling of effort into control rather than teaching was most likely to occur in areas where, as someone in an inner city, multi-ethnic school said, 'You live on a knife-edge, never knowing who will erupt, over what. You have to watch and be ready to intervene every moment of the day — as well as try to teach them something'. Another teacher argued, 'What grinds you down in the end is that everything, even the simplest things, becomes a battle. You never feel you can do a good job, especially for the children'. A woman head put it this way:

> It is so personally and emotionally draining that I think after two years you really have not got anything left to give. You

get very hard and cynical about the demands that people make on you . . . You can see this mostly at case conferences with children at risk — 'never mind it's only a little bruise' — and once you get to that stage you're ready to go somewhere else. What I mean is that a lot of what happens ceases to be shocking, it becomes the norm, and when you recognize that in yourself I think it is definitely time to go.

Environmental conditions such as these were particularly damaging to teachers' morale when they were compounded by staffs who did not 'pull together' (see Chapter 8). Taken together, such conditions made many teachers feel intermittently depressed. All of my interviewees said that they sometimes felt, and about a third argued that it was for much of the time, that no matter how hard they worked, they were failing to do the best that was possible for all their pupils. They knew they were sometimes at fault (e.g. 'When I haven't done the marking the night before and I'm not quite properly organized for thirty-five children'), but their capacity for self-blame exceeded what they knew was reasonable. A man summed it up: 'You blame yourself, even though you know that you can't expect to get it right for everyone all the time, in such a large class'.

Lack of personal extension

Paradoxically, although many of these teachers complained of finding their jobs tiring and stressful, they also expressed fears about becoming 'stale' or 'complacent'. A third were unhappy that they were 'just going through the motions', 'stagnating', 'losing the excitement', 'getting in a rut'. Most of them attributed 'creeping boredom' (as one expressed it) to the influence of their colleagues rather than their pupils and I have therefore returned to this point in greater detail in Chapter 8.

Conflict with individual principles

The biggest reported numerical change was in the number of people who felt that they were ideologically uncomfortable in their schools. With two exceptions, teachers now had a reference group or person in their schools to support their social, political or educational principles (see Chapter 8). Rather than complaining of their isolation, they tended to compare their present situation favourably with a previous one, candidly revealing their own perspectives. For example, one teacher told me:

I'll tell you why I wasn't particularly happy at [that school]
. . . It was all to do with the Asian community. The headmaster and myself had greatly opposing views on the Asians,
whereas [here] the head and I have very similar views . . .
[There] the head bent over backwards to give the Asians their
own culture — if the mosque man said 'don't do it' the
schools didn't do it . . . It was regarded as more important
that the teachers went on courses for Asian languages than
that the children were brought into the English system. I never
felt I did a good job there . . . [Here] it's different.

While another said:

[At that school] I didn't enjoy the sort of con trick that the
children and I had to operate in order to survive. We came to
some sort of working agreement that they would do the
minimum and therefore behave. I didn't like that, though I
think it was fairly common in schools in that area — the
other teachers did it in my school and the standards were
pretty low as a result.

Lack of influence

One in four teachers complained that their job left them feeling
impotent or lacking influence in their schools. This fact may seem
surprising, given the number who had achieved promotion to head,
deputy or curriculum leader. It may, however, be the result of
changing perceptions of how influence is exercised in the educational system (see Chapter 4) and it is certainly related to an
increase among my interviewees in the number of part-time and
temporary teachers, a group to whom I return towards the end of
this chapter.

Lack of autonomy

Although the vast majority now felt that in their schools their most
cherished values and principles as teachers were safeguarded by the
existence of an in-school reference group, they were not so
sanguine about encroachments from outside the school into their
freedom to teach what and how they judged best. Nearly a third
expressed experiences of or anxieties relating to the actions of local
or central government. They talked of school amalgamations, local
authority staffing and curricular policies, parental 'interference',
fears of increasing centralization in the education system: 'I find

restrictions imposed from outside incense me, because I know I'm not doing what I want to do with the children. I have to impose something whether a child is ready for it or not'. A woman said:

The ambitious side of me has always wanted to have its own school but I would never be a deputy or head in a state school. If I had my own school it'd be a private school . . . (Why?) Because there's so much interference — you cannot run the place as you want to. It doesn't matter what your philosophies are or what you believe is best for your children, there's so much interference now, so much administrative work.

A man feared: 'If I was told exactly what to teach and how to teach it and it became an uncreative job . . . then I'd leave'. Since, however, it is hard to distinguish these kinds of concerns from context-related 'dissatisfiers', they are treated more extensively in the next section.

The second decade: 'dissatisfiers'

Although from early to mid-career 'non-satisfiers' remain generally the same, but with different ratings, 'dissatisfiers' change markedly in three ways. First, in the early interviews there was not a great deal of conflict within individuals between job satisfaction and non-satisfaction on the one hand, and job dissatisfaction on the other. In other words, in the mid-1970s most of those who liked their work and wanted to do it well also saw it as offering a satisfactory long-term career. By contrast, in the mid-1980s, a majority loved their work but had serious doubts about their willingness or capacity to sustain a career within the profession. They were, in short, both very satisfied and very dissatisfied, a finding which is strongly confirmed for secondary teachers by Riseborough (1986), Poppleton *et al.* (1987), Poppleton (1988). Second is the related fact that teachers in the early interviews expressed relatively little dissatisfaction with teaching as a career; whereas, later on, their bitterness and frustration in this respect were unanimous and vehement (see also Riseborough and Poppleton who found a similar distinction between the views expressed by 'novitiates' and 'veterans', but who attribute it solely to the effects of national educational policy). On the face of it, these developments confirm Herzberg's hypothesis about the separation of 'satisfiers' and 'dissatisfiers'. However, underlying them is a more general third trend: over time it becomes increasingly hard to classify any aspect of teachers' job dissatisfaction as 'contextual'. Since this progressive broadening of teachers' concerns encompasses and explains the other two points, it forms the heart of the argument in the following section.

Insufficient resources

As they talked, these experienced teachers made little distinction between what they saw happening to teaching as a job and how they perceived it as a profession in which they could with integrity sustain a career. So, to classify large classes or inadequate resources and support services as 'non-satisfiers' (as I did in an earlier section) is unnaturally to divorce them from the political and economic developments which contributed to their existence. The same is true of teachers' comments on the physical conditions in which they worked. Although an increased proportion of my interviewees complained in the mid-1980s about the material nature or state of their schools and classrooms, without exception they related their comments to the effect such conditions had upon their pupils' ability to learn or upon their own health (and therefore upon their efficiency and effectiveness). Sometimes, buildings and furniture had a direct effect upon their physical well-being (e.g. 'It sounds silly but the bending is just at the wrong level for my back and sometimes at the end of a day I could cry with pain'; 'The ventilation [in my new open-plan school] is terrible. Even in moderately warm weather I go home with a headache and in the summer it's appalling. We go out of doors whenever we can'; 'It isn't that the children are particularly noisy, but the space is too small and when there's a run of wet playtimes I get terrible headaches'). More often, however, their effect was indirect; overcrowding and discomfort resulted in increased stress (e.g. 'In the mobile, in the winter, the gas heaters in the ceiling overheat our heads and our feet are like ice. At the end of the day I'm screaming'; 'There's nowhere in the school you can relax even for 2 minutes. The staffroom's so small that we can't all stretch our feet out at the same time without hitting each other. Even the lavatory is full of the caretaker's stores'). In addition, tempers were frayed by equipment (e.g. scissors, glue) which did not work and by the need to economize over basic materials (e.g. 'Nagging about one inch of pencil — it wears you down'). Peeling walls, leaking ceilings, broken windows and vandalism also had an adverse effect upon morale. One woman summed it up: 'At the beginning of term you can cope with these sorts of things, but later on the pressure builds up and you begin to get ill and have to take time off — and what happens to the children then?'.

Teachers were also sharply aware that longer-term developments which they believed were important to children's education were being prevented or retarded by a shortage of money. One teacher complained:

We've got books, I'm not saying we haven't, but they are so old, and so out of date . . . and there's so little money, you can't improve anything. We've started staff discussions on curriculum development, but it's frustrating if we decide we'll do that, that and that and then realize we can't buy anything until this time next year.

Other typical complaints were: 'When we should be talking about curriculum development, we're discussing where to put the buckets when it rains'; 'How can we teach science adequately with practically no equipment and no one on the staff with any qualifications in it?'.

A quarter also told me they found it difficult to live on their salaries. However, as these interviews took place during a prolonged period of dispute with central government over pay and conditions of service, their replies may have been more heavily weighted in this direction than would otherwise have been the case. I have, therefore, chosen not to elaborate this point further, although my judgement was that their complaints about pay were, in general, phrased with moderation, reflected a genuine sense of economic hardship, and expressed a longstanding grievance.

Public image of teaching

A chronic shortage of money for staff salaries, buildings and resources had a further and equally damaging effect upon staff morale. It suggested to teachers, already conscious of working long hours, often in difficult physical conditions, that they were held in low esteem, not just by politicians but by the parents of the children on and for whom they expended energy, time, thought and, on occasion, their own resources. A typical comment came from a male head:

Every now and again I get quite down about it — why the hell do I waste my time, nobody in the government cares, nobody down at the office cares, nobody out there cares, so why should I care?

Another man said:

I think the pay dispute is symptomatic of something a lot deeper seated, like the status teachers have. In a sense, that doesn't particularly bother me personally, because if people around you see the good job you're doing you will be treated in the way that you want. But at a national level, if we don't reward teachers for the hard work and dedication that goes into the job we won't get people coming in who're any good.

His view that the complexity of teachers' tasks was underestimated and their commitment to it undervalued, was echoed over and over again by people at all levels of seniority. Selecting examples has been a difficult task because there were so many of them. Moreover, print gives no indication of the passion and despair with which both men and women spoke:

Basically I am fed up with being attacked. I'm particularly fed up being told I don't have any commitment . . . What really gets to me is the fact that people don't really value the profession and don't trust us and don't think that we care.

You spend lots of time on development in all aspects of the curriculum and then you get criticisms from the Education Secretary, parents, people on the street, who are all telling you how to do your job, as if you aren't a bit interested and you don't care and you have no professional ideas or abilities of your own. I think that at the moment this is the most disheartening thing. Faced with large classes and a large number of difficult children, you're doing your best to do the best job you can for the children . . . And the parents — a lot of them don't care. Yet that doesn't stop people from telling you how to do your job, without them really knowing.

It's making me think twice about, for example, doing a part-time job again — do I really need it? Financially we're not that desperate . . . But do I really need to go in and do a difficult job and then be told by all sides that I'm not doing it properly? When I know how hard I'm working and how much I put into it.

Everyone thinks they can 'do teaching' . . . [It's like] parent governors [who] can demonstrate considerable ignorance of the school, but tell us what we should be doing anyway.

Parents think we are glorified child-minders. I suppose I would carry on simply because we do a good job here, even if no one says so, but it is depressing that we are so badly regarded, because people think teaching young children is so easy.

However, one in six of my interviewees argued that teachers had to some extent brought upon themselves this public underestimation of their work-load and its complexity. Not all teachers, they felt, worked as hard as they did (as one head said, 'The problems of getting all the staff to pull their weight, that irritates the hell out of me. I mean I can see people who are collecting their money virtually without breaking sweat and others who are killing themselves'). Nor did they think that all teachers were as effective as they should be. Indeed, none of my interviewees opposed the idea of teacher appraisal — a third welcomed it — though most voiced anxieties about the way in which it would take place and how the results would be used.

Career concerns

Finally, teachers were anxious about their own careers and especially about their long-term prospects for promotion. Yet even these concerns were often expressed in terms of self-esteem or of perceived constraints upon the realization of personal potential (see also Sikes 1986; Riseborough 1986). Teachers spoke with anxiety of 'good people getting stuck', of 'those who haven't got promotion being bitter and frustrated and worse teachers because of it', of 'good teachers losing heart because they have nowhere to go'. They wanted to take on additional responsibilities, to extend their spheres of influence and were afraid that if their efforts continually met with lack of reward or recognition they would begin to put less into the job. For these teachers diminished career prospects appeared to relate much more closely to an expressed dread of professional stagnation than they did to material incentives.

Women had three additional concerns. Nine commented on the difficulties they had encountered, or were still attempting to overcome, in returning to teaching after child-rearing (see also Biklen 1985; Grant 1986; Acker 1987). Seven reported that they could get jobs only as supply teachers or, occasionally, as part-time or temporary teachers. Eight more, already holding senior management posts, commented on the difficulties which women, especially those with children, faced in obtaining headships, while two Roman Catholics whose husbands had left them felt that they no longer had any future in the voluntary sector in which, they claimed, divorced women would not be promoted. In consequence, several women who perceived themselves as 'having no promotion prospects in schools' had moved or were hoping to move into teacher education. Yet, as one said, 'If I had had any real faith that, as a woman, I would have got a deputy headship, I would certainly have stayed in schools'.

Self-esteem and extension: supply, temporary and part-time posts

Many of the points which were made in the last section are exemplified in the experience of supply, temporary or part-time teachers (i.e. people who do not have permanent full-time posts and who therefore are seen, or see themselves, as peripheral to the main preoccupations of the rest of the staff). In this section I use the experience of seven women, and two men who had full-time 'floating' posts for a year, to illustrate the fundamental importance, as 'dissatisfiers', of low self-esteem and of lack of opportunity to realize the perceived potential of the self.

This is not to suggest that everyone's experience of these kinds of teaching posts was negative. Supply teachers take the place of permanent staff who are temporarily absent from school (e.g. for sickness, on courses). They have the right to decline the opportunity to work in particular schools or areas and, in places where there is a shortage of supply teachers, this gives them considerable power, especially over head teachers. The perceived advantages of supply teaching are: it fits in well with the demands of child-rearing; it enables teachers to gain experience of a number of different age-groups, curriculum materials, types of classroom organization and teaching, staffrooms and schools; and it offers a gradual way of returning to permanent, full-time employment. 'Floating' also provides opportunities for varied experience — a school may decide to release one member of staff from class responsibilities, for a finite period, in order to use him/her for other purposes (usually specialist teaching of classes or small groups) in different parts of the school. Temporary posts are similar to supply teaching in that they involve filling in short-term gaps in a school's permanent teaching staff (caused, for example, by secondment or maternity leave). They are normally full-time but give no security of tenure. Newly qualified teachers unable to obtain a permanent post, experienced teachers moving to a new area, or teachers seeking to return to full-time work (e.g. after child-rearing or a stay abroad) are the most likely candidates for temporary posts. Part-time teaching may be permanent but is, by definition, less than full-time and is often in a specific curriculum area (e.g. music, special needs, or English as a second language). It is possible to teach part-time in more than one school. Like supply or temporary teaching, part-time contracts offer probationers, experienced teachers who have moved house, and would-be returners a foothold in an overcrowded profession. They are also much sought after by people wishing to combine teaching with another career (notably child-rearing).

Given then that these types of post offer some people (especially married women, see Chapter 5) a chance to vary their professional experience and build idiosyncratic careers, it may be surprising to discover how unsatisfying they often are to those who fill them. In general, my interviewees spoke with disappointment, resentment, or frustration about their time as temporary, supply, or part-time teachers. Working in these capacities they found it hard to teach as they wanted to, to think of themselves as 'real teachers', and to participate fully in the wider life of the school. Their most common complaints were not being able to reach the level of performance, for themselves or their pupils, to which they were accustomed and the frustration engendered by the resulting need to accept lower professional standards. As one woman recalled:

During the five years of part-time work, I kept on thinking, 'One day it'll be real again, one day I'll be doing the real thing'. I suppose seeing so many people who don't do it very well, you just keep thinking, 'One day I'll be able to get back in my own classroom and do my own thing and make a good job of it'.

There were two particular obstacles to making 'a good job of it'. In the first place, it was not easy to establish a trusting relationship with children whom individuals saw irregularly or for a short time. As a result, control was often difficult:

They knew I was only temporary; they were used to temporary teachers — why should they bother building up a relationship with me if I was going away like all the rest?

Their attitude towards me is that they just don't care what I think of them and it makes it hard to find any common ground . . . A lot of them just don't care because you're only part-time. In little ways they show, not a lack of respect so much, as a lack of consideration. That makes it more difficult.

Secondly, building a relationship with children could be made more difficult by the absence of physical provision for part-time and 'floating' teachers:

That's where I met my friend who was also part-time. We both sat in the corridor, taking slow readers . . . I suppose my ambition is to have my own class again with the right furniture and the right equipment, instead of other people's cast-offs.

There was one other little set of desks which was right outside my old classroom, but they were surrounded by toilets and cloakrooms . . . you could be moved about all over the place . . . It was a case of just finding a quiet corner and getting on with it.

Until you're on top of it with all the equipment (and it's difficult to get that as a part-timer), you don't feel the children's work is flowing as it should.

The constraints of time and space were compounded by the attitude of some heads and class teachers who, my interviewees bitterly felt, simply wanted them for what they called 'child-minding'. One woman expressed her views:

At some schools, they say, 'Just go along and find something to do!'. That's dreadful. . . . I kept thinking 'This is ridiculous. I'm being paid to do odd jobs'. And being shouted at — 'Mrs. Thingy, would you like to cut out these hand prints'. Two mornings cutting out hand prints. 'Mrs. Thingy, when you've got a minute — sharpen my pencils'. I said 'I'll draw the lines in their books if you like'. 'Oh no, I'll do that'. It was one of those schools, they thought you weren't capable.

In addition, they all felt their previous experience was discounted. A few put it mildly:

Perhaps if people were aware of what responsibilities you'd had in other schools that would help. I think when a member of staff joins a school there could be more of an introduction made, on what they've done in the past. You tend to just start on day one and people find out about you later.

It is frustrating in a way because once you've lost your promotion there's no recognition made of the fact that you ever deserved it. You're then back to where you started, it doesn't count for anything.

Others were more overtly angry:

Well, this girl obviously thought I'd come back to work after a 10-year absence. She said, 'Yesterday we did the Activity Books, today we're doing 'F' but we call it 'f' with infants' . . . And I went back to her classroom and thought, 'I can't take this much longer'.

This job — as a so-called 'remedial teacher' — is the only one I could get. And I had a Scale 3 for language in my last job. So here I am doing things I don't approve of and watching someone else do the language job here that I *know* I could do better. But no one ever asks you what you did before.

I came here first as a supply teacher so no one knows I was a deputy before I had my children . . . They never ask, and if you're an ordinary teacher you can't tell them.

Nor did they feel they were seen as members of their school staffs. Instead they were 'on the periphery', 'just a spare part', 'filling in'. In consequence, they felt undervalued or excluded, either by default or because they were actually prevented from making a contribution to staff discussions:

I tell myself that I don't really mind being left out. I suppose in a way it's a form of defence mechanism against being hurt by not being involved. It's amazing how I can toss things off now that would have mortified me years ago. Like 'you take the school for a long play while we have a staff meeting' — that used to really upset me when I first started doing part-time . . . Now I just think 'Oh here we go again' . . . I do now know how I would never ever treat my own staff.

You don't get told things. You know they don't do it deliberately, it's just that you aren't there when the decision's made and they forget to tell you. In a way you get used to not counting.

It's frustrating in some ways. For example, at staff meetings I know that when we are discussing the curriculum it doesn't really affect me as much as everybody else. But I think it shouldn't be like that really, because although I'm on temporary contract now, I'm still making a contribution and some of the things that they're planning in the curriculum depend on me being there. I don't think that people mean to exclude you but you're not taken into account the same as an ordinary member of staff and that's quite difficult . . . For example, I can stay for staff meetings on a Tuesday and Wednesday but they started arranging them for Monday . . . My protest was noted, but it didn't make any difference, you know. Without meaning to, the staff are excluding you from the group.

The cumulative effect of these working conditions was a damaging loss of professional and personal self-esteem:

My training and skills weren't being used, I didn't feel they were appreciated in supply teaching . . . my self-confidence began to go.

When I was full-time, I was an important person to the kids, but [as a part-timer] I'm just somebody who comes in on Thursdays and they don't care about me.

I can remember that confidence I felt because I'd been [at that school] a long time and I knew all the staff, I knew the children and I knew the parents . . . I would like that feeling back again, not so much that you're important but that you are as important as everybody else.

I find in a lot of schools they tend to think 'Oh great, here's a part-timer, let's give her the riff-raff' . . . I always get on well with the caretakers and the lollipop ladies and the teachers' aides, because they are the lowest of the low, like me.

To these self-doubts was added a sense of injustice, for, as these teachers were quick to tell me, 'I wouldn't be doing much more work if I had a full-time job than I am in a part-time one'. As one reflected, 'No one seems to realize how much thought and effort goes into being a *good* supply teacher . . . In a lot of ways, it's harder than having a class of your own'. Done well, they said, such teaching involved flexibility, sensitivity, vigilance, and a great deal of preparation (e.g. 'That's another thing, every time you come into a school where there's a new reading scheme, or maths scheme or age group, you need new materials'). Yet the circumstances in which they taught tended to leave them feeling not just frustrated, deskilled, undervalued, and impotent, but also lacking the affective and professional rewards of long-term involvement with children and with whole school development. No wonder they felt as one said, 'I wouldn't consider doing part-time again, I would want to do full-time. And permanent too, if I could. I don't want any more temporary posts. It's just not worth it, if you're keen on the job and want to do it well'.

Conclusion

Herzberg's hypothesis was chosen as a framework for analysis of teachers' job satisfaction and dissatisfaction, because his separation of 'satisfiers' relating to 'work itself' and 'dissatisfiers' deriving from the context in which work is set appeared to offer one way of organising teachers' understanding and experience of the job they daily perform. In Chapter 5 I presented evidence which supports his notion that teachers' satisfaction is associated very strongly in both early and mid-career with the nature of the work they do and how they perceive it and very weakly with the conditions under which they work. Support for the idea that dissatisfaction stems from contextual factors is much less easier to find. Indeed, in early career, most of the things that my interviewees 'did not like' about their jobs related to teaching itself. I have called these factors 'non-satisfiers' because, once they were remediated, job satisfaction was increased.

The early interviews also revealed a handful of 'dissatisfiers' which seemed unambiguously contextual. Yet in mid-career even this distinction breaks down. To be sure, in the second set of interviews most teachers voiced many dissatisfactions arising from pay, career structure, and the physical condition of schools. But they made it clear that their major concern was the effect of such conditions upon their standard of work. Their ability to teach well was, they claimed, adversely affected both directly (e.g. through large classes and scarce resources) and indirectly (through lowered self-esteem and reduced opportunities for self-extension). Similar conclusions were drawn by the PSRDG's (1986) survey of 135 primary teachers and by Poppleton's (1988) survey of 700 secondary teachers.

Furthermore, from the teachers' perspective, most of the other factors which Herzberg lists as 'contextual' (e.g. administration, staff relations, institutional policy, supervision of work) are an integral part of work itself. This is in part because, as we have seen, teaching is an activity imbued with individual values which cannot be completely insulated from the principles which inform the work of other teachers. It takes place within a social system (the school) whose culture and history impinge upon both teachers and pupils and whose structures (e.g. of decision-making and resource-allocation) themselves reflect the values embedded in them. So, aspects of institutional life which might in other institutions be deemed contextual are, for teachers, a necessary part of their daily work.

A conscious readiness to see the whole school, rather than just the classroom, as 'work itself' also appears to be associated with the development of personal concerns (see Chapter 4). The later interviews reveal (Table 6.1) that two sources of dissatisfaction are much less frequently mentioned in mid-career than in the early years. These are: 'uncongenial colleagues' and 'aspects of work [which] conflict with my principles' (both of which Herzberg would label as extrinsic, 'hygiene' factors). This trend offers *prima facie* support for the claim made in Chapter 4, that by or towards the end of their first decade teachers find a school in which they have

131

referential support and in which they are therefore ready to stay. Taken with the reported rise in job satisfactions deriving from contact with colleagues (see Chapter 5), it suggests that teachers' relationships with fellow staff members change in nature as well as degree as their experience increases. Or, to put it another way, 'work' comes to mean deliberately relating to and working with adults as well as pupils.

In short, Herzberg's hypothesis cannot be applied uncritically to primary schools. If everything that goes on outside schools as well as within them can affect teachers' satisfaction with, and therefore perception and experience of, their work, it offers an analytic tool too blunt to make much contribution to our understanding of teachers' subjective realities. However, separating 'satisfiers' from 'dissatisfiers' does serve two useful purposes, even though it does not do justice to the complexity of the environment in which teachers work or to the impact of this upon their daily experience. First, it allows us to highlight the continuing importance to teachers of what they do in classrooms; over two decades teaching itself remained both the most satisfying and the most dissatisfying aspect of its practitioners' occupational lives. Second, it emphasizes the importance of the self. Not only were all these teachers' 'satisfiers' and 'non-satisfiers' self-referential but so too were the 'dissatisfiers'. The real salience of the 'contextual' factors causing acute dissatisfaction in the mid-1980s lay not in their effect on personal comfort or material well-being, but in their impact on the teachers' professional values (and thus their self-image), on their sense of self-esteem, and on their desire for autonomy and for self-extension.

It remains to look briefly at the differences in job dissatisfaction which emerge from a comparison of the two sets of interviews (bearing in mind the difficulties outlined in Chapter 5 in making valid comparisons between them). A simple classification of the sources of dissatisfaction in mid-career appears in Table 6.1.

Overall, there was a substantial growth in the level of job dissatisfaction, in almost every category, between the mid-1970s and the mid-1980s. The total number of 'mentions' made by 99 teachers in the first decade was 366. Ten years later it had increased considerably (287), relative to the size of the group (50). Certain categories in particular are mentioned noticeably more often, by more people. These are: stress and fatigue; poor working conditions; and lack of autonomy. Now the increased incidence of the last two factors is, I have argued, largely due to changes in the political and economic climate, and in particular to: falling relative salaries; increased class sizes; cuts in resources and neglect of

Table 6.1 Sources of job dissatisfaction: first and second decades

	First decade			Second decade		
	Numbers % (n = 99)		'Mentions'	Numbers % (n = 50)		'Mentions'
Factors outside the class-room making it difficult to teach well	74		100	67		58
Stress and fatigue	62		79	84		83
Uncongenial colleagues	52		55	20		14
Conflict with individual principles	44		44	2		2
Conditions of work	35		38	86		73
Lack of personal extension	23		23	33		18
Lack of influence	20		20	25		16
Lack of autonomy	7		7	30		25

buildings; and perceived encroachments into teachers' control over classroom practice, staffing, and curricular policies, by parents and by local and central government. All of these factors affect teachers' self-esteem, since each is interpreted as an adverse reflection upon their skills, expertise, commitment, and public value.

Increased stress, however, cannot be so easily attributed to environmental factors. Chapter 5 established that committed mid-career teachers enjoy their work and the evidence presented in this chapter endorses how much of themselves and their lives they give to it. Moreover, a recent study comparing primary teachers in England and France (Broadfoot and Osborn 1986) found that English teachers were more likely to believe they held a responsibility for all aspects of their pupils' lives and to acknowledge the rights of others to make demands on them. In other words, some of the stress and fatigue they experience is undeniably self-induced (an aspect of teaching as work which is explored in Chapter 9). Notwithstanding, the impact of local and central government policies upon the education service during the 1980s also increased the strain upon teachers, and the more involved with their jobs they were, the more they appeared to have felt it. A spiral evidently exists: committed mid-career teachers work hard, to a high standard and, as a result, get very tired. At the same time, they are conscious of being publicly undervalued, underestimated, and under-resourced, all of which adds to the strains upon them. The harder they work to maintain the values, principles and standards they believe in, the more fatigued they become and the greater the discrepancy between their own perception of what they achieve and the public image they experience. Yet they cannot cut themselves off from this image. It daily enters their classrooms through their pupils and the latter's parents, and their schools through parents and governors. Small wonder then that tension from the environment compounds the strains and fatigues of the job, and that ill health results. Small wonder, too, that 'burnout' (Kremer and Hofman 1985) is a growing problem in the teaching profession.

I pick up these strands in Chapter 9. As a prelude to this, I next look at those aspects of the work of teaching which involve contact with head teachers and colleagues. As Table 6.1 suggests, between early and mid-career many teachers are successful in finding a school where they like and can work harmoniously with some or all of their colleagues. At the same time, their felt-need for personal growth increases. Chapter 8 addresses both these developments; Chapter 7 by contrast examines staff relationships solely in terms of support and affiliation.

Chapter seven

Life in staffrooms:
dependence and interdependence

Teachers' continuing preoccupation with pupils should not be taken to mean either that other adults in their schools are unimportant to them or that they have no contact with them. Indeed, the reverse is true. Head teachers and colleagues often help inexperienced teachers to shape and develop the professional competence which they desire to achieve, not simply by providing referential support for their self-defining values (see Chapter 3) but also by offering advice, guidance, assistance, and reinforcement. Practical and emotional support of this kind remains a significant feature of the teacher's life in later years, for not even the skilled and self-confident are immune to the daily ups and downs of classroom life.

In this chapter, I analyse the ways in which teachers use their colleagues as models, as 'professional parents', to provide ideas, information and practical help, for emotional support and for friendship. I also pick out the main factors that seem to prevent the development of whole staff groups among whom individuals can feel personally and professionally relaxed and secure, and from whom they can therefore draw the emotional reassurance and strength which their work demands.

Relevant material came from several places, a fact which itself reflects the important but tangential nature of staff relationships in teachers' lives. I started out with a fairly naïve view of the topic, as my early questions reflect: Did you get all the help you wanted in your first job(s)? From whom? Why not? How did you learn how to behave in this school? Have you at any point consciously used another teacher as a model? But I also found the answers to my questions about job satisfaction and dissatisfaction threw up constant references to head teachers and colleagues, and that some of my most powerful insights into the lives of adults in primary schools came almost incidentally. In the second interviews I chose once again to approach the subject obliquely. So, I asked no direct questions about staff relationships, but instead followed up any references to them which came in other responses (e.g. Which has been your favourite job so far? Why?). The early part of this chapter draws mainly on material from the first interviews, for it was in their first decade of work that these teachers were most aware of needing to learn the knowledge and skills of their craft. The later part uses responses from both sets of interviews.

The fact that teachers appear to become more incisively aware of their relationships with their colleagues as they mature may in itself be a reflection of cognitive development, of a growing capacity to de-centre (see Chapter 4). It may also be that their recurrent search for friendship and reassurance within the staff group points not only to the taxing nature of their work with children but also to their continuing need, particularly in times of stress, for contact with adults who will affirm their self-worth and mirror for them an idealized picture of strength and concern (see Chapter 1). As Kohut (1971) argues, the fact that we are able to revert during periods of tension to child-like levels of self-regard and to a felt-need for the care and protection of a stronger 'other' whom we see as an extension of ourselves, may in the long term help us to fashion more realistic and adaptable 'selves'.

Modelling

No matter how good their pre-service education is, initiates into any occupation experience a 'reality shock' when they take on its full responsibilities. As my interviewees were quick to tell me during our first conversations, no amount of teaching practice adequately prepares a probationer for the reality of class-teaching 5 days a week throughout the year. Few of them felt fully competent when they began and many recalled wanting to know more about other teachers' routines, habits, and ways of behaving. Not surprisingly, it was therefore to their colleagues that they most often looked in their first appointments, for examples of craft skill and knowledge in action.

Unfortunately, such examples were hard to find because teachers in primary schools are seldom visible to one another except 'backstage' (as in the staffroom) or in public places such as corridors and the hall. They found that, apart from in open-plan schools or team-teaching situations, their colleagues' interactions with pupils were normally hidden by classroom walls. As one woman said, 'I don't know how successful teachers behave'. My interviewees overwhelmingly wanted more opportunity than they had been given to watch their colleagues and in the process to learn from the latter's expertise. Deprived of the chance to observe, they relied instead on inference, extrapolation, and imagination in constructing their pictures of 'what real teachers do'. Even so, one in three recalled a teacher, and a few a head teacher, in their first or second school who, they claimed, had had a lasting influence on the way they wanted to teach. If one includes those who remembered such a person from teaching practice or a period of unqualified teaching, the figure rises to nearly half. Yet the main characteristic shared by these models was not a professional one. Time after time they turn out to have shared an open-plan unit with the speaker, to have had an adjacent or nearby classroom and/or to have taught a parallel class. Because they were therefore visible, or at least accessible, my interviewees could hear (if not see) them teaching, borrow or copy materials, gather ideas, plan joint ventures, discuss problems and possibilities.

Lacking such help, a further tenth of the teachers deliberately drew on recollections of teachers whose pupils they had been; for, as Lortie (1975: 64) reminds us, all teachers have themselves been pupils, and so 'many are influenced by their own teachers in ways they do not even perceive'. Past models were recalled from all sectors of education from primary schools to college and university, and appear to have shared no common characteristics. In addition, one or two people had idealized memories of teachers whose classrooms they had visited during their pre-service education. This tendency to draw on personal experience as pupils and students persisted even after many years of experience, particularly when individuals took on roles or responsibilities for which they felt unprepared. Twelve years into his career, one man wrote:

> I have been asked to take over the science . . . I find myself drawing on A-level biology and O-level geology and memories of physics and chemistry which go further back than that . . . It gives me some idea of what I ought to be doing.

Yet, valuable though such recollections evidently are in the absence of actual exemplars, Lortie (1975: 65) is probably right to argue that 'modelling the mentor' reduces the status of the profession by reinforcing the notion that 'those who have been pupils are equipped to be teachers'.

One teacher in five also felt that at some point they had used one or more of their colleagues as negative role models (i.e. as examples of attitudes or practices which they wished to eschew). However, since much of the conduct that they did not wish to emulate was either inferred from staffroom behaviour and from glimpses of teaching, classrooms, or materials, or took place in public parts of the school, their sense of 'the sort of teacher I don't want to be' was based on knowledge as partial as that which informed their choice of positive exemplars.

Setting a standard

Inexperienced teachers sometimes had difficulty not so much in knowing how 'real teachers' behaved, but in sustaining the standards of occupational competence with which they entered the profession (see Chapter 2). So they looked for referential support to their head teachers and, to a lesser extent, senior colleagues. They particularly valued those heads who set a high standard and who displayed considerable personal involvement with the school (e.g. 'The standards of everything in this school come from the head'; 'She had such a high standard herself . . . She was never late, always ready to talk after school, could give you really practical help. If she did anything, like an assembly, you knew it would be well done. There was always something to live up to'; 'The head here is outstanding. His enthusiasm is infectious, he's always around and he sets us a wonderful example of involvement and hard work'). They also praised heads who were accessible (e.g. 'She came in every day, usually after school; she suggested, praised, gave advice. I really appreciated that'), those who worked long hours, who were occupied in school time with school matters (as opposed to professional association activities, or other concerns such as being a JP or a councillor), and those who attended extra-curricular events (e.g. 'To be a good head you have to be totally involved . . . She is, so we all are'; 'It's his school really, but . . . he manages to make us feel it's all of ours'). The memory of such leaders was indelible; as Sikes *et al.* (1985: 133) found to be true for secondary teachers, 'working for a charismatic head is a very special experience, one by which teachers measure their job satisfaction and commitment under other heads'.

Heads helped their less experienced colleagues set and maintain a good standard of classroom performance in other ways: by efficient administration; by ensuring that appropriate resources were readily to hand and that classroom planning could take place within a framework of shared understandings and sound communication; by helping to create a supportive climate for individual control and discipline; and by taking a lead in establishing common aims for the school which enabled individuals to perceive the value of their own contribution in a common enterprise.

'Professional parents'

However inspiring, dedicated or efficient the leadership of their schools, almost every inexperienced teacher at some point also wanted practical help with classroom problems. Yet some felt that this need had been ignored or overlooked by their colleagues: 'My main problem was being entirely on my own, entirely without help'; 'If someone had been there to help me, I might not have made such a mess of my first year'. One teacher who trained for work with older children went straight to an infant school. She left her job after two years with a deep sense of failure and, reflecting on this experience, said, 'I'd go back tomorrow if I could find a head who'd train me on the job. But there aren't many like that, are there?'.

By contrast, in over half the schools to which people went as probationers, help was available. In such schools they received plenty of assistance, especially with the technology of teaching (e.g. classroom organization, display, worksheets, apparatus) and with control. Indeed, nearly half of them attributed their survival in their first posts to help from one or more specific individuals, speaking with profound gratitude of the colleagues who, as one man said, 'taught me the job; I didn't want to be like him . . . but I couldn't have survived without him'. Others recalled: 'She spent hours with me after school sorting out my reading materials, helping me get the room organized and showing me what to do for display', or, 'There was one teacher in particular I leant on very heavily; she showed me all her materials, lent me things, was always ready to help with the difficult children. I couldn't have coped without her'.

Sometimes, rescue was available during the school day. To quote one example:

> One day when the head said he wanted reading tests
> administered by Friday and my class was in its usual uproar,
> another teacher suggested I send my children across to him in
> twos and threes and he'd administer the test. And without
> that sort of help I'd have gone under.

More frequently, help was given in individual classrooms at lunchtime, early in the morning or after school, and was facilitated if the teachers lived in the same neighbourhood or travelled to school together.

The main 'rescuers' were senior teachers. In a few schools (mostly infant or primary) it was the head, as in this example:

> The best thing about him was that he knew how difficult our
> job was. He could tell when you'd had a bad day . . . He did

139

what he could to help, came in a lot and took children out, made you feel you weren't completely alone.

More frequently, it was the deputy, senior mistress, year- or team-leader, although sometimes it was simply an older teacher without formal responsibilities for new recruits. Moreover, in the absence of help from other teachers, some of my interviewees gratefully accepted the support of untrained personnel, such as the secretary:

> Without saying anything, she used to do my register and all that ghastly dinner money . . . She was always ready to help with materials and sometimes, when the head was out, I even used to send a child I couldn't cope with to sit in her office.

Sometimes it was the caretaker ('If it hadn't been for him, I'd have been there till nine every night', or, 'He really helped me to under-stand the children'); or the ancillary staff ('She was much better at a lot of the practical things than I was and she showed me how to avoid confrontations with the kids').

Some teachers needed help so badly that if it was not seen to be available within the school, they would search for it in other places. They recalled: 'There was a college lecturer who had a student in the school and she was ready to help but the head wouldn't let her'; 'There was a terrific row when I went to the adviser and said I couldn't go on without help from someone, so could he please come in and see me'; 'There was a teacher from another school living in the same street and she was more use than anyone'; 'Fortunately we had a good teachers' centre and I used to go there and talk to the warden'. Interviewees also recalled turning to visiting remedial teachers, educational psychologists, and social workers.

Whatever their formal status, these 'rescuers' tended to be perceived as 'middle-aged', 'experienced', 'capable' and were sometimes explicitly described as 'motherly' or 'fatherly'. As one teacher recalled:

> There was a group of older men in that school, willing to give up plenty of time to younger teachers. I still go back and see them . . . They were marvellous. One was almost like a father to me.

The secret of their success seemed to lie in their ability to anticipate when help would be needed and to provide it quietly and sympathe-tically. In short, their role appears to have been that of a 'professional parent'. Years later they were remembered with an almost filial affection, for their kindness, interest, readiness to listen, to offer sympathy and practical help, and for their generosity with time, materials and ideas. As Sikes *et al.* (1985) also found in secondary schools, older colleagues of this kind helped many young teachers to survive their early experiences of the classroom without despair, disaster, or excessive disillusion. Without them, the dropout rate in the first 2 or so years of teaching would probably have been very heavy.

The function of these 'professional parents' is one which, it has been envisaged, would be included in the role of the professional tutor. Four of my interviewees were part of pilot schemes for professional tutors. They could all identify men or women who played the part for them of 'professional parents'; none of these was the officially designated professional tutor. Accessibility, experience, and kindness were more important than formal support from an organized system.

In considering notions of the self in Chapter 1, I suggested that there were two ways of viewing the development of the ill-defined 'I' which, following symbolic interactionism, complements the shifting, socially conditioned 'me'. From a Freudian perspective, maturation is a process during which normal individuals learn to perceive themselves as separate from those who reared and nurtured them in earlier years. Excessive dependency in adult life is therefore regarded as regressive and dysfunctional. By contrast, self-psychology suggests that individuals retain their tendency to relate to other people as if they were part of themselves while also developing the capacity to perceive them as independent beings. Under stress we are likely to emphasise the former element and to treat others as 'selfobjects' (i.e. as people who will love us as we love ourselves, on whom we can therefore rely for nurturance and protection, and yet whom we can control). Our capacity to take refuge in relationships of this kind in times of confusion or distress ensures periods of transition during which we can rebuild our 'selves' in ways that fit our new circumstances. It is tempting to see these teachers' 'professional parents' as providing them with transitional relationships of this kind. As older, more experienced practitioners, they were available, almost on demand, to offer newcomers affection, assistance, reassurance, strength, and in the process to safeguard the latter's self-esteem and self-regard while they forged for themselves the new identities which their work demanded.

Yet there is also evidence that this dependence was neither total nor long-lived. The very nature of the relationship between these older teachers and their younger colleagues limited the help the latter would accept. Although they wanted to do their jobs and therefore welcomed support and guidance, they also cherished their autonomy and the values it enshrined. Just as children distinguish their own 'selves' from those of others, especially their parents, by drawing self-defining boundaries (Winnicott 1955), so new teachers appear gradually to separate their professional lives from those of more experienced colleagues in order to establish their own identities. The language of individuals suggested this. They recalled, for example: 'She really was a terrible busybody. I had difficulty keeping her out'; 'I wish I had had the courage to keep him out. He was a completely different sort of teacher to the one I wanted to be. I think the help he insisted on giving me probably delayed my own development'; 'They pushed their ideas on me even when I didn't want to hear what they said'. In addition, some beginners appeared to feel that if initiation into the status of qualified teacher were made too easy, they would not feel themselves to be 'teachers'. As one woman who taught a class of six physically handicapped children said, 'I don't feel a real teacher yet. I haven't been through the fire of having total responsibility for a large class. I shan't feel a real teacher till I've suffered a bit'. Further, since probationers count for staffing purposes as fully qualified members of staff there is an obvious pressure on them to feel competent and self-sufficient as soon as their employment begins. Many are therefore reluctant to make their inadequacies public, irrespective of how supportive and reassuring their colleagues are willing to be.

'Sharing'

Although greater experience brought more confidence, mid-career teachers continued to need practical help, especially at times when they felt insecure, anxious or ill-equipped for new responsibilities. All too often, however, they felt constrained in seeking it. As one teacher put it:

> If you're feeling ill and can't cope, that's the very time you want someone to come in and help you, isn't it? But if you say you're run down and tired and can't cope, it's not a good thing [in this school], it's a reflection on you.

Another admitted that:

> I learnt to ask the staff, not the head. You don't get any help from him and it only gives the impression you can't manage.

Occasionally, too, individuals wanted assistance but found it was not there. Several said:

The worst thing is feeling so isolated, not having something or someone or some system to fall back on . . . there's no institutional support.

Yet like their less experienced colleagues they were ambivalent about certain kinds of help, discriminating carefully between assistance and intrusion: 'You can always take a problem to her and she's willing to help. But she doesn't push . . .'; [The head] was great. He was always around without being interfering'.

The schools in which teachers did not appear to feel this tension were the ones where all the adults 'shared' — equipment, pupils, rooms, time, ideas, authority, expertise. Many teachers used the phrase 'shared' apparently to indicate the existence within a staff group of a sense of collective responsibility. When this existed, assistance could be taken or given unobtrusively; people did not feel obligated when someone helped them out because they knew they would soon have an opportunity for reciprocal generosity. Tensions (and therefore the need for succour) were reduced because the burdens of, for example, class control belonged to everyone (see also the work of the Primary School Staff Relationships Project, Nias *et al.* 1989). Explaining why she had stayed in one school for eight years, a woman said:

You never feel on your own — you know you can take curricular or other problems to all the other teachers . . . You couldn't ever get a better staff. It isn't one of those schools where everybody shuts their classroom doors and nobody ever sees anybody else except at playtimes and lunchtimes.

Unfortunately such generosity did not always exist. As one part-time teacher said:

I've discovered that teachers are very territorial and materialistic. They like to keep their own books, they like their own rooms, they won't part with equipment, they want to keep 'their' children.

A new head found all the resources duplicated for every class in the school so teachers could be entirely self-contained; another commented on the way the open-plan units had been divided by furniture into 'watertight boxes'. It was a welcome change for some of my interviewees to find themselves, after a move, in a school where they could pass freely in and out of one another's teaching areas, examining displays, borrowing equipment, discussing ideas, feeling confident (as one recalled) that 'you can tell anyone else's child off in public without causing offence'. As the Department of Education and Science (1982, 5.8) reports, 'a general background

143

of support and encouragement from the staff as a whole' makes a critical difference in helping newcomers settle into a school.

Although 'sharing' was an attitude and a set of behaviours which could occur anywhere in the school, it was most visible in the staffroom. Here, in particular, teachers and head teachers could ease the emotional strains of classroom and parental encounters. This was especially important in schools where control was difficult and environmental conditions were stressful. Under such circumstances it was easy for teachers to believe Waller's (1961) proposition that since the relationship between teachers and pupils is inescapably one of conflict, self-interest prescribes the maintenance of staff solidarity *vis-à-vis* pupils. They spoke of 'the Dunkirk spirit', of 'not having to pretend that we're always doing it well . . . we know we're all in the same boat'. One said, 'I've learnt to shut up in the staffroom and not antagonize others. You can't exist solely in the classroom . . . support from other teachers is very important'. One woman summed it up:

> There's an in-built dynamite in teaching because of the
> physical and emotional stress. Here we have a stable staff and
> a friendly atmosphere and people don't very often blow up.
> We help to defuse each other before the flashpoint comes.

Some teachers also needed staffrooms, as Lortie (1975) and King (1978) claim, as places in which they could share their sense of guilt and worthlessness, feelings compounded among teachers in England by the fact that they are expected to like their pupils as well as to ensure that they learn (Broadfoot and Osborn 1986).

In short, this teacher voiced a common feeling when she spoke of her felt-need both to relax and to share failure:

> We've got to preserve the staffroom as a place where we can
> all come and tear our hair and laugh and collapse. If we
> didn't, we'd none of us survive. It doesn't matter whether you
> like them or not. When you're dealing all day with the sort of
> problems we have, you have to get along with other adults in
> the place. So we get on together . . . we have to. You can't
> stand the classroom stress for long if the staffroom's full of
> tension as well. We need each other's support, to keep us
> going, let alone the school . . . Here, we're all failing all the
> time — you can't carry that on your own for long.

Pollard (1987) among others (e.g. Woods 1979; Hammersley 1984), has drawn attention to the relatively low intellectual level of staffroom talk. This characteristic he attributes to the fact that staff 'need each other [even though they] do not necessarily share fundamental values or perspectives'. Pollard also notes that in order to 'strengthen the in-group feeling in the face of perceived external pressure and despite its own underlying tensions', staff talk about topics which constitute 'common denominators of the most immediate and populist sort' (Pollard 1987: 105, 106). His interpretation is consistent with these teachers' complaints in their early years (Chapter 6) about the triviality of staffroom chat and with their use of impression management (Chapter 3) as a means of reconciling membership of the staff group with the preservation of individual perspectives. What it overlooks is the fact that discussion of 'safe' topics is also a way in which staff members can begin to share themselves as people with their colleagues, signalling in the process their willingness to enter into closer forms of collaboration (Nias *et al.* 1989). In other words, staffroom 'chat' is an important part of most teachers' experience of work, but one whose functions may be misunderstood even by those who participate in it.

Sometimes pairs or small groups of teachers offered one another support not only in breaks, but also while teaching was actually in progress. A woman in a school with many social problems explained:

> You go into the classroom next door, if things are getting very bad. Say 'I've just come out to get a breather', then you can go back to your classroom after a couple of minutes, and that teacher can do the same. Children that you are having problems with, you can let somebody else look after for a bit and you'll take on theirs. It's very important.

A man said:

> One of the things I liked about team teaching was that you could catch the other teacher's eye across the room when something awful happened. You didn't have to say anything but you both *knew* and it was reassuring. Sometimes it kept you from going right round the bend.

'Sharing' was, it appears, something which teachers felt as well as experienced in practical ways.

Talking and listening; laughing and praising

The talking and listening implicit in 'sharing' were central in other ways to the professional well-being of teachers of all lengths of experience. The biggest contribution which heads could make to the development of their probationers was to be readily available for discussion: 'The biggest factor in my development has been my talks with the head', said one teacher, while another spoke of 'the key role played by the head in my development; he was always ready to talk'. Heads who encouraged discussion, formal or informal, among their staff were all singled out for praise (e.g. 'I learnt such a lot by talking to the head after school'; 'The head here gives us so much opportunity for discussion, and joins in herself'; 'The head was marvellous . . . He was always ready to talk'.) Such heads were contrasted with those who were seen as obsessed with office routines or as 'hiding in the stock-room', and who, as a result, were 'never available to talk to'. Colleagues, too, were important. Half the mid-career teachers said something like, 'There has always had to be somebody to talk to, or I think I would have cracked up long ago', and a quarter mentioned being part of a pair or group who, typically, 'could meet at the end of the day and just talk things through — unwinding really'.

Laughter was part of this unwinding (though it served other purposes too, such as promoting and maintaining a sense of social cohesion and shared understandings: see Woods 1979; Nias *et al.* 1989). Humour was often mentioned, in both the first and second interviews (e.g. 'Well it's so awful sometimes that if you didn't have someone to have a laugh with you'd give up'; 'I think being able to laugh and joke about what was happening and what ridiculous things the head was making us do helped us all'; 'I shouldn't be marking books outside school, I should be out with the staff having a drink and a laugh . . . It *is* important').

But the interpersonal attribute both most valued and most noticeable for its absence was a readiness to give praise and recognition. Much was expected in this respect of heads. A man commented:

> The head's a tremendous force in the school . . . she can be a real demon and sometimes the tension gets you down because you know she's watching you all the time, but you really feel pleased when she pats you on the back.

A woman in her first deputy headship said:

> The head says he's pleased with what I've done so far and that's given me confidence that I'm on the right tack.

Another told me:

> We have a new head and she's made us all feel much better about things because she takes a real interest in what we're doing — comes round and has a look, talks to the children

about their work, asks us before she buys equipment, all that sort of thing.

Unfortunately, head teachers were often found wanting in this respect. One teacher with fifteen years' experience explained that she had left her previous school because of the head's apparent indifference to her professional practice: 'He never once in 6 years asked what I was doing, came into my classroom or commented on anything he saw'. Others said, for example: 'I feel nobody cares, nobody has ever, ever talked to me about how I feel, about the way I wanted my career to go'; 'The one thing I couldn't stand at [that school] was the head's lack of interest. It drove several of us out in the end'; 'The head didn't give you any feedback . . . I suppose in her way she was pleased with things that were going on and she recognized people's abilities, but she'd never ever let on and tell you'.

Nor did colleagues frequently offer recognition or positive reinforcement to one another. As one woman sadly said:

Everybody goes around patting the children on the back with great enthusiasm and saying how wonderful they are, but nobody pats you on the back and says how wonderful you are, all you get is the flak when things go wrong. I think after a while that's wearing, especially as you give so much of yourself during the day.

Other men and women commented, 'Very occasionally you'll get a person who'll say "I like that" or "What a good idea . . . [but] I've come to the stage where I don't really expect any feedback from adults', or, 'We all need to be told we're doing something well, but it doesn't often happen'. Two heads also remarked on the absence of 'feedback from anyone in this job', and one supply teacher said that she made a point of commenting favourably to head teachers on their ideas and achievements because she had come to realise how little reinforcement they received.

There were isolated examples of peer esteem (e.g. 'As a teacher, you get praised very little, so teachers praise each other sometimes'; 'The head of infants asked me, "I've got to do a language scheme for the school, have you anywhere in your travels come across a language scheme that I can look at and use as a guide?" and I had got one and I felt really good that . . . she was treating me as an equal'; 'She gave me a tremendous amount of backing and straight moral support just telling me I was doing the right thing'). In general, however, the culture of teaching does not seem to encourage its members to praise one another. It seems strange that institutions built upon the rhetoric (and very often the reality) of caring for children should be so poor at giving recognition to adults. In this context, it is probably significant that the Primary School Staff Relationships Project found that schools in which a 'culture of collaboration' existed were characterized by high levels of talk, non-verbal communication, listening, laughing and praising, among all the teaching and non-teaching staff and between head and staff (Nias *et al.* 1989).

Tension in the staff group

The development of an atmosphere in which teachers could relax, find mutual support and prepare themselves emotionally for the next encounter with children was impeded in many schools by one or more of four main causes.

The first has been documented by Hartley (1985), Pollard (1985) and Hargreaves (1986) in case studies of primary and middle schools and sketched less directly by King (1978). All found fundamental splits among teachers or between head and teachers about the social and moral purposes of education and therefore about the aims of the curriculum and the extent to which children should be 'pushed' to learn — as the head at Rockfield Primary School (Hartley 1985) said to his staff, 'Don't flog dead horses'. These studies also found teachers divided from one another by conflicting beliefs about the extent to which children should 'own' or 'construct' their own knowledge and about how they learnt (though King, Pollard and Hargreaves make this division more explicit than Hartley does). It will be apparent that these contrasting educational views are very similar to those noted among teachers in the discussion of reference groups in Chapter 3. They arise from the values (social, moral and educational) which individuals tacitly or explicitly incorporate in their substantial selves, that is from the ways in which they define themselves. At worst, such differences can polarize teachers in a school, especially when they are associated with strong in-school reference groups. Even when subgroups holding different perspectives co-exist peacefully in a single staffroom, by means of the defences described in Chapter 3, of the kind of non-intervention in classrooms practised and promoted by the head of Rockfield Primary School or of the 'coping strategies' described by Pollard, their very existence makes 'pulling together' (see Chapter 8) difficult, if not impossible.

One way or another, provided that they did not confront their educational differences, most of these teachers found it possible to work harmoniously, at a practical, pragmatic level, with heads and colleagues from whom they differed quite radically on educational matters, even though many of them disliked doing this and sought debate in extra-school reference groups (see Chapters 2 and 3). A much more common source of tension was a spirit of competition. One teacher told me:

> You all had to do an assembly and it was awful because the more it went on, the more it got 'mine's got to be better than the one last week' and I hate that sort of thing.

Competition was very often in itself a manifestation of unresolved historical rivalries. Nearly a third of the mid-career teachers described situations in which internal promotion had caused or deepened rifts among the staff. One claimed:

> This used to be a happy staff, very friendly, who worked well together, but this has changed recently with some people wanting to move and not being able to, and some jealousy over internal promotions given without interviews.

A woman referred to her appointment to a senior post 'which caused a lot of bitterness, especially amongst the male staff who felt they should have got the job'. Another commented that, demographically, there were two groups in her school but that they

> get along together because they aren't in competition with each other. There are the older women, mostly married, who don't want promotion and the younger ones who want promotion but only stay for a short time and then move on somewhere else.

She contrasted this situation with her first school and commented: 'College doesn't prepare you for the in-fighting and the nastiness'.

Another related cause of bitterness, more marked in the later interviews than in the earlier, was unequally distributed power. Decision-making often seemed to be in the hands of one group who, typically, made other staff 'too frightened to oppose them' (e.g. 'Well, you know, they sat there in the corner at breaks, talking about their families and their holidays and no one dared go against them'), or of one person (e.g. 'There is a lot of friction and under-current between the deputy head, and the rest of the staff. It's taken me a long time to find this out, but she's definitely the one you avoid — I go straight to the head now and avoid her completely'). Occasionally someone reflected, angrily or sadly, upon the hierarchical nature of the education system:

When you're working in schools . . . it is imposed on you, I mean you see the head walking down the corridor and you're in your room and you think 'Am I doing something he's going to disapprove of?' whereas [my college head of department] will come in and if he disapproves we'll chat about it and that's that, because I feel I'm equal . . . But in school even though I could justify what I was doing, I still felt the head looking over my shoulder. And I think the head feels it as well, because he has the Director of Education, or the advisers, or the HMI looking over his shoulder.

Lastly, staffrooms could be disturbed by interpersonal relationships which violated social norms or, as several people said, 'created undercurrents'. Seven teachers in the later group spoke of schools in which marital breakdown had resulted from a close relationship between the head and another member of staff, particularly the deputy or the school secretary, or in which 'they had this thing going and it never came out in the open but we all knew and it made life very difficult for the rest of us'. Pairing of this sort between members of staff did not seem to unsettle a whole staff group in the way that a head's involvement with a single staff member did.

Whatever the cause, teachers found it difficult and stressful to be in a staffroom whose atmosphere was soured by interpersonal differences. When they could, they moved to other schools; when they could not, their daily experience of work became more tense, and consequently less rewarding. They put it this way: 'When relationships between a few people are bad, it makes things bad for everyone'; 'In some schools . . . if you talk to one person, half the staff will not have anything to do with you', and, 'Working [in that school] was very hard because the atmosphere in the staffroom was so unpleasant. It was fine in the classroom but you had nowhere to go and unwind'.

Friendship

Finally, all teachers come to their work as people. It is, after all, the 'self' who decides to join the profession and the occupational identity which is absorbed (if it is) into the personal. This has implications which go beyond individuals' interpretations of and perspectives on the roles that they occupy. It also means that personal concerns (e.g. health, domestic problems, financial commitments) are not left at the playground gate: despite their 'professional pleasantness' (King 1978), teachers experience negative as well as positive emotions; and that they bring a complex mixture of fulfilled and unfulfilled skills, talents, interests, and aspirations to the task of teaching (see also Yeomans 1986). Now, although many workers of all descriptions have full and satisfying social lives outside their paid occupation, some do not. Such people are more likely, consciously or unconsciously, to look to their work for comradeship, friendship and even love than are those who have alternative sources of affective support. If my evidence is typical, most teachers seem to take up posts (especially first ones) in places where they already have family or friends and they do not therefore look in the first instance to their colleagues for companionship and affection. However, a few people (mostly women) recalled relying entirely on their colleagues for a social life when they moved without partners to unfamiliar parts of the country. In consequence they were often very lonely. As one said, 'Teaching is particularly bad because people do the job and go home whereas in other jobs, like a bank, they have outings together and a fairly mixed staff as well'.

Her remark draws attention to a current aspect of teaching which has received little attention: as an occupation, it disadvantages young people socially, especially those who are looking for friends or future partners of their own age. At the time of the second interviews, five teachers had married one of their colleagues, three had left existing partners to do so. 'Surely', said one, 'it isn't surprising. We saw more of each other than we did of anyone else'. One in three of the men I spoke to in both early and mid-career had at some point been the only male in the staff group; most had felt isolated as a result, especially when they were also by several years the youngest. Several men and women stressed the distance in interest and perspectives created by a 10- or 15-year age gap between themselves and the rest of the staff, while for others it was a financial question. One said, 'All the rest were older married women. It wasn't that they were unpleasant or anything, but their salary wasn't essential to their families and they couldn't understand my situation', and an older man singled out as divisive the fact that he could afford 'a different type of housing from anyone else'.

In general, women, especially those who had been at home for some years with young children tended to get the most enjoyment out of the comradeship of the staffroom. Typical remarks were: 'I like coming to school and being with the other teachers. They've become friends now. I'd miss them if I left to have a baby'; 'I look on all the staff in this school as my friends. They don't feel like "colleagues" — they're part of my life'. 'They were a very generous staff, more like a family really'; 'We get on, we are a very relaxed group, we can chat to one another'.

Moreover, some of the more experienced teachers, especially heads and deputies, felt that their staffs ought to be aware of one another as people, not simply as co-workers. The welfare of the children, they argued, was intimately bound up with the well-being of the adults. If the latter did not feel personally accepted in the staffroom they would not be at ease in the classroom. Besides, it was philosophically inconsistent to treat children as 'whole' and 'individual' and not to relate to their teachers in the same way (see also Nias *et al.* 1989). One head put it forcefully:

> Teaching isn't just working with children, it's enjoying the staffroom and the laughing that goes on there. This needs to be built up if it doesn't exist. If you find other teachers dull then you shouldn't be in teaching. They probably are narrow and boring and conformist, but then so are most accountants and most plumbers. If you feel that way about your colleagues then you are better out of the profession. Schools need their staffrooms.

Conclusion

Several familiar strands emerge from this chapter. First is teachers' desire to perform with high levels of professional skill and to become, as soon as they can, very competent as practitioners. As probationers and for as long as they feel insecure or inexperienced, they therefore look to their head teachers and colleagues to provide models of appropriate behaviour. Second, however, they are selective in the help that they accept, welcoming sympathy, advice and practical assistance (especially from 'professional parents'), but rejecting ways of teaching or relating to children which appear to run counter to their view of themselves as people and practitioners. Third, therefore, they are happiest in a social environment characterized by mutual dependence, in which 'sharing' is the norm and individuals do not feel ashamed to admit to failure or a sense of inadequacy. Fourth, teachers' experience of schools as organizations of adults as well as children is coloured by their experience in them as people as well as role-occupants. Sometimes they make friends, share interests, enjoy companionship and find mutual affection. At others, their staffrooms are poisoned by rivalry, jealousy and suspicion, making it difficult to secure any remission from the pressures of classroom work. Yet teachers need this relief, especially in schools where children have many social problems and within which teachers therefore work under considerable strain. Lastly, relationships between staff — who can and do help each other, provide one another with oases of calm in a long and frenetic day, set one another high but attainable standards for professional performance, and provide a mutually supportive social environment — are characterized by: personal accessibility; plenty of opportunity for discussion; laughter; praise; and recognition.

It would, however, be over-simplistic to infer from these generalizations that the teacher's experience in a staffroom is simply that of anyone who works in a small, relatively informal group of adults. Rather, collegial relationships appear to feature more prominently in individuals' professional lives as they become older and more experienced. Perhaps surprisingly, teachers seem to become more aware of such relationships at a time when they might be expected to need them less (i.e. when they have become more self-confident, less dependent on support from within the staff group, and more established in their private lives). To understand this apparent anomaly, I look in the next chapter at the scope the staff group provides for the task and impact concerns of the mature teacher.

Chapter eight

Life in staffrooms: wider horizons

In the previous chapter, I presented evidence to suggest that, despite the privacy, loneliness and individualism of primary teaching, becoming and remaining a skilled classroom practitioner is a process in which individuals' head teachers, fellow teachers and other adult colleagues are often closely involved. I have also suggested that this involvement is, to a large extent, controlled and monitored by the individuals themselves as they selectively watch, talk to, lean on, imitate, learn, and borrow from their peers and seniors. In this chapter, I take these two arguments further, to show that, once they are assured of their professional competence, many teachers look to the other adults in their schools to increase their sense of personal efficacy and influence. They seek promotion to posts which give them wider responsibilities, participate in teams and whole-school activities, look to their colleagues for stimulation and challenge. The self is fulfilled and extended through and by means of the ideas and actions of adult as well as child others. This does not however always or easily happen. All too often the culture and structure of primary schools impede the development of either collaboration or constructive disagreement.

Yet it is possible for pairs or groups of teachers to work together in ways which allow and encourage them to experience simultaneously a sense of common achievement, an awareness of mutual influence and a sense that they are learning from one another. Moreover, it is clear from the accounts of such groups with which I finish the chapter that their members also support and help one another in the ways suggested in Chapter 7. In the process they come to like and often to care about one another. Although groups like these (with members who simultaneously meet all one another's felt-needs) occur relatively rarely, and often by chance, they have a powerful and enduring effect upon those who participate in them. Working together towards the fulfilment of the same ideals, stimulated by forthright but positive debate, bound together by intimate knowledge of and affection for one another as persons, and with communication between them eased by common understandings born of shared experience, they find new levels of self-extension and of fulfilment in their work, moving beyond pleasure and satisfaction to an all-absorbing delight, in each other and in the task. For some teachers, working in schools can be 'the best experience of all'.

To be sure, not all the teachers in my study became members of working groups such as these. Nor was this simply because they did not have the good fortune to meet at some point in their professional lives what one described as 'a collection of twin souls'. It appears also to relate to the development of personal concerns discussed in Chapter 4. Building on Fuller's proposition that teachers become in turn interested in 'self', 'task', and 'impact' (Fuller 1969; Fuller and Bown 1975), I suggested that these concerns can also be construed as a preoccupation with survival, a search for identification, an interest in consolidation and extension (either within or outside teaching) and a desire for increased influence within the educational system. In the first two phases, the individual is centred on 'self', and in particular with securing a sense of fit between choice of career and the substantial self. In the third, the search for personal extension shown by those who choose to remain within the profession may be seen as a concern for 'task', and in particular for the performance of that task. Lastly, teachers develop a concern for 'impact', (i.e. for making a lasting impression upon pupils, colleagues and/or the educational system as a whole).

There is no suggestion in Fuller's work or mine, however, that these phases are normative, irreversible or mutually exclusive, or that teachers do or should move through them at an even pace or at the same time as one another. Certainly, not all the teachers whom I interviewed either in early or in mid-career were interested in their potential effect upon other adults. Some seemed content to retain the classroom as their centre of gravity and interest for most of their working lives. Moreover, individuals appeared to develop a concern, for 'impact' after very different lengths of service. Some of my interviewees began to want influence, even leadership, after less than 8 years, others after 12 or more. The picture is complicated in two additional ways.

First, married women returners with fewer years of classroom experience than their male contemporaries were nonetheless often anxious after a career break to extend their sphere of influence in their schools. Second, what teachers described as 'pulling together' — working in teams or whole staff groups towards the realization of shared aims — satisfied both task and impact concerns. To be a member of a team enhanced individuals' sense of task-accomplishment by endowing their work with significance beyond their own classrooms. At the same time it increased their interdependence with their colleagues and thereby their influence over them. Similarly, teachers who 'stimulated' or extended one another's professional thinking were sometimes interested in teaching better, sometimes in affecting others. The pace and lineaments of teachers' professional development are evidently as individual and idiosyncratic as teaching itself.

The evidence used in this chapter is taken mainly from the second set of interviews, though I have used material from the first set as well when it seemed appropriate. This imbalance was dictated by the teachers' own preoccupations. They talked of their colleagues less frequently and less favourably in the first decade of work than they did in the second. In particular, in mid-career they often mentioned the latter in the context of job satisfaction, though this hardly ever happened in the early years. The exceptions were head teachers who were often and spontaneously the focus of people's attention in the early interviews, much less so in the later ones, with the exception of deputies who made frequent reference to them.

The search for influence

Although I have argued that impact concerns tend to develop later rather than earlier in teachers' careers, I have also suggested that development is neither uniform nor clear cut, as the experience of these teachers suggests. Even at the beginning of their careers, while their main preoccupation was survival, most of them reacted strongly against heads who denied them any part in decision-making:

> It was impossible to disagree with our last head teacher. But I'm happier now. There's more open discussion, and people are more involved in the school.

> We all have to follow directives from the head . . . All she wants from the staff and the children is obedience. That's really why I'm giving up. I don't feel any more that I have anything to contribute.

> I used to smoulder in silence in staff meetings . . . He wasn't interested in anything we had to say.

Moreover, they were quick to spot, and to resent, what one described as 'mock democracy, based on length of service', or, as others put it, 'The staff can talk, but the school is run the head's way', and, 'Staff meetings are disguised dictatorship'. A woman said:

I find it very hard to cope with messages sent from heads and deputies, where they're asking you to implement things but there's been no discussion and no feedback . . . basically they're treating you as a second rate citizen, using you but not listening to you. And the other thing I don't like is in staff meetings . . . where, if you're asked your opinion, the head seems to be listening, but then it has no effect on the ultimate outcome. You know — 'Yes, but this is how we're going to do it'.

In addition, some teachers began to look beyond their classrooms from early in their careers (as some secondary ones also did, Sikes *et al.* 1985; Riseborough 1986). They wanted not only to feel that they could display 'competent membership' (Denscombe 1980a) of their organizations but also that they had a say in goal-setting and the formation of school policies.

It's good here, because you can work out with the head and the staff what the goals are.

We have staff meetings every week, and we really feel that we can have a say in what the school is about . . . Mind you, it's hard work, but it's worth it. Everyone pulls together, whereas at [her previous school] we all went our separate ways.

There's no conflict in this situation, but plenty of discussion. That's due to the head. He started us all talking to each other, and although he makes the decisions, he listens to what we have to say.

However, as Belasco and Alutto (1975) show, one must not assume that all teachers want to be involved in this way. They advance evidence to suggest that age, sex, marital status, social and economic status, and type of school all affect the extent to which teachers want to participate in decision-making and that some teachers do not welcome the opportunity to spend time and energy on wider school matters.

In my group a few of those who did wish to exert influence beyond their classrooms were able to do so informally. As a mathematics teacher explained:

I like talking about maths and teaching, so I do that naturally. Similarly, trying to introduce people to new ideas,

I've done that naturally because I like to see whether other people will enjoy [certain activities] as much as me, as well as the children.

Most, however, had to wait for some time (minimally 2 years) before they took on formal responsibility for advising or leading their colleagues in a particular curriculum area. Once in post they often began to 'enjoy the feeling that I'm training my colleagues in [science] teaching'. They spoke of 'the extra feeling of pride, the sense that I have something worth telling other people', the satisfaction they experienced when 'people discuss [your area] and ask for advice . . . and when the things that one has been trying to achieve for a long time are suddenly fitting into place', and the pleasure of 'occasions when I go into classrooms and see that [the other teachers] are all stuck into something, enthusiastically, that I've suggested'. Nor were the satisfactions of teaching one's peers the sole preserve of curriculum co-ordinators; a deputy said, 'I like working with the staff — talking to them, helping them find ways round their difficulties, suggesting ideas'.

Indeed, several people made it clear that a major reason for seeking promotion was to secure more direct influence over their colleagues than they currently had (a form of motivation shared by secondary teachers, Sikes 1986). They felt, as one said, 'I want to affect all the children, through my colleagues, rather than just the ones who are sitting in front of me all day'. Some came to realize that 'if you want to change things, you've got to have a say in how the money's spent', others that 'I had people in charge of me who weren't as competent and, even worse, weren't as interested [as I was]'. Not surprisingly, all five heads spoke of their desire to exert influence, talking with evident pleasure of 'the time I spend with students', or of 'bringing the staff round to my way of thinking', of enjoying 'the whole process of communicating with people, influencing the way they say things', or of 'training my deputy so she can move on to a headship herself'.

Unfortunately, many of my interviewees experienced as much dissatisfaction as they did satisfaction in the posts to which they were promoted. Frustrated expectations about the likely extent of personal influence could, and did, cause a good deal of discontent. As a head remarked:

People write lists of good practice and 'this is the way to encourage people'. I find the trouble with that is that we're dealing with human beings, and human beings with all their frailties, and I'm not convinced that the sort of approach which is encompassed by 'good practice' necessarily accepts that human beings have got frailties.

Five co-ordinators talked with vivid frustration about the impossibility of the task they had been given, emphasizing that 'you want to do things but [because of time shortages, industrial action, a heavy work load] you just can't get round to it', or complaining that 'the success or failure of achieving your goals is dependent upon an awful lot of people'. One said:

> It worries me sometimes when my job is to advise and I go to a lot of trouble to do that and then other members of staff perhaps haven't understood or worse still, go their own way anyway and don't do what they've been advised . . . I'm fairly flexible, but usually at the end of term when I'm feeling tired I get uptight about it.

Campbell (1985) and Taylor (1986) also stress the difficulties encountered by curriculum co-ordinators, emphasizing in particular how little time they have available in which to fulfil their duties, and the Primary School Staff Relationships Project (Nias *et al.* 1989) noted similar anxieties, frustrations and self-doubt among those with formal curriculum responsibilities. The quest for influence over one's colleagues is obviously not brought to an end simply by promotion to a more senior post.

At the time of writing it is too soon to tell whether the new pay scales and Conditions of Service introduced in 1987 will encourage or discourage primary teachers from looking for greater influence within their schools. On the one hand, the abolition of Scale 2 posts (in favour of a Main Professional Grade) has removed a financial and status incentive for the assumption of school-wide responsibilities. On the other, all teachers are now required to take on oversight of at least one curriculum area, a fact which may encourage some to move sooner than they otherwise might from 'task' to 'impact' concerns. However, unless everyone is now given some resources (especially non-contact time) with which to carry out these new curricular responsibilities, little may change; or, what change does occur may be in the direction of disengagement from the school.

For some heads and deputies the urge to make an impact on staff as well as children combined with a fondness for organization, for its own sake. One head said, 'I love my systems', and another explained 'It was a total muddle when I got here, but I like setting up systems — and that's what I think I like doing best of all — to get all those plates spinning. I'm not quite so keen on plate-spinning maintenance, but sussing out what's needed and getting it sorted out — I love that'. One deputy described herself, as several others did, as a 'person who loves organizing things. I like doing lists and seeing things work. If the school runs better because I've organized people, then I'm happy', while another woman, re-starting her career and looking for a headship, said, 'One reason is, I'm fascinated by organization. I'd really like to have the chance to set up a school and make it work'.

'Pulling together': groups and teams

There was another, less formal way of making an impact upon the practice of one's colleagues — to work alongside them. Now, I have argued (Chapter 2) that teachers' values are central to their self-image as people and as teachers, and are therefore the bedrock of their practice. So, they cannot work closely together with others who have different educational goals or views on how to achieve these, for to do this would create an uncomfortable dissonance between their actions and their view of themselves. Indeed, the very attempt would be self-defeating, because people who are going in different directions (i.e. who are pursuing divergent aims, deter-mined by incompatible values) cannot, by definition, pull together. My interviewees reported that the people with whom they did work closely 'thought the same' (as several put it) — i.e. had the same frame of reference in relation to learning, teaching, and the aims of schooling as they did. This fact enabled them to share with one another the act and context of teaching because they had sufficient common understanding of what 'teaching' was to make team-work possible. Put another way, they felt that they could co-operate with (in the sense of being considerate towards) people whom they did not perceive as part of their own self-confirming reference group, but that they could not collaborate with them, either in the formation of common curricular or disciplinary policies or in translating these into action (i.e. in teaching).

Hartley's (1985) study of Rockfield Primary School clearly illus-trates this point. One group of teachers (the 'stabilizers') followed the head in aiming to provide a caring stability for their pupils, whom they saw as coming from an educationally under-privileged background. Another group (the 'stretchers') felt that the only way out of this environment for some children was through academic success. A third group (the 'straddlers') attempted to bridge these two positions, and a fourth (the 'poor relations') who worked in what was called the 'Immigration Department' had a distinctive set of aims and concerns, deriving from their work with children from ethnic minority families. Each of these groups defined in different ways the purposes for which they, as teachers, were in school. Accordingly, they set different standards for their pupils, expected different behaviour from them, and treated them, as classes and individuals, differently. In consequence, they could not work together as a whole staff, a situation which was made worse by the fact that the head and his newly appointed deputy belonged to different groups. Outside their sub-groups, staff seldom spoke to one another, there were no staff meetings and no school-based in-service work in which divergences on policy and practice could have been aired. Archetypally, Rockfield was a primary school in which the existence of different staff reference groups made it possible for individuals to collaborate within cohesive sub-groups but impossible for them to work together as a whole staff (see also Nias *et al.* 1989).

Unfortunately, despite the obstructive effect of such groups upon the growth of whole staff collaboration, individuals have a number of incentives to create or join them. Group members confirm one another's perspectives, they learn from one another, they have a sense of exerting influence over each other and group membership is affectively satisfying. Moreover, work undertaken jointly can be easier and more enjoyable than the same tasks tackled in isolation. So, many of my interviewees actively sought, in their schools, not only for reference groups but also for opportunities to work in teams or, as they said, to 'pull together'. Indeed, half of those interviewed in early career and over three-quarters in mid-career spoke glowingly of the pleasures and rewards they had derived from collaborative work of this kind.

To emphasize the importance to teachers of their reference groups is not to suggest that they hold lengthy philosophical discussions. Teachers in primary schools decide whether or not they have enough in common to be able to work together by, for instance, watching each other's actions, looking at children's work, holding brief conversations about common interests, not by seeking the articulation of deeply-buried beliefs (King 1978; Pollard 1985; Nias *et al.* 1989). The kind of team to which my interviewees referred was usually formed when two or more teachers sensed (through casual conversation, discussion, or observation) that they shared compatible aims or principles, and felt, therefore, that they could enhance each other's work. They then decided, often quite tentatively, to undertake a joint venture of a limited kind (e.g. a visit, a project, a school production). They pooled or exchanged resources, planned together, co-operated in the conduct of the work, and discussed one another's pupils. Finding these activities valuable and reaffirming for themselves and fruitful for their pupils, they repeated them, slowly increasing the scope of their collaboration and the numbers of teachers involved.

Proximity obviously facilitated such developments; indeed 'teams' often grew up in open-plan units or schools. Over a quarter of those interviewed in mid-career mentioned that they had worked at some time in an open-plan school. Many of them spontaneously said that they liked the design because it facilitated contact between adults. Typical comments were: 'It was a very close-knit, pleasant staff to work with . . . we worked together well as a team. I think we had to in an open-plan situation'; 'All the staff worked together. I think it had something to do with the fact it was an open-plan school'; 'I started off in a large teaching area (with two other teachers). They gave me a room with a door, but gradually the door opened and I became part of the unit'; 'It was working [in an open-plan school] that helped us. You do develop more of a relationship, get to know one another on a personal level . . . you were all there working together, able to chat and help each other's children'.

'Camps', 'factions', and the difficulties of 'building bridges'

Despite the manifest attractions of working in cohesive sub-groups, many of my interviewees felt, from the start of their careers, a sense of 'commitment' (Chapter 2) to their schools as well as their classes. They wanted to teach in schools, not just teams, which had agreed aims and policies. When they found such contexts, they typically felt: 'It gives you a sense that your own work isn't wasted'; [My greatest satisfaction] was getting the feeling I had clicked in and become part of an organization which was doing something worthwhile'; 'That was the important thing at that school — we all pulled together. Everyone had different styles and approaches but we were going in the same direction'; 'I like [my present] school . . . Everyone deals with all the children, so things can be discussed and school-wide policies worked out to give a consistent approach. You get more sense of achieving something'. Two women summed up contrasting experiences. One said:

> You've got to have some sort of consensus within the school. If everybody else felt that (after discussion) this was the way we should be doing things and I was left out of step, then I would adapt myself as far as I could rather than expect everyone else to adapt to me.

The other described her current school as

a nightmare. The head is past it, really, and the staff don't get along together . . . Basically, it's a difference of opinion between them about how much direction she should give. At the moment, everyone just teaches what they want to and it's chaos. And because it's so fragmented and bitty, no one gets much satisfaction from it . . . You don't get any sense of achieving much as a whole school.

Unfortunately, all too often the development of whole-school approaches was obstructed by the existence of conflicting reference groups — i.e. of 'camps', 'factions', or 'divisions'. In general, the more senior my interviewees, the more definite they were about the destructive nature of such groups. A deputy said:

Staff relationships are much more important to me now I'm in a school where there are rival camps. I didn't realize [in my last school] how lucky I was to be working in a year group where we all felt the same way about things.

Another told me that he had been frustrated in one school by the presence of staff with different aims from his own and, finding that he could not alter their views 'without a constant head-on collision the whole time', had successfully applied for another job. A third spoke of an 'aggressive minority' who had made his designated task of creating curriculum cohesion very difficult and it was with relief that he, too, moved to another school. Looking back, a head reflected on a group to which he had belonged in his previous post, 'We must have been unbearable, setting the world to rights and presenting our ideas to the head, pre-packaged, in a way I would hate if it was done to me now'.

There are many reasons why teachers find it hard even to start the difficult process of bringing sub-groups constructively together, or, as one put it, of 'building bridges'. My interviewees identified some of them. All but five of them mentioned lack of time to talk to their colleagues and therefore of opportunities to tackle directly differences of policy or practice. Typically, 'There really was no time to talk about anything but who was going to do playground duties and what some child had just done'. These and similar difficulties, now well established in the educational literature (see, e.g., Fullan 1982; Campbell 1985), were exacerbated by the effects of industrial action. In many schools all formal meetings had ceased and, because many staff left the premises at lunchtime, scope for informal discussion was also reduced. I asked my interviewees if they could see anything positive coming out of the 2 years of action. Many replied, as one did, 'Yes, I think it has made us realize how much we need to talk to one another . . . I never thought people would be glad to have meetings again, but we have got to that point'. Physical isolation imposed by the traditional architecture of 'box' classrooms was also seen as contributing to lack of discussion.

So, too, were head teachers who did not consciously promote it. One teacher said:

> When I was given a Scale 2 post for Maths I tried to devise a record-keeping system for the whole school, but I could never pin the head down to a discussion of it, and in the end I gave up trying.

Another, describing an abortive attempt to introduce team-teaching, said:

> We never see him; as long as he can tell visitors to the school that we've got team-teaching, I don't think he's interested in whether or not we actually achieve anything . . . He certainly never encourages us to talk about policies or curriculum.

Another perceived obstacle was the fact that many staffs included teachers at different stages of life and professional development (see Riseborough 1986, for a description of secondary schools in which staff of different lengths of experience retreated into conflicting groups, so preventing effective school development). Seven mid-career teachers, anxious to involve other people in curriculum planning, remarked how hard it was to get some of their colleagues interested in the idea of collaborative decision-making or action. Probationers and newly appointed teachers tended to spend all their time in their classrooms. Those whose main preoccupation was with the roles they played outside work (e.g. as daughter, parent, magistrate) did not appear to want closer involvement with the school. As 'privatized workers' (Goldthorpe *et al.* 1968), they earned a living by their profession but felt that their chief interests and loyalties lay elsewhere. They therefore resisted closer involvement with the school. As one teacher said:

> They spend all their breaks and lunchtimes marking, and then — off they go the moment school finishes, with empty briefcases. They don't care what reading scheme we have or whether the school visit is to Timbuctoo as long as they're not expected to put more time in. It's impossible trying to get them to come to meetings and they don't want to talk about the job.

All the heads spoke feelingly of the difficulty of creating unity of purpose in divided schools. Looking back on his early months in his first headship, one man confessed:

> I came to the realization that you can't just go treading all over people all the time . . . You learn as a head that you can't do it on your own, you try but you can't do it.

A relatively experienced head summed it up:

> It's all very well having theories about discussing and agreeing your curriculum with staff . . . it's a very slow process bringing that about, especially if you've got people who are diametrically opposed on an issue.

(See also Nias *et al.* 1989.)

When a staff is divided, primary heads traditionally look to their deputies for referential and practical support and the heads among my interviewees appeared on the whole to receive it. The deputies' viewpoint was, however, a different one, especially when new head teachers were appointed to schools in which they were already teaching. On a recent management course, a deputy was talking about the apparently irreconcilable conflict between herself and her newly-appointed head. The suggestion was made that, being unable to move schools, she might treat the situation as an 'arranged marriage' and simply try to make it work. Her reply was succinct: 'Arranged marriages are between people with the same value-system. We have different values'. Three deputies in this study told the same story. One felt: 'I was taken in by [the head] at my interview', and, as a result, found that to obtain credibility with the rest of the staff he had to behave in ways which violated his sense of personal and professional integrity. At the end of three years he succeeded in finding another post, but not before he had begun 'to feel like a prisoner facing a life sentence, without remission'. A woman, who had also moved, told me, 'The problem with my head [teacher] filled my life for three years after he came to the school. It's only now that I've left that I can start to think again about where I want to go'.

'Bounded professionals'

Where whole-school curriculum or disciplinary policies did exist, it was usually heads rather than individual teachers or sub-groups who had initiated them. As one said:

> On the whole [the staff] know that the school has been a somewhat chaotic place . . . One or two of them are coming

165

round to the notion that everybody is lacking in guidance . . .
As long as I don't do anything stupid . . . I think they'll go a
reasonable way with me . . . I feel that once they start
[making whole-school plans] they might feel caught up in it
and there will be more sense of achievement for everyone.

Sometimes they encouraged collective decision-making among all
the staff (e.g. 'I think that almost every change we've made took a
lot of discussion . . . The head would make sure we'd talk around it
for a week or two, and then we'd decide'). At others, responsibility
was devolved to year- or team-groups (e.g. 'A lot of decisions
about the curriculum are made by year-groups and we have to
reach a joint decision'). In either case, however, the development
of a whole-school approach seemed to depend in the first instance
upon the head teacher's initiative (see Nias *et al.* 1989).

By contrast, in activities which spanned the curricular and the
extra-curricular there was scope for leaders other than the head to
pull the whole staff together. A woman who had left teaching for
family reasons confessed that she had missed school very much at
first, particularly 'at Christmas, I wanted to go to all the school
concerts and get involved in everything'. Another said:

There was a lot of going back and forth to school at
weekends, but it was great fun . . . For example, there was
one term where we turned the school into a ship — we
painted all the doors and windows and all the children had a
naval hat, and one area was pirates, so we changed all the
names. That involved a lot of work from the teachers, we
spent a lot of time doing that. If we had plays or assemblies,
even, we'd all get together and make the clothes and things.

A man in a small school where teachers 'stayed in their rooms'
nostalgically recalled the annual musical in his last school: 'All
eighteen of us pitched in and helped, rolled their sleeves up . . . it
was great'. He went on to say how difficult he found it to work now
in an atmosphere where 'they don't seem to work as a team.
They're quite content to get on with it by themselves'. In addition,
several schools had regular staff outings, usually meals, for, as one
teacher explained, 'I'm keen on the social bit. We need to be a
school, an overall unit and it's one way of helping that to happen'.

These kinds of concerns — for the learning and welfare of all
pupils, for the future of one's own class and therefore for the
educational coherence of the whole school, for the social cohesion
of the staff — go beyond what Hoyle (1974: 77) calls 'restricted

professionality' (i.e. an atheoretical, pragmatic concern for the effectiveness of one's own classroom practice). Yet the teachers who expressed them were not, according to some of his criteria, 'extended professionals'. Only a minority were interested in theory, were highly involved in non-teaching professional activities, read professional literature regularly, or were involved in in-service work. Furthermore, Hoyle argues that 'extended professionality is associated with a career orientation rather than with expertise where it ultimately matters — in the teaching situation itself' and that it is achieved 'at the cost of effective restricted professionality at the classroom level' (Hoyle 1974: 19). Now this was clearly not the case with the teachers I interviewed. They took on some of the characteristics of 'extended professionals' — they perceived classroom events in relation to school policies and goals, placed value on professional collaboration, compared their methods with those of colleagues — not so much in pursuit of a managerial career but in order to become better 'restricted professionals'. This is not to argue that the two categories in Hoyle's seminal typology do not exist. Rather it is to suggest the need for a new one — 'bounded professionality' — which falls between the other two. Teachers in this group have whole-school perspectives and an interest in collaboration and collegiality but are largely atheoretical and school-bounded in their approach to other educational issues. Like 'extended professionals' they derive satisfaction 'from problem-solving activities and from a greater control over their work situation' (Hoyle 1974: 18), but like 'restricted professionals' they also find great rewards in successful classroom practice.

Learning from one another

'Pulling together' is not the only form of staff interaction which allows individuals to concentrate upon becoming better teachers while also offering them opportunities to influence one another. My interviewees also looked, especially in mid-career, for situations in which they could learn from their colleagues as well as teaching them. That they were aware of the differences between the two types of relationship is clear from the language that they used in speaking of them. They described teamwork in terms (e.g. 'putting one's shoulder to the wheel'; 'no one's out of step') which suggested that they saw it as a productive but relatively unexciting experience. By contrast, they used metaphors of energy and movement when referring to groups or staffrooms which provided their members with mutual stimulation. They spoke of head teachers or colleagues who would 'pump one another up', 'soak each other's ideas up', 'spark each other off', 'recharge each other', 'keep us all on our toes', 'help us to generate energy', 'bounce ideas off you and you could do the same'.

One woman put it this way:

> I worked in [that school] with two girls that I got on really well with, sharing ideas . . . there's nothing like that, nothing to beat it for keeping you going.

Another said:

> The environment isn't stimulating any more, the school is dying on its feet and that's what's prompting me to move. Because you're not getting stimulation and it's all very well reading the latest reports, going on courses — if you've got no one to talk to and to get feedback from, you don't really grow . . . You can get that stimulation, once you've got the correct balance of staff, very much so. A good staff can stretch you in all directions . . . That's another change that's happened in school: we used to regularly go into each other's rooms and talk about things, swap ideas . . . and we don't have that now. The door tends to be closed and you rarely get a spark from other members of staff; even the head doesn't come in now.

Altogether, two-thirds of the mid-career group had at some point worked, however fleetingly, with people who had 'stretched' or 'recharged' them. They recalled these encounters with animated faces and, often, a smile. Moreover, the memory of them was lasting; one in three of those who had this experience were now working in a different kind of staff group, of whose likely impact upon them they spoke with anxiety and dread: 'I can feel', said one, 'all the enthusiasm draining out of me'. Hewitt (1978) claimed that staleness, questioning the validity of one's work and a desire to update one's knowledge were profound concerns of older secondary teachers. These concerns are certainly echoed by the primary teachers in this study.

One of the main antidotes to the 'boredom' of the staff group was in-service courses, held outside the school. Only two of my interviewees had much experience of school-based INSET; the rest had reservations about it, due, they claimed, to their fear that it would not result in any 'new ideas', 'fresh ways of doing things', 'exciting new developments'. The majority of the group already made good use of local authority in-service provision, looking particularly for practical courses 'with ideas I can use tomorrow morning'. But they did not want only to add variety to their daily practice. They also sought exposure to people who would, as one woman said, 'Gee me into looking at things from a new angle . . . I want to, but it is difficult to do it for yourself'. Most of those who had experience of advanced diploma or higher degree courses tended to find them 'just what I was looking for — not practical, but you really had to think', or 'very stimulating, and useful too because we had to look at what *we* were doing'. Some indeed saw them as 'my salvation', the place where 'I could get my head stretched on a Thursday evening and it kept tingling in school almost till Tuesday'. It remains to be seen whether school-based activities undertaken through Grant-Related In-Service Training (GRIST) will provide teachers with the professional and intellectual stimulation that many of these teachers felt that they needed.

Lack of challenge

A minority of both men and women wanted 'challenge' from their colleagues as well as stimulation. They tended to describe this relationship in confrontational terms, typically using verbs such as 'hammer', 'thrash' or 'hack'. A man said:

> I'd like to be feeding ideas and people picking me up on them, saying, 'Hey, you've not read this, let's talk about this, why can't we do this, I think you're wrong'. But people don't say that. . . . I want a system to challenge me so that I've got to show that I'm right. I want them to say 'You're wrong. Make yourself a case and prove it'. . . . I produced a thirty-page suggested scheme for language about twelve months ago that formed the basis of six staff meetings, and not a word of it was changed, which upset me . . . It should have been thrashed out and hacked about, but . . . nobody stood up and said 'Wrong. The way to teach English is this way or that way'. . . . I'm not challenged, made to question what I'm doing, I do it automatically and easily, which is no stimulus to do the job.

Yet few people worked in staff groups in which this kind of professional confrontation was the norm, a phenomenon which has also been noted in the studies by Jackson (1968), Lortie (1975), Sharp and Green (1975), King (1978), and Pollard (1987). Many reasons have been advanced for the absence of open debate among primary teachers. My interviewees were aware of several. They talked of teachers' isolationism and individualism (see Chapter 1). As a deputy said:

> People tended to keep themselves to themselves. . . . If they
> had a good idea, they didn't want anybody to share it. I think
> this is typical of many teachers, particularly those who've
> been doing the same thing for years, they live in their own
> little worlds and feel protective of them.

In this kind of situation (as another teacher said) 'doors are closed,
sharing ideas is "stealing"; the only place you ever meet is the
staffroom'. A supply teacher argued, 'Most teachers want to get
[the resources] and the children into their rooms and keep everyone
else out'. Her view was confirmed by the teacher who complained:

> The majority of them know how to get through a day,
> through a year, achieve reasonable results without having to
> put in any extra effort, they've got all the resources and
> things in their room and that's it. There's no coming together
> for planning, you don't get any stimulation from other
> people's ideas.

They also felt constrained by the absence of a tradition within
their schools which encouraged debate about ideas. In Nias (1978c)
I have argued that the traditional roots of English teacher education
are unhelpful in this respect. Teachers can learn from the natural-
ism and pragmatism of Rousseau, Froebel and Dewey, as they
would not from the continental dialecticism and debate of Hegel
and Marx to eschew open intellectual conflict. As a result, there is a
tendency for them also to proscribe the expression of negative
emotions (such as jealousy and anger) among adults as well as
children and therefore to regard potential conflict as a pathological
symptom rather than as a natural phenomenon, the resolution of
which can lead to personal and collective growth. King (1978)
further suggests that the particular culture of infant teachers may
serve to repress potential conflict among them. Their acceptance of
the myth of 'childhood innocence' leads them to frown upon disagreement, as being a dangerous and potentially destructive force
in school environments which should be kept as free as possible
from violent and divisive attitudes, words or actions, on the part of
adults as well as children.

The fact that teachers implicitly accept that they are what they
believe (see Chapter 1) may also explain their reluctance to face
intellectual conflict. As one of my interviewees said:

> The most frustrating thing is the level of staffroom chat —
> but perhaps it's a substitute for talking about what we're
> doing, and we don't want to do that; it might be too chal-
> lenging if people started to knock each other's beliefs about.

If her interpretation is right, it is not surprising that English primary teachers find it hard to challenge one another's ideas without at the same time seeming, to themselves and to their colleagues, to be mounting a personal attack. There are schools characterized by inter-personal and inter-professional openness, but Nias *et al.* (1989) suggest that views and opinions can be freely exchanged within them because the staff hold common beliefs about the social and moral purposes of education. In other words, even in these schools there are limits to what teachers may call in question without offending against school norms.

Whatever the reasons, primary staffrooms, as Pollard (1987) points out, tend to be used for friendship, company and conversation, a convention which often inhibited my interviewees from expressing opinions or raising contentious issues (e.g. 'I've got to work with these people. What would have happened if I'd alienated them by going too fast?'; 'It would have meant a head-on collision and I can't work that way, so I backed off'; 'If I'd stayed, I'd have wanted to exchange ideas more and not be afraid [of disagreement] — but it would have taken courage to do that. They weren't used to it'.) It was not surprising, therefore, that they more often found their colleagues 'supportive', 'friendly', and 'helpful' than 'dynamic' or 'exciting'.

Their reluctance to challenge their colleagues was perhaps due to three other common characteristics of primary teachers and schools (Nias 1987c). First, teachers are often authority-dependent, a tendency which is promoted by the widespread prevalence in English society of two largely unchallenged assumptions about knowledge: that those in authority possess it and that learning therefore passes downwards (Abercrombie 1981). Second, the hierarchical nature of many schools and educational systems encourages belief in these assumptions. Lastly, teachers tend to talk more and more skilfully than they listen, perhaps as a result of socialization into these beliefs and structures. Certainly, my interviewees seldom tried to provoke debate in the staff group unless they felt someone would listen:

I think the thing to do is to keep in touch with people who are like-minded. That's the way to survive . . . and if you find yourself in a school with lively, interesting people, stay there and you'll re-charge each other.

If I was in a school where no one would listen and it was just me and a class of children I think I'd lose a lot [of my enthusiasm].

They mentioned two further features of many primary schools which tended to encourage consensus rather than divergence among the staff. The first was smallness. My interviewees commented, for example:

In most village schools there is not the vivacity, the drive, the career enhancement which has geed me up [in my other jobs]. There are not people driving you to go on this course, do that.

I'd like to try teaching in a bigger school with more ideas and different types of people.

The second was stability; for this, too, could easily lead to inertia. As one teacher remarked:

I've worked with them as colleagues for 10 or 11 years, and many of them are personal friends, but I think perhaps . . . you see the same ten people, day in, day out . . . you know each other too well.

A married woman said:

Too many teachers fall into schools where it's cushy for some reason or another, like being near home, so they can put the washing out at dinnertime and they don't want to be lazy, but it's comfortable, so they stay there, and they've got things to think about that seem just as important as teaching.

To the points they raised I would also add teachers' perpetual lack of time and their tendency to spend what time they do have for interaction in the company of those who reinforce rather than challenge their perspectives (see Chapter 3) and the divided, isolated, and bureaucratic nature of many schools (Nias 1987c).

To sum up, many of my interviewees valued staff groups which gave them 'stimulation' (that is, a sense of mutual teaching and learning) because this helped them in pursuit of both 'task' and 'impact' concerns. For similar reasons, a minority also looked to their colleagues for 'challenge' but, for a number of reasons relating to the occupational culture of teaching and the structure of schools, seldom found it in their staffrooms.

'The best experience of all': bringing it all together

In Chapter 7, teachers emphasized how important it was to them to work in an adult environment in which they received help, sympathy, guidance and friendship. Yet, in this chapter, they have spoken of their wish to influence and be influenced by others, to work with them towards common ends, to extend their professional thinking and practice through contact, and sometimes through disagreement with their colleagues. Is there then a tension between what teachers want of one another? Is it possible for teaching staff to help newcomers become technically competent, to give one another practical and emotional guidance and assistance (i.e. to encourage dependence) while making room for dispersed leadership and displays of initiative (i.e. by fostering independence and collegial influence)? How far is it the case that a staff which is socially agreeable is also professionally static? Can staff members who work well together because they share the same perspectives also disagree constructively with one another in ways which promote growth or does consensus lead eventually to stagnation?

To provide a tentative answer to questions like these I turn to the accounts of four teachers who chose to describe in detail to me what one described as 'the best experience of all'. Notwithstanding the formidable obstacles to constructive disagreement discussed in the previous section, some teachers apparently do find within their schools deeply satisfying social contexts which combine support with stimulation, unanimity with challenge, interdependence with a high degree of mutual influence. Teachers who have been able to share not just beliefs, practice and ideas, but also constructive disagreement and mutual concern, find it a potent and heady mix. It was clear from the manner in which the teachers spoke that the adult relationships which they experienced were of profound and lasting emotional significance to them as people and had made a powerful contribution to their thinking as teachers. I let them speak for themselves.

A male deputy, with 15 years' experience in junior schools, who is now married to Sue, said:

> [In my first school] I formed a relationship with a colleague which was very close . . . We had a first and second year, which in total was only really two classes, so I suggested to the head that we put the two classes together and team-teach the two because we related to each other and we had similar outlooks, though she was well-organized and I was intuitive. I played it by ear and she had it on paper. We did it for about ten months and it was probably the most rewarding teaching experience that I've had . . . we stayed in school every night till we were locked out, then we went to a pub and stayed till seven or eight, sometimes nine, preparing work for the following day. We also introduced parents into the classroom

one day a week . . . the parents stayed all morning, and halfway through the morning the kids went out and made coffee and the parents helped the kids out . . . And that worked great — it stopped because I left, but I would have liked to have pursued it. She and I worked very well together on a personal level, and it came across. And in the same way, several years on, Sue and I related in a similar way, we worked together . . . it was a rounded family unit, and that was important for us and the kids.

A married woman with fifteen years' service, interrupted by child-rearing, in primary and special schools, told me:

It started with the head, though she didn't seem to do much — indeed in some respects she seemed quite lazy, but that was good because it made us take the initiative and get on with it. Then she just let it happen. What she did, though, was always to support us — she made us feel secure. She made us feel good about ourselves; it was the first time I'd ever met anyone who said teaching was important and teachers were great.

There were six of us, seven with the head, and although she was head of the whole school she seemed one of us. We all worked down the same end (of the school building) to start with, but not afterwards. I can't remember how we came together as a group, but I'm sure it's important that none of us was hung up on status or role. One of the people we learnt most from was a welfare assistant . . . we were all willing to learn from each other, ready to take on other people's roles and to try and see things from their point of view.

It was very important that we didn't feel the need to compete. Somewhere along the way we lost the need to defend ourselves to each other, our egos stopped being important. You weren't afraid any more of making a fool of yourself and you could admit when things were going badly. I felt absolutely secure in that group. I suppose we all did which is one main reason why it was so important. You could be completely open.

I can't really say how it worked — it was 'organic'; if that doesn't sound silly. It just happened. It was important that we all shared certain values — mostly that we all took the job seriously and wanted to do it well, but also that we have the same basic idea about, for example, how the children should be treated. But we didn't agree about everything. You influence each other. I changed my views on corporal punishment, but stuck my ground on competition and brought

the others with me — which was hard because we were all
brought up to be competitive and our children are competitive
too.

I suppose that's where the openness comes in. If you're a
group, and one or two members change their minds or have a
new idea then you all change a little, otherwise you don't stay
a group. That's why it is good if new people come in . . . [a
new teacher] joined us one year, and she was very different to
the rest of us in her views on teachers always being right. We
had to accept her ideas a bit but you could see her changing
her ways within months of arriving. If you don't change a
little, you ossify. But we did need to keep changing — if that
had stopped happening, and nobody had changed we could
easily have all stopped growing. It didn't happen, but you
could see that it could have done.

We didn't meet as a whole group very often. There wasn't
time, though sometimes after school we'd all sit down for half
an hour or so, and occasionally we went out for lunch all
together and had longer for talking. Somehow the ideas
seemed to move between us by osmosis. But we did talk a lot
in overlapping twos and threes, yes, a lot, about all sorts of
things, as they came up. That was terribly influential. It was
the constant talking, and the openness that helped me to
change.

It made us feel very together, because we knew each other
so well, and gave each other so much support. We didn't see
much of each other outside school, but if there had been more
time we could have been friends and done things together as
well . . . It was a tremendous feeling, I missed them terribly
when I moved on. I still think about it. We really changed
that whole school in the time I was there, and the parents
changed too because we spent a lot of time talking to them as
well. We couldn't any of us have done it on our own . . . It
was probably the most important and formative experience
I've ever had.

A man, now married to Sarah and recently appointed as a head
teacher after ten years in the classroom, recalled:

Working with Sarah and Alan was my first experience of team
work . . . It changed an awful lot of my outlook . . . I
honestly don't know [how it happened]. Partly to do with the
building — it was an open-plan unit of four classes and we
had three of them. The other person — the fourth person who
changed a couple of times — never entirely fitted into the

175

group . . . We were always talking, putting the world to rights
. . . It did me a lot of good. It persuaded me — it got me
listening to other people and it got to a stage when I was
secure with them, in particular to take their criticisms. I can
remember vividly being told by Sarah in a friendly way, long
before we were anything other than friends, 'Look, you're not
going to make any progress while you're continually putting
backs up left, right and centre, couldn't we try it this way?'
and my reply was 'no' but she repeated the exercise and it did
me a lot of good . . . Alan was like that too. We all fitted in
together, though it wasn't always easy. Like me, he was pretty
neurotic to start with. We very quickly realized that we had
things to learn from him as well. I think that's what made the
difference. In certain areas he was clearly the leader and it
provided him with a degree of security, that we were willing
to listen to him too . . . We didn't meet formally, there was
no need to — it was the usual times, mostly after school,
lunch times, in the morning, sometimes whenever we felt the
need to, but working together, there's always something that's
happened or some child or an idea that one of you wants to
talk about.

A woman teacher with eight years' classroom experience
reflected:

[In my first school, the head] had a definite philosophy about
the way he wanted his school to run . . . If he didn't agree
with you, he'd tell you, often in a public and rude manner,
but you could take that because . . . he didn't bear any
grudges, and let you carry on expressing yourself the way you
felt was best, and you could talk to him, too. I think the
energy [in the school] — came from having a body of
professional people who were interested and did things
together . . . There was a lot of talk . . . I miss it . . . We
didn't always agree, but we spent a lot of time doing things
for school together and we learnt from each other . . .
Perhaps we'd make it a social occasion too — we were always
going out together. [By contrast, in this job] we're finding the
need more and more for young teachers to get together, to
give each other ideas, to spark off from one another. In fact
we're trying ourselves . . . to develop [part of the school]
where we can meet and be together.

In my first school, you could talk about philosophy and
argue about it and if your view was different from somebody
else's you could have an argument. In this school you can't

really have any views at all because you're not sure whether anyone will agree with you and if they don't agree with you they hold it against you. So if it's part of you, something you've believed in all your life and you're holding it in all the time, then you have problems, don't you, if you can't express yourself? Then Beth came along and she isn't like that at all, so we huddle in little corners and talk about things we feel passionately about. I go home to her house in the evening if there's a problem we really want to thrash out. She's brought me out a lot . . . made me realize the ways I can change and helped me to do it . . . I wish there was a group of us, like there was in my first school . . . [if I could change one thing here] it would be to make the staff be far more open and honest about teaching and while they're actually at school, to work as a team. We're just not benefitting from everybody's experience and ideas and they're too isolated, everybody is and nobody's happy because there isn't unity, we aren't a group . . . I think we'd benefit an awful lot if it opened up and we could talk to each other. I think the rest would follow then.

It would obviously be unwise, methodologically and substantively, to build too much upon four accounts. Moreover, they leave many questions unanswered. For example, who decided that these particular teachers should be so accessible to one another? If it was the head, did he/she intend that individuals should work so closely together? Who are the 'fourth teachers' in the third account and why did they not become members of the group? Did all four groups impose a joint perspective upon newcomers rather than freeing them to discover and modify their own? Was Beth (in the fourth account) helping the speaker to change or confirming her in her existing viewpoint?

Notwithstanding such gaps in the available evidence, and the attendant difficulty in drawing valid conclusions from it, these accounts confirm that it is possible for teachers to work in situations in which one or more colleagues enrich each others' daily contact with children, confirm yet challenge each other's basic assumptions about education and its purposes, widen each others' professional horizons and responsibilities, and offer one another interest, attention and esteem as people. Members of the pairs or groups which these teachers described offered one another help and recognition in the daily tasks of teaching, took one another's ideas and expertise seriously and built upon them, and spent time in the give and take of professional discussion. In the process, each member developed an awareness of increased influence over the others which offset any perceived decrease in autonomy. Further, while shared perspectives reinforced the individual self-concept, there was enough difference within the group to ensure that, within an overall atmosphere of acceptance and concern, members were challenged as well as affirmed.

At the same time, the groups gave their members a sense of belonging and stability as a counterpoise to the recurrent emotional switchbacks of classroom life, making it possible for interpersonal liking to develop and even to grow into love. No wonder that those who had been part of these groups remembered them, and the teaching with which they had been associated, as 'the best experience of all', reminiscent of the 'peak experience' described by Maslow (1973: 177). This state, he argues, earns its description because through it (however induced) we transcend the inner contradictions and conflicting urges of our human natures and discover what and who we are. In a similar fashion teachers in these collegial groups transcended the contradictory requirements that they had of each other, discovering in the process a sense of personal identity as part of a whole which was, indeed, greater for its members than the sum of its parts. It is perhaps in such experiences that teachers become aware of their identities, going beyond the socially-conditioned 'me' which governs much of their daily work to the autonomous 'I' which simultaneously creates and rebels against it (see Chapter 1).

Because of the importance of such groups to those who were or had been part of them, it is worth briefly drawing attention to their characteristics (for a fuller discussion, see Nias 1987c). First, relationships within them were non-competitive and relatively egalitarian. Each group had a leader, in the sense that someone took the initiative in starting discussions, but he/she then became a member of the group, allowing and encouraging leadership to move between the others as seemed appropriate to them all. Second, despite their differences, members had enough in common to start talking to each other and, once the habit of talking had been formed, they found it so valuable that they made time for it whenever they could. Third, their discussions were similar in several ways: members of each group felt secure with one another, so they talked very openly; topics for discussion arose spontaneously and naturally among members and were not imposed upon them; no firm boundaries were drawn between personal and professional concerns; differences of opinion were sanctioned, even welcomed; individuals were willing to learn from one another. Fourth, as a result of all these other characteristics, the groups acquired a life and identity of their own which served not to enforce conformity upon their members but to enrich their thinking and behaviour, individually and collectively. Through groups of two, three, or more, members found 'a new kind of stability based on the recognition and acceptance of ambiguity, uncertainty and open choice' (Abercrombie 1969: 171). Such groups were a means of achieving growth as well as a source of security.

Conclusion

Building and sustaining adult relationships are, then, increasingly salient parts of the job of primary teaching, for, as teachers mature, they develop the capacity to see their classroom tasks in the context of whole-school goals and policies. Such relationships offer individuals a wider arena in which to operate and an opportunity to exercise greater influence, as they advise and guide their colleagues and actively participate in school-wide decision-making. More importantly, in some respects, they affect the extent to which teachers see their own values and their aims for children's education reinforced or undermined by other's efforts (i.e. by the way in which the staff do or do not 'pull together'). They are also crucial in preventing professional stagnation and in providing opportunities for individuals to extend and develop their occupational knowledge and skills.

Put another way, whereas Hoyle (1974) felt that school staffs could be divided into classroom-focused 'restricted professionals' (with an atheoretical, pragmatic concern for the effectiveness of their own classroom practice) and career-focused 'extended professionals' (with an interest in wider educational issues and a career orientation) many of the teachers I interviewed could be described as 'bounded professionals'. Their interests were the children, their horizons were the school. For them, work could not be confined to interaction with pupils in teaching areas, even though the craft of teaching and the personal relations it involved were of central importance to them. Instead, their work necessarily involved contact with, dependence on, and influence over, other adults. In Fuller's terms, their concern was neither narrowly one of 'task' nor simply one of increased, career-based 'impact'. Rather, they construed their interest in 'impact' in terms of 'task'; they felt that they would be better teachers if they could persuade their colleagues to work together and then help them to do so.

For a few people, relationships with other teachers could also become an end in themselves, providing a yeasty mixture of vision, endeavour, self-extension and affection which leavened the whole

179

task of teaching and filled the lives of those affected by them. Those who had been touched by the excitement and intimacy of such a pair or group could not define teaching merely as work with pupils, or its rewards only in terms of mastery over classroom activities. Nor could they see it simply as involvement with and influence over colleagues in the interests of children. Instead, for a time it became life itself, a highly-charged, intense, all-demanding discovery of personal identity through absorption into the common purposes of the group.

It is this experience that leads into the final chapter, which attempts to explain both what teaching means (in an existential sense) to its practitioners and what is the essential nature of the primary teacher's skill.

Chapter nine

'Feeling like a teacher'

In Chapters 2 and 4 I showed that it is possible to teach for years, successfully and with the affirmation of one's head teacher and colleagues, without incorporating 'teacher' into one's self-image. As several of my interviewees said in their first decade of work, 'I teach, but I do not feel like a teacher'. However, by their second decade most of those whom I interviewed had incorporated their professional identity into their self-image (i.e. they 'felt like teachers'). Clearly, in any attempt to understand the nature of teaching as work, it is important to include the affective reality of experienced, committed teachers. Accordingly, this chapter is built around an analysis of conversations with fifty people in mid-career of whom I asked, 'Do you feel like a teacher?', and explained why I wanted to know. If they said they did, I then requested an explication. In addition, I have used comments they made when they were talking more generally about their work.

What emerges from this analysis is the contradictory nature of the feelings associated with teaching. Various reasons can be adduced for this. The outcome of all of them, for the successful teacher, is mastery over a complex and difficult skill: the theme of 'balance' runs through the latter part of this chapter and, it can be argued, accounts for the sense of fit between identity and work which, at its best, characterizes 'feeling like a teacher'.

Eight of my fifty interviewees did not see themselves as teachers. One man and one woman had drifted into it and were trapped by financial pressures and lack of alternative employment. Three women (one a college lecturer) and one man enjoyed some aspects of teaching but rejected what they saw as the socially imposed role of the primary teacher. The two adult education tutors felt in their new jobs, 'You can go in as yourself, not with that teacher-person to hide behind', or, 'There is no switch of personality, I am the same person while teaching as I am outside'. Two men, though enthusiastic about teaching, felt all adults were teachers and

181

preferred not to split their occupation from their other roles. I have used the responses of all but the first two of these people.

'Being yourself'

Most of the remaining forty-two believed that to adopt the identity of 'teacher' was simply to 'be yourself' in the classroom. They expressed this idea in three similar but slightly different ways. Some stressed a sense of fit between self and occupation (e.g. 'I feel as if I've found my niche'; 'However annoyed I may be at the end of a day in school . . . I still feel I'm in the right job for me'). Others saw little distinction between their 'selves' at work and outside it; as one said, 'What's happening to you as a person can't be separated from what's happening to you as a teacher'. Similar responses included: 'I've mellowed as a person so I've mellowed as a teacher'; 'For me, being happy in teaching was a question of realizing what sort of person I was'; 'I don't think you're any good as a teacher if you're no good as a person'. Lastly, some felt, as one said, that they 'would have been the same person no matter what job I went into'. For example, they saw themselves as 'Christians', 'organizers', 'workaholics'.

Two people stressed how important it is for teachers to have a strong sense of personal identity. One said, 'If teachers are going to be any good, they've got to have a really strong concept of what they are themselves. Fortunately, I have'. The other who had left primary teaching recalled:

> I just wanted to get out. I was asking too much of myself. I couldn't give what I hadn't got inside me to give and I felt that having gone from school straight into university and back into school again, I had not had the opportunity to explore life and certainly not to explore my own creativity. And there I was trying to get the children to be creative individuals and doing all the things I seemed never to have done at school . . . I wanted to sit down and make puppets and play with paint and put my fingers in. I loved just playing with children . . . I felt I needed to become whole and find out who I was and . . . become a personality in my own right.

'Being whole'

Many teachers linked, as this one did, the notions of 'being yourself' and 'being whole'. Some achieved 'wholeness' by blurring the boundaries between their personal and professional lives. A woman said:

I tend to bring a lot of my personal life into school with the children. They know a lot about what I'm doing all the time, so in that way teaching is never separate from my personal life. They know all about my cat, everything that happened to me the previous evening, they know that I sail, they know that I paint, they know what my house is like, so they're not separate lives at all.

A man recalled:

Before I was married, what I did during the day followed through, automatically, into the pub. So if I went for a drink, all I talked about was school. It was a town pub with a wide range of people — actors, bus drivers, postmen, alcoholics. I fulfilled the role of the educationist . . . and I'd go into school the following morning and I'd talk in assembly about the guy I'd met in the pub last night who had real tales to tell. There wasn't any conflict between my two lives.

Many more experienced a sense of unity in school, particularly with their classes. Typical comments were: 'I enjoy doing drama with them, especially if it's some sort of work that means . . . the whole class working together so that we're all swept along'; 'I like the class response when we feel as if we're a class and "our Miss is doing this" or "with our Miss we did so and so" '; 'It's a feeling that at the end of the day, at the end of a year, at the end of a project you . . . can look back and say, "Yes, we all, as a class, found it satisfying" '. A secondary teacher was trying to create a remedial unit, 'seen as having a oneness it never had before'. A head teacher confessed:

I think I'm trying, probably unwisely, to build up the same sort of thing I had with a class. I'm regarding them as my class of 220 and I'm hoping I can go at least part of the way [towards] that sense of oneness.

Other heads, recognizing that they had permanently lost this aspect of 'feeling like a teacher', nevertheless regretted it and repeatedly referred back to it as they talked.

What these excerpts do not convey is the non-verbal signs which every teacher used when they were talking about the 'wholeness' of class teaching. Without exception, when they tried to explain what it was to feel at one with a group of children, they cupped their hands or made enfolding movements with hands and arms. They spoke eagerly, enthusiastically, often leaning forward, their faces animated. In displaying what Biklen (1986: 506) has called a 'passion for teaching' they seemed to me, as a listener, to be describing what they experienced as a deeply satisfying sense of belonging. Certainly, their response to my questions was an affective rather than a cognitive one, as is further shown by the difficulty they had in reflecting analytically upon the notion of 'wholeness'.

There were two teachers, however, who did manage to explain, in some way, why 'wholeness' was important to them. Both talked about it in terms of feelings. Commenting upon the introduction of specialist teaching into a pair of classes, a man said:

> I began to feel . . . there's something wrong here . . . I
> thought to myself, 'But we can do that [building a link
> between subjects], that can't be the problem. We can do that
> quite easily . . . There's something else that must be missing
> . . . There is a mood the children have; individuals are
> different and we don't think about it very much because it's
> not one of those things that we actually plan and mark like a
> piece of work, but it's there, and the child's mood from one
> day to the next is different and it carries him through the day
> . . . Normally . . . his mood comes from the previous piece of
> work and there's a psychological strand running through the
> day. By psychological I'm talking about his feelings. If we
> split the day in half, there is a rupture . . . and the child has
> to start anew in the afternoon.

A woman suggested:

> Having that [sense of 'we're a class'] isn't to do with
> curriculum, or the integrated day or anything . . . it's about
> feeling you're together . . . What goes on in a classroom is
> mostly about feelings, just as it is in life generally. Feelings
> are infinitely more important in guiding how people act than
> ideas are. You have to accept the importance of feelings, your
> own and theirs, or you will never be happy as a teacher.

The desire to create 'wholeness' also showed itself in attempts to soften the barriers of role, age and status and to prevent the erection of new ones (particularly those of curriculum or timetabling). Several teachers attacked what they described as 'fragmentation' or 'splitting' of their pupils' learning experiences. Many talked enthusiastically and, in the case of some heads, nostalgically, about their involvement with children in extra-curricular activities, clubs, on field trips and school journeys, and in residential study centres. At the time of the interviews, most had abandoned such activities because of their support for industrial action. Many regretted this curtailment of their roles and looked forward to a resumption of those activities which blurred the boundaries between the instructional and other aspects of their jobs.

The urge to work in an environment characterized by unity, not division, extended to staff relationships as well (see Chapter 8). In the words of a head, 'The school was a part of me, the staff were a part of me . . . I couldn't separate myself from them'. Similarly, several spoke warmly of schools in which they 'felt part of the community', or were 'very much part of a great, big unit, we are rooted in the history of the place, we've got parents who came to the same school'. Two had taken jobs in village schools, one because in such a school 'we're constantly working towards a oneness with the community', the other for 'the sense of community intimacy which attracted me to a small school'. Four had chosen to move to 4–11 schools because in them they could be with the same children for most of the latter's school career and, 'if you're lucky, they come back from the high school to see you sometimes so you see them as they get older, too'. Three of the five people who had moved to jobs in pre-service education made a point of telling me that their main aim was to try and bring theory and practice together for students. Asked to describe things he enjoyed doing as a teacher, one person replied, 'I find that very difficult — it's the wholeness of the thing, I think, the total experience'.

'Being natural'

Feeling 'whole' was very close, for many teachers, to being 'natural'. Several saw school as being 'unnatural' and wanted to find ways of 'having a compromise between letting [pupils] be childish and childlike and saying "When you're here . . . this is how we do it" '. Two men rejected the designation 'teacher' because, as one said, 'In any relationship between an adult and a child, teaching is a natural role to play'. Nearly a third used the family as a metaphor or an analogy for their favourite schools. One described working with her welfare helper in a special school as 'we're almost a mummy and daddy, with a family'; another said he treated the children in his class as he did his own children, 'behaving like a dad to them'. In several other teachers' minds small village schools offered a 'natural', 'family' form of education. Indeed, four confessed, as one said, to 'having a pipe-dream about ending up in a village school where I can make education into a natural thing and my part in it a natural one . . . The more you can equate the classroom to a family the more effective the education'. Others spoke graphically of the 'natural feel' given to

185

their work by the temporal rhythms of the day, the week, the term, seasonal celebrations, and the start and end of the year (see also Lieberman and Miller 1984).

'Establishing relationships with children'

Embedded in the notions of belonging, and of education as an extension of family life, is a belief that to teach one must 'establish a relationship with pupils'. Several people were explicit about this:

> I've met kids that I taught when I first went there who are now working . . . They don't just say, 'Aren't you Mr Jones?', they say, 'Alright Sir?' and that's the difference. It's not a question of education, it's a question of relationships.

> One of the problems of being a part-timer is that you can't build up that relationship with them. You never say to a child, 'Carry my bags'; you offer to carry theirs . . . and you make sure the teachers never sit while the children are standing. But it works both ways, I used to get them together and say 'We're going on holiday this week, I'm going on holiday as well, don't spoil it for me'.

They described their work in terms such as 'getting co-operation from the children', 'it's a joint effort between you and them', 'what a teacher is to any individual child could be something totally different, it's a function of the two personalities involved'. One put it very strongly: 'If you actually reach the level where you see yourself as an hourly-paid imparter of knowledge to whom relationships are unimportant, I think that is when you cease to be a professional'. Several others made similar references, to 'passing on information, not teaching' or 'telling them things, rather than teaching'. If my interviewees said that they liked their work, I asked them to imagine that I knew nothing about schools, and to name several things which they did that they enjoyed. Only two could do this; the rest described their satisfactions in terms of relationships with individuals or groups. By contrast, no one had difficulty in naming things that they did which they did not enjoy. In other words, they all had difficulty in conceptualizing the pleasures of the job in instrumental terms. In the same way, most found it hard to think in terms of external measures for their success or failure. One said, 'You can look at it in terms of results, but you can also look at it in terms of your gut reaction to the class as a whole and how they feel about you and you feel about them'. Although they knew it existed, my interviewees found it hard to describe what they meant by their 'relationship' with children. Occasionally it was seen as playing a parental role, sometimes as relating to peers — e.g. 'It can be as close as another friend', 'Some of those children I'd really like to keep as friends' (see also Woods, 1987a). Very frequently it contains a marked element of humour, often based on shared understandings (Walker and Adelman 1976; Woods 1979). Many teachers appear to gauge the state of their relationship with a class by the extent to which 'we can all have a laugh together', 'I can be myself, laugh and joke', or, 'we can share a joke and then get down to work again'. However, to many teachers the relationship is more than being either a parent or a friend. Several people described teaching as 'communication with another human being' or 'learning to communicate with other people'. A woman reflected:

I've come to realize that if you really want to educate children you've got to share yourself with them, as a person. They've got to know about you, your interests, your life out of school, the sort of person you are. But most of all it means being open to them as a person, and that makes you vulnerable. Yes, being a teacher is being ready to be vulnerable.

A man put it bluntly, even angrily:

To talk of teaching as having a relationship with children isn't a cosy thing, it doesn't mean 'having a nice time' with them. It means committing yourself as a person.

Control

To the person who undertakes to build this relationship, it has three main characteristics: control, responsibility and concern. Virtually every teacher responded to my request to explain what it was to 'feel like a teacher' by saying that it was to be in control (e.g. 'It's doing things you're in control of to a large extent'; 'It's being in control of what goes on in the classroom'; 'To start with, it's your will against theirs'). However, people had different reasons for making this response. Ten teachers (five men and five women) were explicit about their felt personal need to control their lives and environments. Two spoke of local political developments (e.g. amalgamations, curriculum initiatives) making them feel that 'instead of me having control over what I'm doing, the outside situation is taking over'. Most talked of the personal satisfaction they derived from being able to control and influence children and other adults, although I also spoke to three people who found the

187

exercise of classroom control inconsistent with their self-image. One reflected:

> Feeling like a teacher can have a negative side to it — unless you're careful you can find yourself taking advantage of the situation, because you have tremendous power over children.

The others said: 'Sometimes I feel like Billy Liar or Peter Pan in that I have to pinch myself to think that I'm 36 and people call me "Sir"; and "Mr Brown", when I feel just like a big soft kid half the time', and, 'With teaching you're sort of God, aren't you? I find that very hard'. Further, even those who did not feel this way hated 'being a policeman', the times 'when you can't do any teaching because you spend all day just keeping them down', or 'children who force you to act in ways you know have nothing to do with teaching'.

A few, echoing Geer (1968), felt that teachers and learners can never be equal, that the act of teaching necessarily involves the exercise of power. This tacit assumption was voiced in both negative terms (e.g. 'That's why I should be paid the same as a police inspector — I do the same job') and positive ones (e.g. 'Feeling like a teacher is feeling as though you're in control, that you know what response is right for you to make').

Whether or not they enjoyed the exercise of control, they all accepted that, as a teacher, 'You have to exercise authority. Treating children like human beings and yet maintaining discipline is a constant challenge'. Indeed, being willing to exercise authority was widely seen as the one necessary condition for 'feeling like a teacher'. Two teachers suggested:

> A teacher's relationship with children is quite distinctive. However much you care and however much you share with them, you assume an air of authority. I didn't have any authority for a couple of years, partly because I didn't really have any conviction that I was doing anything right.

> There is no way round it. If you want to be a teacher you have to find a way of establishing your control because it's a sort of barrier you have to get through. If you want to do the job you have to do that because it is part of being a teacher. You cannot do the rest of the job, which I wanted to do, without getting over the first barrier.

In a study of teachers in an alternative school, Swidler found that those who tried to assume responsibility for pupils without recourse to formal authority had to fuel their teaching with their private

lives — relying on 'personality, charm and interests' — and that
they found this too exhausting to sustain for long (Swidler 1979:
181). My interviewees, too, had come to realize that the authority
implicit in the teacher's role was a necessary condition for the
exercise of their pedagogic skill.

The related idea that teachers have constantly to strive for a
balance between authority and friendliness recurred over and over
again. For example:

> [In my first school] you could have a joke with them, you
> could be friendly up to a point, as you wanted to be, but
> beyond that they would show you some respect. I found that
> quite different from where I am now.

> Being new it was hard trying to be approachable and yet
> getting the children to realize that there had to be a certain
> amount of distance. That was awfully hard, but then I think
> towards the end I got it reasonably right. The children could
> always come and speak to me and they would never be turned
> away, and yet they knew I was the teacher and they were the
> pupils.

> It's the times when you're with a class, with discipline, and
> they know how far they can go with you, and you can laugh
> and joke and have fun with them, both in and out of the
> classroom — that works best of all.

Closely related to feeling in control was the sense of being well-
organized and purposeful — 'having specific ends in view, not
muddling through, knowing what you're about', 'knowing what
you want from and for children', 'being organized, so that in any
teaching situation you have a sense of direction'.

Responsibility and concern

Assuming responsibility for children was also seen to be linked with
feeling in control. People believed that, as teachers, they must
'accept the children's dependence on you', 'feel a great responsibility for every child in my care', 'accept that you will influence
them by what you are, whether you want to or not'. One man
claimed:

> It means that you have got to accept them for what they are,
> and if an 8-year-old says 'I love you, Mr Smith' she means it,
> and you can't play with that, you cannot dismiss it, you
> cannot turn round to her and say 'I love you as well, Sarah' if

you don't mean it. And I think that's what feeling like a
teacher is: when you realize what an awesome responsibility
you bear. . . . If teachers realized just what influence they
have on children, I think then they'd realize what being a
teacher was.

Another man said:

I feel privileged, I suppose, to belong to the teaching profession which I really do believe is perhaps the most important
profession for changing the future — the future is really in
our hands, so to speak . . . I feel a great responsibility in
being a teacher. I don't think about it every minute of the
day, but when I do, I handle this relationship I'm being given
with great care because it's a very precious profession. I'm
not involved in making money for anybody, not involved in
running a big organization, or the country, I'm involved in
running an organization to nurture children, which must be
the most important function in the world. So I accept the
responsibility of being a teacher as important.

Related to both control and responsibility, but less detached than
either, is affection. Many teachers emphasized the caring aspects of
their role, using such terms as 'being prepared to put their interests
first', 'doing your best for all the children in your class'. Five, four
of them men, put it more strongly than this. One said:

There are one or two children that I love very dearly. There
have been one or two children in the past twelve years I have
loved totally . . . only one or two. The difference that having
my own son has made to my relationships at school has not
been that strong. I still have one or two children I'm really
fond of, not as pupils, but as people.

Another said:

I really loved them until I had my own children. Once I
started having my own children, my relationship changed with
the classes I taught. But up to my little girl being born I used
to love the children in my class, I used to get very close to
them. At the end of the summer term I used to be sad at
losing them and having to pass them on to someone else.

One woman felt:

Love comes into it too, that's part of what you experience as
a teacher.

Another could not face these demands:

> It was giving, giving, giving all day long . . . it drove me round the bend.

In whatever way these teachers expressed the essential characteristics of their relationship with children, they became, in the words of one man, 'more intuitive, relaxed and spontaneous' as they came to 'feel like teachers'. Individuals repeatedly spoke of being more relaxed in the classroom and the staffroom, of feeling more able to be 'adaptive and flexible', of 'being less of a worrier', 'more laid back', and above all more self-confident. As one person crisply responded, 'Feeling confident in what you do, that's what it all hinges on'.

At this point the circular nature of what they were saying becomes apparent: to 'feel like a teacher' is to feel you can be yourself in the classroom; to be yourself is to feel whole, to act naturally; to act naturally is to enter into a relationship with children, a relationship in which control makes possible the exercise of responsibility and the expression of concern; together, these states enable you to 'be yourself' in the classroom and therefore to 'feel like a teacher'.

Living with tension, dilemma and contradiction

Yet this sense of 'wholeness' and fit between self and occupation is dearly bought. As Chapters 5 and 6 make clear, there is little consistency in the lived experience of primary teaching. To 'be' a teacher is to be relaxed and in control yet tired and under stress, to feel whole while being pulled apart, to be in love with one's work but daily to talk of leaving it.

There are three inter-related sets of reasons for this contradictory state of affairs: socio-historical, psychological, and philosophical. Sociologically, the teacher's role is ambiguous and ill-defined, hedged about with uncertainty, inconsistency, and tension. Primary teachers occupy many roles, some (e.g. instructor, parent, judge, friend) perpetually at war with one another (Blyth 1967; Woods 1987a). The essentially conflictual nature of the job is emphasized by teachers' inescapable obligation to control children. The American sociologist, Waller, has made a powerful case for the view that 'the teacher–pupil relationship is a form of institutionalised dominance and subordination . . . Teacher and pupil confront each other with attitudes from which the underlying hostility can never be removed' (Waller 1961: 195). The need for teachers to exercise power stems from the fact that adult groups (of whom in school the teacher is representative) and the formal curriculum, which offers children 'dessicated bits of adult life' (ibid.) confront pupils who are 'interested in life in their own world' and 'striving to realize themselves in their own way' (ibid.). Education cannot escape from being a process in which the older generation (represented by teachers) force-feeds the younger. In the clash of interests which follows, teachers have to use every resource they can muster to curb and harness children's energies, to render the 'desiccated bits of adult life' palatable to classes full of the richness of their own experience. Add to that the fact that in England this process of compulsory socialization is invested in teachers who, with negligible adult help and relatively few resources, daily face large numbers of physically active children, and it is inevitable that control becomes for them a central issue in school and classroom life (see also Woods 1977; Denscombe 1980b).

Lieberman and Miller (1984: 14) put it this way:

> Once inside the classroom, a teacher knows that all control is tenuous. It depends on a negotiated agreement between students and the teacher. If that agreement is violated, a teacher will subordinate all teaching activities to one primary goal: to regain and maintain control . . . when one loses control, one loses everything.

Since the exercise of dominance by one person over others can never be without strain, stress is therefore built into the teacher's job. Moreover, as studies of teacher–pupil interaction from Jackson (1968) onwards have shown, control is often exercised in a face-to-face manner. However skilled or subtle the negotiation or oblique the exercise of control (Lortie 1975; Sharp and Green 1975; King 1978; Pollard 1979, 1980, 1985; Woods 1987a), primary teachers' relationships with young children are daily, frequent, direct, sometimes conflictual, always central. There is no escape from the interpersonal tension which characterizes the exercise of their authority.

Furthermore, the teacher's work is riddled with uncertainties. The goals of their schools and the values which underpin these are conflicting (Blyth 1967), and, in an attempt to reduce the impact of this conflict, have often become imprecise, ambiguous, and unattainable (Alexander 1984). The resulting vagueness masks a number of dilemmas which teachers' daily practice expresses, even if they do not themselves voice them (Berlak and Berlak 1981). These authors vividly portray dilemmas-in-action in English primary classrooms, showing how teachers resolve, on a minute-by-minute basis, conflicting expectations about, for instance, their role, the curriculum, their teaching methods and response to pupils' work. For example: how can the needs of individuals be reconciled with those of the whole class group? Should the teacher or the pupil control the content and pace of learning and determine the standards by which it is judged? By what criteria should particular elements be included in or excluded from the curriculum? Some of the mutually incompatible preoccupations which teachers therefore experience enter the classroom with them, the product of their own social and educational experience and of their professional beliefs and aspirations. Other dilemmas which they face stem from views expressed directly or indirectly by outside forces, such as parents or local and central government. Either way, teachers' inevitable inability fully to satisfy their own consciences and their wider audiences leaves them feeling simultaneously under pressure, guilty, and inadequate.

Vagueness on goals (and therefore responsibilities) is coupled with the absence of clear or valid criteria by which teachers may be judged. This ambiguity itself rests on insecure foundations, since little is known with certainty about the connection between teaching and learning. Nor is there any consensus about the knowledge base of teaching as a profession (Lortie 1975; Hargreaves 1980; Alexander 1984) and therefore about what teachers should know. Since 1986, attempts have been made in England and Wales to introduce systems of teacher appraisal into schools, but they have so far met with little success, not so much because of opposition within the profession to the notion of quality control, but because of the chronic difficulty of agreeing criteria on which judgements may be made. As Lortie (1975) repeatedly argues in his cogent chapter on the 'endemic uncertainties' of teachers' work, the view from outside the profession is complex and ambiguous, while, even from within, many teachers find it difficult to rate their own performance. Yet the very absence of clear feedback about their effectiveness can spoil the pleasures of teaching for them.

Further, the many roles which teachers already occupy are currently expanding. In the past two decades these roles have grown to include work (of many sorts) with parents, governors, outside agencies, support services, and colleagues (Campbell 1985; Acker 1987). In the 1990s, these demands are likely to be augmented by the need for teachers to assume greater responsibilities for school-based in-service education, and national assessment, and for head teachers of larger schools to take on, with their governors, the running of their school's finances and physical plant — and all this on top of English teachers' documented tendency to assume a very wide range of moral responsibilities for their pupils

(Osborn 1986). Nor has there ever been any guarantee that the interpersonal skills which allow many teachers to work wonders with children will enable them to work smoothly and with political acumen among such a variety of different adult groups. Yet the requirement to assume all these additional roles and responsibilities has been placed upon primary teachers at a time of deep, acute professional frustration (Primary Schools Research and Developmental Group 1986).

Psychologically, the job itself is not only 'incredibly, unexpectedly demanding' (Fuller and Bown 1975: 48) but also shifting and elusive. It rests upon relationships with pupils whose attendance may be erratic, even arbitrary (Duke 1986). The time of day, the weather, children's moods, staff illnesses, break-ins, visitors from medical and other support services, and a myriad of other minor alterations in the teachers' context and programme mean that they experience continuous and endemic change, in circumstances already characterized by uncertainty and unpredictability (Nias *et al.* 1989). The classroom is never the same place from one day to the next, often it can alter radically from one moment to another. Yet teachers are expected to maintain throughout an aura of 'professional pleasantness' (King 1978) and to 'correct for the capriciousness of students with the steadiness, resolve and sangfroid of one who governs' (Lortie 1975: 156).

The warmth, patience, strength and calm thus required by tradition and circumstances cannot eradicate teachers' fiercer and more negative emotions; for teaching is, in Connell's words, an 'emotionally dangerous occupation' (Connell 1985: 121). Harrison (1983) talks of the 'daemonic power' of love in institutional life, and although educationalists seldom use 'love' in describing teacher–pupil relationships, teachers themselves are aware that it exists. For example, Jackson (1968: 139–41) gives a sensitive and insightful account of American elementary teachers' 'love' and 'respect' for their pupils. The intensity of such emotions is balanced by anger (Connell 1985; Blase 1986; Duke 1986), and by the shame which accompanies the uncontrolled expression of this rage (Lortie 1975).

The 'erratic selves' of teachers have to exercise self-control as well as holding their pupils and their shifting circumstances in check (Lortie 1975: 155). Moreover, they want to: Smith *et al.* (1986) and Alexander (1988) both see the professional maturation of teachers in part as a process of coming to terms with the tensions of the psyche. Teachers as people, Alexander argues, need to try to resolve internal uncertainties, ambivalence and dissonance; it is a natural instinct, to try 'to make the jungle into a garden' (Alexander

1988: 44). It is thirty years since Gabriel (1957) wrote a book entitled *An Analysis of the Emotional Problems of the Teacher in the Classroom*, and, apart from the work of Richardson (1967; 1973) and Salzberger-Wittenberg *et al.* (1983), little has been published in the intervening years to remind us that 'teachers face themselves' (Jersild 1952), not just their pupils. In particular, as I suggested in Chapter 1, attempts to understand the psychological strains of teaching have paid little attention either to Freudian notions of repression or to Kohut's legitimation of self-love and love of pupils as an extension of the self.

Living with paradox

Finally, the varying philosophical roots of primary teaching contribute to its stresses. Not only is there an unresolved tension between the 'elementary school tradition' (with its emphasis on the mass instruction of a narrow curriculum to large classes) and the 'developmental tradition' (Blyth 1967; Alexander 1984) but, within the latter, different influences bear upon teachers, all of them giving encouragement to the idea that teaching is 'building relationships'. So, the emphasis which the teachers in this study laid upon being 'natural' and 'whole' echoed the prescriptions of Froebel and Rousseau. At the same time, their concern with individual relationships owed much to Buber, the existential philosopher and educational thinker; many tried, without using his phrase, to establish an 'I–thou' relationship with the children in their classes, making themselves available as resources for and facilitators of the development of each unique personality. Even the agnostics and atheists appeared also to be influenced by the Christian tradition. They spoke of their pupils as human beings of equal worth to themselves, cared for and accepted moral responsibility for them. Elliott and his colleagues (1981) found this emphasis upon moral responsibility to pupils, and through them to parents, when they explored the ways in which teachers conceptualize 'accountability'. As Brown and McIntyre (1986) indicate, teachers want to ensure that children are actively involved in learning and are making progress. They therefore see discipline and order as complementary to concern.

Now these ways of thinking about teaching impose both practical and philosophical strains on the teacher particularly in the light of the Education Act, 1988. In practical terms, the contemporary debate on the primary school curriculum (especially as it relates to specialist teaching of a subject-based National Curriculum), on exigencies of cost and staffing, on assessment, on accountability, and on enrolment policies make it increasingly difficult for teachers to work in environments which are not competitive, constrained, or divided (in terms of time, curriculum, and personnel). The aftermath of industrial action, and continuing debate about teachers' roles, responsibilities, and duties, challenge those who see learning as extending outside the classroom and beyond the limits of the school day. The impact (e.g. school closures, teacher re-deployment) of falling rolls and financial cuts reduces teachers' emotional and financial security and breaks up established relation-ships with parents, pupils, and staff. Further, as the Oracle Project (Galton *et al.* 1980) has made abundantly clear, the managerial difficulties of relating to and answering the learning demands of each individual within a large class places impossible demands on the teacher. Small wonder, then, that teachers feel under stress, when the conditions of their working lives prevent them from behaving in ways that they perceive as 'organic', 'natural' or 'right'.

More fundamentally, however, primary school teachers in England appear to have a conception of teaching which imposes upon them the need continually to live and work with paradox. The very nature of teaching, as they experience it, is contradictory. Teachers must nurture the whole while attending to the parts, liberate their pupils to grow in some directions by checking growth in others, foster and encourage progress by controlling it, and show love and interest by curbing and chastising. Indeed, there is some evidence that these teachers were themselves aware of the paradoxi-cal nature of their task. In particular, they saw themselves facing three quandaries, each of them relating in some way to their perception of themselves.

First, they could not become the sort of teachers they wanted to be without also accepting the need to behave in ways they found disagreeable. One talked of 'learning that you've got to establish yourself and your authority first — let them dislike you so they can like you later'. Another said, 'I have learnt that you must dominate the children in order to free them . . . I quite accept that now, it's just the pain of doing it'. A third explained, 'What I offer the children is the possibility of using the security of my control to try and develop themselves', while someone else argued, 'The only way to stop the teacher–pupil relationship being a negative one, based on power, is to make sure that it's you who has the power'.

Second, they could encounter children as individuals and care for them only if they were also aware of and valued themselves. One of them put it this way:

I don't think anyone could teach young children unless they're both egocentric and selfless. You've got to be very sure of who you are yourself and yet quite prepared to forget who you are, not forget it, but put who you are second to who the kids are.

Similarly, they could meet the children's personal calls upon them only if they had something left to give (i.e. if they safeguarded opportunities out of school to replenish the 'selves' who went to work).

Third, they could not be fulfilled by their work unless they allowed themselves to be depleted by its demands. I asked several people, 'Why do you let the school take so much of you?'. The typical reply was: 'I enjoy giving it'.

My claim is, therefore, that to adopt the identity of an English primary school teacher is to accept the paradoxical nature of the task and inexorably to live with tension. Those who claim that they can be themselves in and through their work — i.e. that they can 'feel like teachers' — are signalling that they have learnt to live not just with stress but with paradox. To define teachers' learning goals and conditions of service, to increase training and funding, to improve the management of schools may all reduce the practical burden on teachers, but they do not alter the nature of the work itself. Nor, unless we change the philosophical bases of primary teaching — the apparent, though often unacknowledged influence of Rousseau, Pestalozzi, Froebel, Buber, Rogers, and the Christian tradition — are we likely to do so.

Craftsmanship and artistry

Primary teaching is, then, an occupation which requires the ability to live with, and handle constructively, a multitude of dilemmas, tensions, contradictions, uncertainties, and paradoxes. As the all-party Select Parliamentary Committee Report on Primary Education (Education, Science and Arts Committee 1986: 1, 2) reported:

> [Our comments] are made in the context of . . . our high regard for the skills of good primary teachers and our recognition of the complexity of their work.

This ability to work productively with complexity depends in turn upon the exercise and refinement of highly developed expertise in four areas, the first three of which make possible the fourth.

First are interpersonal skills. Some of these are almost intuitive, such as the 'pedagogic tact' described by Van Manen (1984: 2), a quality of 'sensitivity, founded in love, which enables one to do what is pedagogically the right thing for a child'. Others are based on the ability to acquire, store, retrieve, and interpret accurately information about all the children in a class (Doyle 1986). Together, they enable teachers to win the confidence of, control, laugh with, listen, and talk to children of all ages.

Second, there are the pedagogic skills of observation, interpretation, organization, management, and communication (see, e.g. Smith and Geoffrey 1968; Jackson 1968; Bennett *et al.* 1984; Doyle 1986). Together these require, as Desforges and Cockburn so clearly illustrate, personal resources, qualities of insight, hard work, and the capacity to act as a 'ruthlessly efficient quartermaster' (Desforges and Cockburn, 1987: 55).

Underlying, and in some senses, enabling both these sets of skills is the ability to adapt to circumstances and constraints through the use of 'coping strategies' ('a type of patterned and active adaptation to a situation by which an individual copes', Pollard 1982: 155). Pollard (1985) describes in detail various ways of adapting used by teachers and pupils to obtain a 'working consensus' in the classroom which will protect and enhance the self-interests of both. 'Open negotiation' and 'manipulation', in particular, require of the teacher a high degree of practised ability in observation, interpretation, and sensitive responsiveness. The resulting 'negotiated system of behavioural understandings' (Pollard 1985: 160) enables both teacher and pupils to safeguard their interests, reduces the stress under which they work and allows teaching and learning to proceed with the minimum of disruption and the maximum goodwill. To survive, then, teachers must also be expert classroom negotiators.

Each of the three sets of skills that primary teachers use in classrooms is impressive to watch in action. However, it is when they are operated together or 'orchestrated' (Woods 1987a: 135) that competence becomes craftsmanship. Shifting swiftly between instruction and affection, management and laughter, teachers 'display a superb feel for moving back and forth between familiarity, liking, caring, warmth and a more detached teacher-like stance' (Lieberman and Miller 1984: 20). To this highly-developed capacity to switch instantly and smoothly between the personal and the professional, experienced practitioners add other abilities: for instance, the ability to handle variety and complexity; to juggle priorities; to resolve dilemmas; to process densely-packed information reaching them simultaneously on many channels; to respond to it with sensitivity and accuracy; and to adjust their intentions, plans, and actions without disrupting themselves or others. This composite skill has been noted and admired by many classroom observers (e.g. Jackson 1968; Smith and Geoffrey 1968; Kounin 1970; King 1978; Berlak and Berlak 1981; Lieberman and Miller 1984; Pollard 1980, 1982, 1985; Hartley 1985; Duke 1986; Desforges and Cockburn 1987; Woods 1987a). It has also been noted in studies of inter-adult relationships in primary schools (Nias 1987b; Nias *et al.* 1989). Although each of these studies has a slightly different focus, they all single out for special attention a capacity to do what is most often described as 'balance'.

Now what is truly remarkable about experienced primary teachers' pedagogic 'balancing' is not so much that they achieve it, but that they do so in the face of unremitting pressures towards disequilibrium. The craft of such teachers is epitomized in their capacity to bring their own emotions and the social systems within which they work into harmony and then to refuse to be disrupted, unbalanced, torn asunder, blown off course, or put out of step (one can use many metaphors, all of them appropriate) by the historical, social, emotional, philosophical, or practical tensions which form the context and backdrop of their work.

There are acknowledged pleasures in the exercise of craftsmanship, and the successful performance of this complex, demanding act of balancing might in itself explain the fact that accomplished classroom practitioners often feel purposeful and satisfied. To handle smoothly the essentially conflictual nature of their work is an expression of practised abilities in which they can justly take pride. The resulting sense of equilibrium may also account for why they feel 'whole', 'natural' and 'in control'. However, this is not the whole story, for successful balancing also brings its own affective rewards; a finely-tuned, well-equilibrated relationship between teachers and pupils is, for all its tensions and intricacies, a warm and even a loving one. The intrinsic pleasures of skilled performance are complemented by the giving and receiving of affection. Teaching offers its 'joys' and 'thrills' (Jackson 1968: 134, 137) as well as its sense of mastery.

Some people would go further than this, however, claiming that teaching is an art rather than a craft (e.g. Eisner 1979; Stenhouse 1980; Lieberman and Miller 1984; Woods 1987a). Certainly, the creative endeavour needed to transcend its dilemmas, contradictions and paradoxes can result in the exhilaration, intense joy, even 'ecstasy' (Woods 1987a: 142) of the artist:

> People who have not taught can have little idea what it is like to have *taught well* [author's italics], to be buoyed up and swept along by the response of students who are learning. One

> reaches for metaphors: chemical reactions, currents, setting
> alight, taking fire. But however difficult to describe . . . it is
> something that most teachers . . . have, at least some of the
> time.
>
> (Connell 1985: 127)

Now Connell's description is not unlike that of William James
(Chapter 1), in which he writes to his wife of the moments in which
he feels 'most deeply and intensely active and alive [when] there is a
voice inside which speaks and says, "This is the real me!" ' (quoted
in Erikson 1968: 19). Perhaps it is in the precious moments when
primary teachers become creative artists that they transcend the
contradictions of the job and achieve the 'peak experience' of
which Maslow (1973: 177) writes and in which they, like James,
become aware of their full identity.

The notion that primary teachers achieve 'balance' through the
exercise of a complex and demanding skill, which at times becomes
a creative act, puts a different complexion upon the often-repeated
accusation that they are middle-of-the-road, moderate, realistic,
pragmatic (see, e.g. Waller 1961; Lortie 1975; King 1978; Connell
1985; Pollard 1987), preferring consensus to extremism, compromise to controversy, the immediate to the remote, the concrete to
the abstract. To be sure, some of them do answer this description:
in any craft-based occupation some people perform less well than
others, and teaching is no exception. The skill of balancing requires
attributes and qualities — for example, adaptability, flexibility,
good information-processing abilities, swift reflexes and responses,
physical and emotional energy, perseverance, concentration, self-
control — which not everyone possesses in equal measure or all the
time. But there is no escaping the need to keep the primary classroom in equilibrium. Consequently, some teachers achieve a type
of balance which satisfies them and their pupils by reducing the
number of components with which they have to juggle, or by
simplifying the relationship between them. Others slow the whole
process down or deal with only one part of it at a time. Whatever
the strategy they select to retain control over the act of teaching, it
may (and sometimes does) lead to a sluggish, unresponsive form of
equilibrium characterized by dullness, inertia, complacency, or
stagnation.

But it is easy to confuse the calm counterpoise of an experienced
teacher with mediocrity. It is a truism that a good craftsman or
woman makes the job seem easy. The balance and rhythm which
many teachers achieve, in the face of considerable and growing
difficulties, can readily be mistaken for stagnation or complacency.

Judgements about the skill of teachers should therefore be made only by those who understand the subtleties and nuances of what they observe. Moreover, teachers put 'off balance' by, for example, a particularly disruptive child, an acerbic colleague, a shortage of essential resources, or a deep sense of professional frustration, are likely to search for a new equilibrium which contains but does not redress the cause of the imbalance. Over time, such adjustments may render the craft performance of skilled practitioners heavier, less responsive, and more sluggish. Furthermore, since to 'feel like a teacher' is to feel 'in balance', and this sense in turn carries with it great affective rewards, one can speculate that teachers who believe that they can no longer — for whatever reason — achieve the difficult feat of holding tensions in balance and transcending contradictions, may choose to leave the profession, either literally or by withdrawing their interest and commitment from it (Chapter 4). When either of these developments takes place, the education system is deprived of its most skilled and experienced practitioners.

Conclusion

In this chapter, I have explored four themes. An empirical analysis of what it is 'to feel like a teacher' (for committed, experienced and successful teachers) suggested that it is to have learnt to feel relaxed, whole, natural in the exercise of one's job, and that these states in turn rely upon a sense of being in control (of oneself, one's pupils and their learning, one's environment, one's destiny) which enables one's relationship with children to be responsible and loving. Yet these states are attained in the face of endemic dilemmas, tensions, uncertainties, inconsistencies, paradoxes, and contradictions. Primary teaching at its best is a complex and highly skilled activity which holds in balance, and occasionally transcends, the historical, sociological, philosophical, psychological and practical tensions and constraints of the work itself. As a craft, and sometimes as an art, it deserves recognition in its own right. Observers who wish to discern the beauty and the skill inherent in the work of successful teachers must first learn something of what it is they do.

Chapter ten

Conclusion

No book about teachers written in 1988 can ignore the political and economic changes which have affected the profession in the past decade. Yet the latest date at which the evidence used here was collected is 1985 and the full consequences of the 1988 Education Act have yet to be felt. Over-much speculation about its effects would not therefore be fruitful.

Accordingly, this chapter falls into three loosely linked parts. In the first I draw out three main themes which have run throughout this study. In the second I plait them together with the notion of motivation, while in the third I use the ideas underlying one theory of motivation to comment upon the impact, and possible consequences, of national developments in the past decade on teachers' continuing willingness to give more of their 'selves' to their work than they are minimally required to do.

The most pervasive and persistent theme to emerge from this study is the centrality to individual teachers of their sense of *self*. In interpreting this fact, one has three choices. One is to assume that all workers discuss their work in terms of its impact upon their 'selves' and that teachers are in this respect no different from any other occupational group. The second is to accept that teachers are peculiarly and abnormally egocentric, a hypothesis which it would be impossible to substantiate and difficult to sustain. The third is to argue, as I have throughout, that teaching as work requires its practitioners to be self-conscious.

For a number of historical, philosophical, psychological, and cultural reasons, teachers in English primary schools are socialized (from their pre-service education onwards) into a tradition of isolation, individualism, self-reliance, and autonomy — in which high value is attached to self-investment and the establishment of a personal relationship with pupils. The teacher as a person is held by many within the profession and outside it to be at the centre of not only the classroom but also the educational process. By implication, therefore, it matters to teachers themselves, as well as to their pupils, who and what they are. Their self-image is more important to them as practitioners than is the case in occupations where the person can easily be separated from the craft.

It follows that an understanding of primary teachers must rest upon some conceptualization of the notion of 'self'. I have accepted the formulation offered by symbolic interactionism which sees the 'self' as, simultaneously, socially constructed (the 'me') and autonomous (the 'I').

The 'I' is an elusive concept, more widely addressed in poetry or psychiatry than in science or sociology. We cannot reflect upon or examine it; instead we sense its existence in moments when we break through our social conditioning and act in accordance with the dictates of an inner prompting of which we are not consciously aware, or when for reasons that we cannot fully explain, we feel, 'this is the real me!'. In both these senses, the 'I' of symbolic inter-actionism has much in common with the Freudian 'id' or the Kohutian 'self'. All three have been largely ignored in studies of teaching, either because they are deemed to be too ill-defined to be much use to practitioners, or because pedagogic theoreticians have been unable to fit the untamed emotions of Freud or the self-love of Kohut into predominantly cognitive models of teaching and learning.

By contrast, I have argued throughout this book that no account of primary teachers' experience is complete if it does not make room for potentially dangerous emotions such as love, rage, and jealousy, on the one hand, and intermittent narcissism and out-breaks of possessive dependence on the other. Although much of this book focuses upon teachers' socially-regulated 'selves', their own descriptions of their feelings about pupils, and their relation-ships with them and with their colleagues, reminds us that the regressive, passionate and unruly aspects of human nature are always present in the classroom and may sometimes escape from rational control.

The 'me' is a less slippery concept than the 'I', in part because we create it by self-reflection and are therefore conscious of its existence and nature. In other words, it *develops*, as from child-hood we respond to the actions and expectations of 'significant' and 'generalized' others. Because it may alter as we interact with different people in varying contexts, we can be said to have multiple, 'situational' selves. But part of the 'me' is not susceptible to environmental influences. The 'substantial self', a set of self-defining beliefs, values and attitudes, develops alongside our situational selves and is highly resistant to change. Our most salient beliefs about 'the sort of person I am' are deeply internalized, and are not easily altered. In consequence, the core of our self-image is well-defined and stable.

Although by definition each substantial self is unique, the teachers whose views form the basis of this book tended to see themselves as the same 'sorts of people' (i.e. their substantial selves were similar in significant ways). They thought of themselves as: 'caring' people (i.e. sometimes as loving, and always as prepared to put the interests of children before their own); people who were concerned to achieve a high standard of occupational competence; people who placed a high value upon autonomy and scope to use their manifold talents; and people who were interested in educational ideas as well as practice.

However, at the start of their careers, most of them did not define themselves as 'teachers'. Indeed, once they had survived their induction into the job, in ways which were consistent with their view of themselves as successful or tenacious, they set about searching for a school or phase of education in which they felt that they fitted. Unless they found this, after a search which often lasted for as long as 4 years, they generally moved into another career (usually parenthood). Those who decided that they were prepared to identify as teachers put their energies into improving their craft knowledge and skill and often, in due course, into influencing others within the educational system. Their development as practitioners cannot be separated from the ways in which their attitude to their work changed, for the latter determined their personal preoccupations and the direction in which they channelled their effort and attention. 'Staff development' programmes and initiatives which overlook the effect which personal concerns can have upon the individual adult's motivation to learn and to change in particular directions obviously do so at their peril.

Although the professional focus of individual teachers altered over time, they were always at pains to protect their substantial selves from change, avoiding the necessity to behave 'in ways I don't believe in' and the company of those who 'think differently from me'. From the start of their careers they developed strategies which protected their 'selves' from situational influences while at the same time allowing them to draw upon the support and companionship of the rest of the staff group (particularly that of kindly older colleagues, whom they cast in the role of 'professional parents'). The most effective of these forms of self-protection was the reference group. Regular contact with other people who shared their beliefs about the social and moral purposes of education and about how children learnt, not only reinforced their view of themselves but also enabled them to filter and even distort messages reaching them from other sources. Reference groups which were located within individuals' schools were particularly potent in protecting them from situational influences, but discussion with like-minded people outside the school also had the effect of stiffening their resistance to change within it. In many cases it also helped them make up their minds to leave the profession.

The second major theme to emerge from this study overlaps with the first, for the people about whom it is written were not simply unique, self-protective individuals. They were also teachers, and conversations with them revealed the centrality to them of their *task*. To advance this proposition is to do more than to reiterate the argument that primary teaching makes unusually heavy claims upon the person who is the practitioner, and therefore that the latter 'is' in large measure what he/she does for a living. It is also to suggest that teaching as an occupation has certain characteristics. First, it involves affect as well as cognition and practical activity. The day-to-day work of classroom teaching involves emotional highs and lows; as an occupation it is felt as well as experienced. Second, it calls for a large number of cognitive, practical and inter-personal skills, and to do it well requires that these be carried to a high level of 'balance', a form of craft performance which at times becomes artistry. Third, for all these reasons, to teach well is extremely demanding. The costs of primary teaching are physical — mental and emotional exhaustion, constant self-examination, and self-doubt. By the same token, its potential rewards are high — warmth, acceptance, exhilaration, self-extension, fulfilment, and the satisfactions which come from doing a difficult job well and, sometimes, superbly. Fourth, it is in essence a private activity: teacher–pupil encounters which lead the latter to learn are exchanges between two or more people. No matter who else is present, their unique quality cannot be shared. It follows therefore that, fifth, teachers rely in the last resort for recognition upon their pupils, for no one else knows, or can know, how effectively they have taught.

What all these characteristics of teaching have in common is their capacity to affect the individual teacher's self-image. This fact is compounded by the existence of historical and cultural traditions in England and Wales which require primary teachers to accept a wider range of responsibilities — moral, social, affective, physical as well as cognitive — for their pupils than is the case in many other countries, and to make most of the resulting curricular and pedagogic decisions unaided. In addition, they are assumed to be capable of fulfilling these responsibilities in respect of large classes, with relatively few material resources, in physical isolation, and with little guidance or support from other adults. In other words, they are required to perform complex and demanding tasks under conditions which constantly underline their loneliness and individual accountability, and yet which remind them that failure is a reflection upon their own worth as people. It is small wonder that teachers so often externalize the reasons for their pupils' bad behaviour or failure to learn. Nor is it surprising that teaching, as work, occupies a central place in the waking minds and hearts of its practitioners and often disturbs their sleep.

It may seem contradictory, therefore, that the third notion to permeate these teachers' accounts was the importance to them of their schools as well as their classes. There was one obvious reason for this: the ways in which schools were run, their routines, institutionalized practices, systems of decision-making and communication, customs, and accounting procedures all affected children's behaviour, their interpretations of adults' aims and priorities, and the levels of constraint or support which teachers themselves experienced. The task of classroom teaching cannot be divorced from the context of the school.

There were, however, other things about schools as work places which made them significant to these teachers. Buildings and equipment affected physical comfort, levels of tension, and states of health. Head teachers and colleagues could offer kindness, laughter, friendship and, sometimes, love; or could fail to notice and respond to their colleagues' needs for acceptance and belonging. Staffrooms could be reassuring, relaxing places, or riven with interpersonal competition and unresolved tensions. Similarly, teachers could enhance or undermine one another's self-esteem by giving or withholding praise and recognition. The dominant values of the institution could reinforce or undermine the self-defining values of the individual, and its staff provide (or fail to provide) a reference group to affirm the individual's sense of worth, integrity, and even reality. Above all, perhaps, an awareness of shared aims and the assumption of collective responsibility for the education of pupils reduced teachers' sense of isolation and relative impotence. It gave them a feeling that they were 'pulling together', instead of being divided into 'camps' or 'factions'. Teachers who took a school-wide view in order to become better classroom teachers are described, in an extension of Hoyle's (1974) seminal typology, as 'bounded professionals'.

For mid-career teachers, in particular, schools were significant for three further reasons. The institution presented individuals with a broader canvas than the classroom upon which to paint their

desires and aspirations. The assumption of school-wide responsibilities gave some people opportunities for self-extension which
they no longer found in the classroom and confirmed for them the
sense that, as practitioners, they were still capable of growth.
Others were reassured by discussion with colleagues whom they
found 'stimulating' or 'challenging' that they were still men and
women of ideas and lively intellects. For these and other teachers
the staffroom or the school provided a forum in which they could
feel that they were influencing adults as well as children, that their
ideas or abilities were having an *impact* upon the wider educational
scene.

By the same token, of course, schools could frustrate teachers
who were anxious for opportunities such as these, but unable to
obtain them. Not all teachers secured the promotion that they felt
they deserved, or found that their colleagues shared their interest in
professional growth or vigorous debate, or worked in staffrooms
where other people were open to their influence. The more anxious
they were for extension into these areas, the more depressed or
embittered they became when they found that their growth beyond
the classroom was stunted and their influence restricted.

A handful of teachers were successful in finding, usually by
chance, a school in which everything that they wanted from their
colleagues came together in one staff group. Such groups were rare,
but the degree of commitment, enthusiasm, and satisfaction which
membership of them engendered indicates how much potential
exists within them for liberating and harnessing the task-focused
energy of classroom teachers, at all levels of experience.

There is an obvious sense in which one cannot separate these
three central themes — i.e. teachers' concern for their substantial
selves, their preoccupation with the task of teaching, and the significance to them of their schools — since the last two were important
only to the extent that they impinged upon the first. From whatever
angle these teachers reflected upon their work, they were
persistently self-referential.

This fact may also throw some light on the importance which
they attached to talking, because it is through interaction with
others that individuals test and affirm their self-conceptions. More
particularly, it is by verbal interaction with others that people
negotiate and agree shared meanings and eventually forge a
common language which enables further communication to take
place. The more people talk to one another, the more likely they are
to understand one another's realities and, provided they confront
the differences which divide one person's perspective from
another's, to create a shared experience in and through which they

can communicate further. So, once staff members had begun to talk with one another, their conversation could also perform other functions — i.e. showing sympathy and understanding; giving support; helping the process of reflection upon, and learning from, experience. The more often services of this kind were exchanged, the easier mutual understanding became, and the more likely it was that open discussion would develop. Talking was, then, an essential tool for the creation of a shared reality within staff groups, and it was this reality which in turn enabled individuals to seek and find, through interaction with others, confirmation of their 'selves'.

However, in pressing home the central importance of teachers' sense of personal and professional identity, one should not lose sight of the fact that school teaching is work, in the particular sense that people are paid to undertake it and that they are, in consequence, under a contractual obligation to perform specific duties and responsibilities, whether they feel like it or not. Yet, as I pointed out in Chapter 1, primary teaching has a bottomless appetite for the investment of scarce personal resources, such as time, interest, and energy. The more of these resources that individuals choose to commit to their work, the better for pupils, parents, and fellow staff, and the more rewards the individual teacher is likely to reap, in terms of appreciation, recognition, self-esteem, and, perhaps, self-extension. Therefore, it could reasonably be argued that children, teachers, and parents will all benefit, if teachers are motivated to give more to their work than simply the physical presence and minimum level of occupational competence required by the 1986/7 Conditions of Service.

'Motivation' to work, in this sense, is whatever persuades individual teachers to put more of their 'selves' into their work. This proposition goes further than Herzberg's fairly simple (and highly normative) assumption that people will work hard to achieve that which they find satisfying at work. In any case, as Chapters 5 and 6 make clear, the distinction which he draws between 'hygiene' factors ('dissatisfiers') and motivating 'satisfiers' breaks down when it is applied to primary teachers. For them, there is little which, in time, does not become 'work itself' and, therefore, a potential 'satisfier'.

Instead, it is tempting to perceive motivation as the drive to satisfy 'needs' (as does Maslow 1954). However, this concept also rests upon insecure foundations, since it is extraordinarily difficult to say what human needs are, beyond the satisfaction of basic physiological requirements which must be met for the maintenance of life. For one thing, we lack an adequate definition. If we take that offered by the Oxford English Dictionary ('circumstances requiring some course [of action]') we are left with further questions of definition, particularly of 'circumstances' and 'requiring', since both these latter terms are open to individual interpretation. Further, we have the problem of whether 'needs' are consciously or unconsciously determined and experienced; and the fact that individuals are themselves shaped and conditioned by the cultures within which they live. 'Needs', therefore, must always be dependent — not only upon individual but also upon cultural perceptions. Nor does any of this resolve the question of when 'needs' should be seen as 'wants' and vice versa.

The picture becomes even cloudier when one tries to apply the concept of 'needs' to that of 'work', since there is no agreed understanding of the latter term, particularly when one attempts to distinguish it from 'play' or from 'non-work' activities which an individual would want to undertake, whether or not they were required to do so. (As one of my interviewees, a late entrant who had tried other occupations, said, 'I can remember coming home one night in my first year of teaching and saying to my wife, "To think that they actually pay me to do this. I love every moment of it!"'.)

Notwithstanding all these doubts and reservations, there is a close resemblance between what these teachers said about their job satisfactions and dissatisfactions and the categories used by Maslow in his well-known formulation of human motivation. Maslow claimed that the impetus to action in men and women comes from their desire to satisfy their needs. These can be classified into one of six categories and arranged in a hierarchy (the alternative labels given in brackets are those commonly used in discussions of Maslow's work). They are, in order of appearance: physiological (physical); safety (security); belonging and love (social); esteem and status (ego); autonomy (self-determination); and self-actualization. Before a particular class of needs becomes important, those below it in the hierarchy must be satisfied. So, to a starving or homeless person, esteem needs will be unimportant — someone who lacks friendship, affection and a sense of belonging to an identified group or who feels undervalued or unesteemed by them will not seek to act independently; only those who have had the opportunity to develop and act in accordance with their own values and standards will feel the urge to fulfil their talents and potential.

To be sure, there is an initial intuitive appeal to Maslow's conceptualization, because much of our daily experience confirms its validity, particularly in relation to the satisfaction of lower-order (physical and safety) needs before higher-order ones. It has not, however, received much support from social scientists (especially those who have attempted to test it in industrial settings), and it does not stand up well to rigorous semantic analysis (how much, for example, does it take to 'satisfy' any particular need?).

Moreover, it appears in two main ways to be inconsistent with the evidence presented in the previous chapters. First, teachers' descriptions of their work do not reflect a hierarchy of needs (e.g. some showed a desire for autonomy and for self-actualization long before they felt liked or esteemed by their colleagues, while others achieved a sense of self-esteem through feeling loved by pupils). Secondly, Maslow's categorization does not allow for teachers' evident need to feel in control of themselves and their environments. Even if room is made for this in Maslow's list, as an aspect of autonomy, its presence cuts across his hierarchy because it appears from the start of teachers' careers — unless we trivialize this dimension of their work by thinking of it as a 'safety' need.

For all that, Maslow has much to offer anyone seeking to understand teachers and their relationship with their work, particularly if one is prepared to elide 'needs' and 'wants'. To adopt a needs-based view of their motivation helps one to understand the intensity of their rewards and frustrations and the way in which they often appear to accept severe demands on their time and energy as an inevitable part of their job. It also explains why teachers attach more importance to the intrinsic than the extrinsic rewards of their occupation and why their job dissatisfactions and satisfactions are, in general, not separate coins but two sides of the same one. Finally, the categories of needs which Maslow proposes match almost exactly the rewards which my interviewees found in teaching: a sense of belonging and of being valued for their competence and efficacy; opportunities to act in accordance with their own standards and values; and a feeling of fulfilment and of self-extension.

There are grounds, then, for applying a modified version of Maslow's hypothesis to motivation in teachers. We do not have to accept his version of a hierarchy to find useful the notion that at any given moment an individual may find some needs more potent (i.e. unsatisfied) than others and that their efforts will be directed, for as long as this state continues, to the satisfaction of them. In other words, although the rewards to be found through work may be arranged in a hierarchy (some being more important than others), the nature of this hierarchy will differ from one person to another and within a particular person from one period of their lives to another. Moreover, there is no reason to suppose that needs are satisfied only at work. This being the case, needs satisfied outside work will be less potent within it, and vice versa. This, in turn, allows us to understand why teachers' involvement with their jobs, and with different aspects of them, varies over time.

There is, however, another way of looking at the topic of need-fulfilment through work. It is possible to accept the fact that people have latent 'needs' of many kinds but that these are activated by circumstances. So, for example, sub-aqua divers are probably more conscious than many other people of their need for oxygen, or, at a different level, we may all need to feel esteemed or recognized for our skills but not become aware of this until we have no job through which to display them. To view teaching from this perspective is not to ask 'what needs does teaching as work fulfil for individuals?', but rather, 'what is there about the nature of teaching as work which makes people aware of their needs?', and, 'of which needs are they made aware?'. If we ask these questions, it is easy to see how the pressures of classroom and staffroom life stimulate in teachers, at different times, a felt-need to experience: the sensation of belonging; self-esteem; a feeling of control, or of influence over, others; or a sense of fulfilment arising from self-expression and personal development. To view needs as activated by life circumstances, of which work is only one, enables us to take a less normative view of human desires than Maslow did, and to explain why they do not appear to operate in a hierarchical fashion for teachers.

It also opens the door to an alternative formulation of teacher motivation which not only accepts the meeting of needs, however triggered, as a satisfaction or reward, but also considers the effort which is needed to achieve that reward. Where likely effort is perceived to outstrip either the value of the reward or the probability of receiving it, effort will be diminished. To put it another way — for people to be positively motivated, they must judge that in a personal and subjective analysis of cost and benefit, the balance is tilted in favour of the latter.

In organizational theory, a complex version of this relatively simple view of motivation is discussed as 'expectancy-valence theory' (Porter and Lawler 1968). In essence, it argues that the amount of effort that individuals put into pursuing a reward will depend on two main sets of expectations which will themselves be shaped by past experience. These expectations are: that their effort will be rewarded and that they will value the reward. The theory also argues that effort expended in work and performance attained in it are not the same. It posits a complex relationship between the two which feeds back into the expectations which individuals have about the extent to which they will be rewarded.

To apply this theory of motivation to primary teachers offers an explanation for why many of them are apparently prepared to live with a high level of fatigue, stress and self-expenditure on the one hand and substantial ego-rewards on the other. The value to them of the latter justifies the effort they know they must make in order to achieve them, since they can be reasonably certain that if they make this effort they will receive its rewards. In other words, they risk, even invite, the lows of their work because they can be almost certain that these will be balanced by highs. The cost may be great, but so too is the benefit; further, the benefit follows with reasonable certainty upon the cost.

Viewed this way, primary teachers' reactions to the political and economic changes of the decade up to 1986, and their anxieties about developments since then, make good sense (in terms of their own subjective accounting system). My interviewees provide evidence relating to two such developments; about two others I can only speculate and therefore have chosen to deal briefly with them.

In the experience of my interviewees, cuts in public expenditure since 1979 have led to larger classes, poorer provision of appropriate materials, equipment and facilities, and lack of maintenance for buildings. In addition, the 'mainstreaming' of children with special educational needs (in response to the Education Act, 1981), often without an adequate compensatory increase in ancillary help, has increased control and pedagogical problems for many teachers. Singly and together, these changes have substantially increased the amount of effort teachers must expend in order to help children learn, and have decreased the quantity and quality of time they have available for the professional development of themselves and their colleagues. In other words, although the potential rewards of teaching children remain the same, the costs to teachers of achieving them have spiralled upwards. Fatigue and strain have multiplied and often been compounded by lack of opportunities to seek help or stimulation from colleagues and by the frustration of not being able to achieve the highest possible professional standards (sometimes, indeed, to attain even a satisfactory one).

Secondly, these teachers were aware of repeated attacks upon them from politicians, in the media and, though much less frequently, from individual parents and governors. This barrage of ill-substantiated complaint made many of them feel that they were not receiving the recognition and esteem which they felt to be their due professional reward for demanding work well done. Why then, they asked, should they continue to invest a great deal of their 'selves' in their work, especially when the material rewards which they received were also paltry? From their viewpoint, the rewards available from teaching children and, for some people, from working in schools, were still high, but the likelihood was much diminished that their equally potent need for status and self-esteem would be publicly met.

Two further developments have taken place since 1985, each of them with the potential to tilt teachers' cost–benefit analysis towards cost and away from benefit, and each therefore likely to reduce the effort and self-investment which teachers make. The first is the imposition in 1986/7 of a new 'flatter' salary structure and of Conditions of Service which specify, among other things, the minimum hours which teachers should work. The former reduces the financial and 'impact' incentives which in the past encouraged many teachers to take on additional work. The latter (coupled as it is with the loss of teachers' bargaining rights) appears to reduce their professional status and to devalue their client-centred commitment.

The second is the Education Act of 1988 whose proposals are so far-reaching that I can only sketch them here. The likely costs to primary teachers are loss of freedom (arising from the introduction of a national curriculum and national assessment) and erosion of their sense of professional integrity (should they be required to work in ways which they feel to be educationally improper). It is also possible that the increased powers which the Act gives to governors (especially parent governors) will threaten teachers' sense of autonomy and, in the case of larger schools, that their attention will be taken away from teaching by the demands of 'local financial management'. Together these provisions could reduce the satisfactions of the job (especially as they relate to affective relationships with pupils, control, autonomy, influence, self-extension and self-esteem), while at the same time multiplying potential sources of tension for teachers and therefore the costs to them of their work.

Earlier I argued, following a simplified version of 'expectancy-valence theory', that effort will be reduced, sometimes to nothing, if rewards are perceived to be smaller and/or the likelihood of achieving them is seen to be diminished. At their worst, therefore, both the financial settlement of 1986/7 and the Education Act, 1988, could have the effect of reducing teachers' motivation and with it their self-investment in their work.

However, one must not take a wholly pessimistic view. Viewed positively, the Act, taken together with the new Conditions of Service, might have two beneficial effects. First, by defining teachers' responsibilities and hours of work, it might reduce their chronic tension, self-doubt and fatigue. Second, by spelling out more clearly than is presently the case their pupils' learning goals and the means of assessing these, it might increase their sense of pedagogical efficacy. In addition, it is not yet certain that loss of autonomy will necessarily result, either from the introduction of a national curriculum and assessment or from vesting more powers in parents and governors.

One can only hope, and trust in the professional skill and commitment of the teachers whose experience is reported here, as well as in their capacity to defend the values they prize most highly. But the costs to the nation's children of a reduction in teachers' willingness to give generously of their 'selves' to their work would be formidably high. The satisfactions of teaching itself will presumably always remain as I have described them in this book. But if teachers themselves come to feel that they cannot, with integrity, achieve these rewards or that the effort required to do so is too great, their motivation will certainly decrease. In other words, if they cannot satisfy the needs which they are daily made aware of in their work in classrooms and schools (i.e. if they are not rewarded), then the effort that they make through their heavy investment of self in work will eventually decline.

Can we afford to take that risk?

References

Abercrombie, M. L. J. (1969) *The Anatomy of Judgement: an Investigation into the Processes of Perception and Reason*, Harmondsworth: Penguin.
—— (1981) 'Changing basic assumptions about teaching and learning', in D. Boud (ed.) *Developing Student Autonomy in Learning*, London: Kogan Page.
Abercrombie, M. L. J. and Terry, P. M. (1979) *Aims and Techniques of Group Teaching*, 4th edn, Guildford: Society for Research and Higher Education.
Acker, S. (1987) 'Primary school teaching as an occupation', in S. Delamont (ed.) *The Primary School Teacher*, Lewes: Falmer Press.
Alexander, R. (1984) *Primary Teaching*, London: Cassell.
—— (1988) 'Garden or jungle? Teacher development and informal primary education', in W. A. L. Blyth (ed.) *Informal Primary Education Today: Essays and Studies*, Lewes: Falmer Press.
Argyris, C. (1964) *Integrating the Individual and the Organisation*, New York: Wiley.
Ashley, B., Cohen, H., McIntyre, D., and Slatter, R. (1969) 'A sociological analysis of students' reasons for becoming teachers', *Sociological Review*, 18: 53–69.
Ashton, P., Kneen, P., Davies, F., and Holley, B. (1975) *The Aims of Education: a Study of Teacher Opinions*, London: Macmillan.
Aspinwall, K. (1986) 'Teacher biography: the in-service potential', *Cambridge Journal of Education*, 16: 210–15.
Ball, S. (1972) 'Self and identity in the context of deviance: the case of criminal abortion', in R. Scott and J. Douglas (eds) *Theoretical Perspectives on Deviance*, New York: Basic Books.
Ball, S. and Goodson, I. (1985) 'Understanding teachers: concepts and cultures', in S. Ball and I. Goodson (eds) *Teachers' Lives and Careers*, Lewes: Falmer Press.
Barnard, C. (1938) *Functions of the Executive*, Cambridge, Mass.: Harvard University Press.
Becker, H. S. (1960) 'Notes on the concept of commitment', *American Journal of Sociology*, 66: 32–40.

Becker, H. S. (1976) *Sociological Work: Method and Substance*,
New Jersey, New Brunswick: Transaction Books.
Bee, H. and Mitchell, S. (1984) 2nd edn, *The developing person: a life-span approach*, London: Harper & Row.
Belasco, J. and Alutto, J. (1975) 'Decisional participation and teacher
satisfaction', in V. Houghton, R. McHugh, and C. Morgan (eds) *The
Management of Organisations and Individuals*, London: Ward Lock
Educational.
Bennet, C. (1983) 'Paints, pots or promotion: art teachers' attitudes
towards their careers', in S. Ball and I. Goodson (eds), 1985,
Teachers' Lives and Careers, Lewes: Falmer Press.
Bennett, S. N., Desforges, C., Cockburn, A., and Wilkinson, B. (1984)
The Quality of Pupil Learning Experiences, London: Lawrence
Erlbaum Associates.
Berlak, A. and Berlak, H. (1981) *The Dilemmas of Schooling*, London:
Methuen.
Berman, P. and McLaughlin, M. (1977) 'Federal Programs supporting
Educational Change', vol. 8: *Factors Affecting Implementation and
Continuation*, Santa Monica, Calif.: The Rand Corporation.
Bethell, P. (1980) 'Getting away from it all', *The Times Educational
Supplement*, 21 March.
Biklen, S. K. (1985) 'Can elementary schoolteaching be a career? A
search for new ways of understanding women's work', *Issues in
Education*, 3 (3): 215–31.
—— (1986a) 'Good morning, Miss Munday: fictional portrayals of
young female teachers', paper presented at American Educational
Research Association Conference, San Francisco.
—— (1986b) 'I have always worked: elementary school teaching as a
career', *Phi Delta Kappa*, March, 504–8.
Blase, J. (1986) 'A qualitative analysis of sources of teacher stress:
consequences for performance', *American Educational Research
Journal*, 23: 13–40.
Blyth, W. A. (1967) *English Primary Education*, 2nd edn, vol. II,
London: Routledge & Kegan Paul.
Bown, O., Fuller, F., and Richek, H. (1967) 'A comparison of self-perception of prospective elementary teachers', *Psychology in the
Schools*, 4: 21–4.
Broadfoot, P. (1985) 'Institutional dependence and autonomy: English
and French teachers in the classroom', *Prospects*, 15: 263–71.
Broadfoot, P. and Osborn, M. (1986) 'Teachers' conceptions of their
professional responsibility: some international comparisons', paper
presented at British Educational Research Association Conference,
Bristol.
Brown, S. and McIntyre, D. (1986) 'How do teachers think about their
craft?', in M. Ben-Perez, R. Broome, and R. Halkes (eds) *Advances
in Research on Teacher Thinking*, Amsterdam: Swets and Zeitlinger
BV.
Burgess, R. (1984) *In the Field: an Introduction to Field Research*,
London: Allen & Unwin.

Burns, R. (1982) *Self-concept Development and Education*, London: Holt, Rinehart & Winston.

Bussis, A., Chittenden, E., and Amarel, M. (1976) *Beyond Surface Curriculum: an interview study of teachers' understandings*, Boulder, Col.: Westview Press.

Calderhead, J. (1987) *Exploring Teachers' Thinking*, London: Cassell.

Campbell, R. J. (1985) *Developing the Primary School Curriculum*, London: Cassell.

Christensen, J., Burke, P., and Fessler, R. (1983) 'Teacher life-span development: a summary and synthesis of the literature', paper presented at American Educational Research Association Conference, Montreal.

Cohen, A. (1976) 'The elasticity of evil: changes in the social definition of deviance', in M. Hammersley and P. Woods (eds) *The Process of Schooling*, London: Routledge & Kegan Paul.

Cohen, L., Reid, I., and Boothroyd, K. (1973) 'Validation of the Mehrabian need for achievement scale with college of education students', *British Journal of Educational Psychology*, 43: 269–77.

Connell, R. (1985) *Teachers' Work*, London: Allen & Unwin.

Cooley, C. (1902), *Human Nature and the Social Order*, 1983 edn, New Brunswick, New Jersey: Transaction Books.

Coulter, F. and Taft, R. (1973) 'Professional socialisation of teachers as social assimilation', *Human Relations*, 26: 681–93.

Delamont, S. (1987) 'The primary teacher, 1945–1990: myths and realities', in S. Delamont (ed) *The Primary School Teacher*, Lewes: Falmer Press.

Denscombe, M. (1980a) 'The work context of teaching: an analytic framework for the study of teachers in classrooms', *British Sociology of Education*, 1(3): 279–92.

—— (1980b) 'Keeping 'em quiet: the significance of noise for the practical activity of teaching', in P. Woods (ed.) *Teacher Strategies: Explorations in the Sociology of the School*, London: Croom Helm.

Department of Education and Science (1982) *The New Teacher in School*, HMI Series: Matters for Discussion, 15, London: HMSO.

—— (1983) *Teaching Quality*, London: HMSO.

Desforges, C. and Cockburn, A. (1987) *Understanding the Mathematics Teacher: A Study of Practice in First Schools*, Lewes: Falmer Press.

Doyle, W. (1986) 'Classroom management and organization', in M. Wittrock (ed.) *Handbook of Research on Teaching*, New York: Macmillan.

Duke, D. (1986) 'Understanding what it means to be a teacher', *Educational Leadership*, 44: 27–32.

Dunham, J. (1984) *Stress in Teaching*, London: Croom Helm.

Ebbutt, D. (1982) *Teacher as researcher: how four teachers coordinate action research in their respective schools*, TIQL Project, Working Paper 10, Cambridge Institute of Education.

Education, Science and Arts Committee (1986) *Select Parliamentary Committee Report: Achievement in Primary Schools*, London: HMSO.

Eisner, E. (1979) *The Educational Imagination*, London: Collier Macmillan.

Elbaz, F. (1983) *Teacher Thinking: A Study of Practical Knowledge*, London: Croom Helm.

Elliott, J. (1976) *Developing hypotheses about classrooms from teachers' practical constructs*, Ford Teaching Project, Cambridge: Cambridge Institute of Education.

Elliott, J., Bridges, D., Ebbutt, D., Gibson, R., and Nias, J. (1981) *School Accountability*, London: Grant McIntyre.

England, H. (1986) *Social Work as Art: Making Sense of Good Practice*, London: Allen & Unwin.

Erikson, E. (1950) *Childhood and Society*, New York: Norton.

——— (1968) *Identity: Youth and Crisis*, 1983 edn, London: Faber & Faber.

Fessler, R., Burke, P., and Christensen, J. (1983) 'Teacher career cycle model: framework for viewing teacher growth needs', paper presented at American Educational Research Conference, Montreal.

Festinger, L. (1957) *A Theory of Cognitive Dissonance*, Stanford, California: Stanford University Press.

Finlayson, D. and Cohen, L. (1967) 'The teacher's role: a comparative study of the conceptions of college of education students and head teachers', *British Journal of Educational Psychology*, 37: 22–31.

Floud, J. (1962) 'Teaching the affluent society', *British Journal of Sociology*, 13: 299–308.

Foulkes, S. H. (1975) 'A short outline of the therapeutic process in group-analytic psychotherapy', *Group Analysis*, 8: 59–63.

Fullan, M. (1982) *The Meaning of Educational Change*, New York: Teachers' College Press.

Fuller, F. (1969) 'Concerns of teachers: a developmental characterisation', *American Educational Research Journal*, 6: 207–26.

Fuller, F. and Bown, O. (1975) 'Becoming a teacher', in K. Ryan (ed.) *Teacher Education*, 74th Yearbook of the National Society for the Study of Education, part 2, Chicago: University of Chicago Press.

Gabriel, J. (1957) *An Analysis of the Emotional Problems of the Teacher in the Classroom*, London: Angus & Robertson.

Galloway, D., Boswell, K., Panckhurst, F., Boswell, C., and Green, C. (1982) 'Satisfaction with teaching', *National Education*, December, 206–12.

Galton, M., Simon, B., and Croll, P. (1980) *Inside the Primary Classroom*, London: Routledge & Kegan Paul.

Geer, B. (1968) 'Teaching', in N. Bennett and D. McNamara (eds) *Focus on Teaching*, London: Longman.

Gehrke, N. (1982) 'A grounded theory study of beginning teachers' role personalization through reference group relations', *Journal of Teacher Education*, 32: 34–8.

Gibson, T. (1973) *Teachers Talking: Aims, Methods, Attitudes to Change*, London: Allen Lane.

Glaser, B. and Strauss, A. (1967) *The Discovery of Grounded Theory*, London: Weidenfeld & Nicholson.

Glassberg, S. (1980) 'A view of the beginning teacher from a developmental perspective', paper presented at the American Educational Research Association Conference, Boston.

Goldthorpe, J., Lockwood, D., Bechofer, F., and Platt, J. (1968) *The Affluent Worker: Industrial Attitudes and Behaviour*, vol. 1, Cambridge: Cambridge University Press.

Gould, R. (1978) *Transformations: Growth and Change in Adult Life*, New York: Simon & Schuster.

Grant, R. (1968) 'A career in teaching: a survey of middle school teachers' perceptions with particular reference to the careers of women teachers', paper presented to British Educational Research Association Conference, Bristol.

Hall, G. and Loucks, S. (1979) *Staff Development: New Demands, New Realities, New Perspectives*, New York: Teachers' College Press.

Hammersley, M. (1984) 'Staffroom news', in *Classrooms and Staffrooms: the Sociology of Teachers and Teaching*, Milton Keynes: Open University Press.

Hammersley, M. and Atkinson, P. (1983) *Ethnography: Principles in Practice*, London: Methuen.

Hampson, S. (1982) 'The construction of personality', in P. Barnes, J. Oates, J. Chapman, V. Lee, and I. Czerniewska (eds) 1984, *Personality, Development and Learning*, London: Hodder & Stoughton/The Open University.

Hannam, C., Smyth, P., and Stephenson, M. (1971) *The First Year of Teaching*, Harmondsworth: Penguin.

Hanson, D. and Herrington, D. (1976) *From College to Classroom: the Probationary Year*, London: Routledge & Kegan Paul.

Hargreaves, A. (1986) *Two Cultures of Schooling: the Case of Middle Schools*, Lewes: Falmer Press.

Hargreaves, D. (1978) 'Whatever happened to symbolic interactionism?', in L. Barton and R. Meighan (eds) *Sociological Interpretations of Schooling and Classrooms*, Driffield: Nafferton.

——— (1980) 'The occupational culture of teachers', in P. Woods (ed.) *Teacher Strategies: Explorations in the Sociology of the School*, London: Croom Helm.

Hargreaves, D., Hester, S., and Mellor, F. (1975) *Deviance in the Classroom*, London: Routledge & Kegan Paul.

Harrison, R. (1983) 'Strategies for a new age', *Human Resource Management*, 22: 209–35.

Hartley, D. (1985) *Understanding the Primary School*, London: Croom Helm.

Havinghurst, R. (1953) *Human Development and Education*, New York: Longman.

Herzberg, F. (1966) 'Motivation-hygiene theory', in D. Pugh (ed.) 1971, *Organization Theory*, Harmondsworth: Penguin.

Hewitt, F. (1978) 'Teacher participation in planning and provision: the identification of pertinent factors', *British Journal of In-service Education*, 5: 50–53.

Hitchcock, D. (1982) 'The social organization of space and place in an urban open-plan primary school', in G. Payne and E. Cuff (eds) *Doing Teaching*, London: Batsford.

Holland, R. (1977) *Self and Social Context*, London: Macmillan.

Hoyle, E. (1974) 'Professionality, professionalism and control in teaching', *London Educational Review*, 3: 13–19.

—— (1986) *The Politics of School Management*, London: Hodder & Stoughton.

Huberman, M. (1974) 'Looking at adult education from the perspective of the adult life-cycle', *International Review of Education*, 117–37.

Huggett, F. (1986) *Teachers*, London: Weidenfeld & Nicholson.

Ingvarson, L. and Greenway, P. (1984) 'Portrayals of teacher development', *Australian Journal of Education*, 28(1): 46–65.

Jackson, P. (1968) *Life in Classrooms*, New York: Holt, Rinehart & Winston.

Jersild, A. (1952) *When Teachers Face Themselves*, Columbia: Teachers' College Press.

Johnson-Laird, P. and Wason, P. (eds) (1977) *Thinking: readings in cognitive science*, Cambridge: Cambridge University Press.

Kanter, R. (1986) 'Commitment and social organization', in D. Field (ed.) *Social Psychology for Sociologists*, London: Nelson.

Katz, D. (1960) 'The functional approach to the study of attitude change', *Public Opinion Quarterly*, 24: 163–204.

Kearney, G. and Sinclair, K. (1978) 'Teacher concerns and teacher anxiety', *Review of Educational Research*, 48: 273–90.

Kelly, A. (1968) *Knowledge and Curriculum Planning*, London: Harper & Row.

Kimmel, D. (1973) *Adulthood and Ageing*, New York: Wiley.

King, R. (1978) *All Things Bright and Beautiful: a Sociological Study of Infant Schools*, Chichester: Wiley.

Klein, L. (1976) *New Forms of Work Organization*, Cambridge: Cambridge University Press.

Kohut, H. (1971) 'The psychoanalytic treatment of narcissistic personality disorders: outline of a systematic approach', *Psychoanalytic Study of the Child*, 23: 86–113, London: The Hogarth Press.

Kounin, J. (1970) *Discipline and Group Management in Classrooms*, New York: Holt, Rinehart & Winston.

Kremer, L. and Hofman, J. (1985) 'Teachers' professional identity and burnout', *Research in Education*, 34: 89–95.

Kuhn, D. (1979) 'The application of Piaget's theory of cognitive development to education', *Harvard Education Review*, 49: 340–60.

Kyriacou, C. and Sutcliffe, J. (1977) 'Teacher stress: a review', *Educational Review*, 29: 299–306.

—— (1978) 'Teacher stress: prevalence, sources and symptoms', *British Journal of Educational Psychology*, 48: 159–67.

—— (1979) 'Teacher stress and satisfaction', *Educational Research*, 21: 89–96.

Lacey, C. (1977) *The Socialisation of Teachers*, London: Methuen.

Laughlin, A. (1984) 'Teacher stress in an Australian setting: the role of biographical mediators', *Educational Studies*, 10: 7–22.

Levinson, D. *et al.* (1978) *The Seasons of a Man's Life*, New York: Alfred Knopf.

Lewis, M. (1979) *The Culture of Inequality*, New York: New American Library.

Lieberman, A. and Miller, L. (1984) *Teachers: their World and their Work*, Alexandria, Va.: Association for Supervision and Curriculum Development.

Lintott, W. (1986) 'Group work in a course for teachers', mimeo, Cambridge Institute of Education.

Lortie, D. (1975) *School Teacher: a Sociological Study*, Chicago: University of Chicago Press.

Lyons, G. and McLeary, L. (1980) 'Careers in teaching', in E. Hoyle and J. Megarry (eds) *World Yearbook of Education: Professional Development of Teachers*, London: Routledge & Kegan Paul.

McDonald, F. (1982) 'A theory of the professional development of teachers', paper presented at American Educational Research Association Conference, New York.

McLaughlin, M. and Marsh, D. (1978) 'Staff development and school change', *Teachers' College Record*, 80: 69–94.

Marris, P. (1968) *Widows and Their Families*, London: Routledge & Kegan Paul.

—— (1974) *Loss and Change*, London: Routledge & Kegan Paul.

Maslow, A. (1954) *Motivation and Personality*, New York: Harper & Row.

—— (1973) *Further Reaches of Human Nature*, Harmondsworth: Penguin.

Mead, G. H. (1934) *Mind, Self and Society*, Chicago: University of Chicago Press.

Merton, R. and Kitt, A. (1950) 'Contributions to the theory of reference group behaviour', in R. Merton (ed.) 1957, *Social Theory and Social Structure*, Glencoe, Ill.: Free Press.

Morgan, V. and Dunn, S. (1978) 'Why choose primary teaching?', *Durham and Newcastle Research Review*, 8: 44–50.

Morrison, D. and McIntyre, D. (eds) (1969) *Teachers and Teaching*, Harmondsworth: Penguin.

Newcomb, T. (1943) 'Attitude development as a function of reference groups: the Bennington Study', in E. Maccoby, T. Newcomb, and E. Hartley (eds) 1966, *Readings in Social Psychology*, London: Methuen.

—— (1950) *Social Psychology*, New York: Dryden.

Newman, K., Burden, P., and Applegate, J. (1980) 'Helping teachers examine their long-range development', mimeo, Kent State University.

Nias, J. (1980) 'Leadership styles and job satisfaction in primary schools', in T. Bush, R. Glatter, J. Goodey, and C. Riches (eds) *Approaches to School Management*, London: Harper & Row.

—— (1981) 'Commitment and motivation in primary school teachers', *Educational Review*, 33: 181–90.

—— (1987a) 'Learning from difference: a collegial approach to change', in W. J. Smyth (ed.) *Educating Teachers: Changing the Nature of Pedagogical Knowledge*, Lewes: Falmer Press.

—— (1987b) 'One finger, one thumb: a case study of the deputy head's part in the leadership of a nursery/infant school', in G. Southworth (ed.) *Readings in Primary School Management*, Lewes: Falmer Press.

—— (1987c) *Seeing Anew: Teachers' Theories of Action*, Geelong: Deakin University Press.

—— (1988) 'Informal education: teachers' accounts', in W. A. L. Blyth (ed.) *Informal Primary Education Today: Essays and Studies*, Lewes: Falmer Press.

Nias, J., Southworth, G., and Yeomans, R. (1989) *Staff Relationships in the Primary School: a Study of Organizational Cultures*, London: Cassell.

Noad, J. (1979) 'Maslow needs hierarchy related to educational attitudes and self-concepts of elementary student teachers', *Educational Review*, 31: 51–7.

Oja, S. (1981) 'Deriving teacher educational objectives from cognitive-developmental theories and applying them to the practices of teacher education', paper presented at the American Educational Research Association Conference, Los Angeles.

Open University: Introduction to Sociology Course Team, D207 (1981) *Self in Social Context*, Milton Keynes: Open University.

Osborn, M. (1985) 'Profiles of a typical French and English primary teacher', mimeo, Teachers' Conceptions of their Professional Responsibility Project, Bristol University.

Otto, R. (1982) 'Occupational stress among primary school teachers from seven schools in the metropolitan area of Melbourne', mimeo, Department of Sociology, La Trobe University, Victoria.

Pajak, E. (1981) 'Teaching and the psychology of self', *American Journal of Education*, 9: 1–13.

Peterson, A. (1979) 'Teachers' changing perceptions of self and others throughout the teaching career', paper presented at Southwest ERA, San Francisco.

Peterson, W. (1964) 'Age, teacher's role and the institutional setting', in S. Delamont (ed.) 1984, *Readings in Interaction in the Classroom*, London: Methuen.

Pollard, A. (1979) 'Negotiating deviance and "getting done" in primary school classrooms', in L. Barton and R. Meigham (eds) *Schools, Pupils and Deviance*, Driffield: Nafferton.

—— (1980) 'Teacher interests and changing situations of survival threat in primary school classrooms', in P. Woods (ed.) *Teacher Strategies: Explorations in the Sociology of the School*, London: Croom Helm.

—— (1982) 'A model of classroom coping strategies', *British Journal of Sociology of Education*, 3(1): 19–37.

—— (1985) *The Social World of the Primary School*, London: Cassell.

—— (1987) 'Primary teachers and their colleagues', in S. Delamont (ed.) *The Primary School Teacher*, Lewes: Falmer Press.

Poppleton, P. (1988) 'Teacher professional satisfaction', *Cambridge Journal of Education*, 1: 5–16.

Poppleton, P., Deas, R., Pullin, R., and Thompson, D. (1987) 'The experience of teaching in "disadvantaged" areas in the United Kingdom and the USA', *Comparative Education*, 23: 303–15.

Porter, L. and Lawler, E. (1968) *Managerial Attitudes and Performance*, Homewood: Irwin-Dorsey.

Primary Schools Research and Developmental Group (1986) *The Primary School Teacher: a profession in distress*, Birmingham: University of Birmingham.

Razzell, A. (1968) *Juniors: a Postscript to Plowden*, Harmondsworth: Penguin.

Rich, R. (1933) *The Training of Teachers in England and Wales in the Nineteenth Century*, Cambridge: Cambridge University Press.

Richardson, J. E. (1967) *Group Study for Teachers*, London: Routledge & Kegan Paul.

—— (1973) *The Teacher, the Task and the School*, London: Methuen.

Riseborough, G. (1985) 'Pupils, teachers' careers and schooling: an empirical study', in S. Ball and I. Goodson (eds) *Teachers' Lives and Careers*, Lewes: Falmer Press.

—— (1986) ' "Know-alls", "Whizz-kids", "Dead Wood" and the crisis of schooling', paper presented at British Educational Research Association Conference, Bristol.

Rogers, C. (1982) *A Social Psychology of Schooling*, London: Routledge & Kegan Paul.

Rokeach, M. (1973) *The Nature of Human Values*, New York: Free Press.

Ryan, K. (1979) 'The stages of teaching and staff development: some tentative suggestions', paper presented at American Educational Research Association Conference, San Francisco.

Salzburger-Wittenburg, I., Henry, G., and Osborne, E. (1983) *The Emotional Experience of Learning and Teaching*, London: Routledge & Kegan Paul.

Sarason, S. (1982), revised edition, *The Culture of the School and the Problem of Change*, Boston: Allyn & Bacon.

Sharp, R. and Green, A. (1975) *Education and Social Control*, London: Routledge & Kegan Paul.

Sheehy, G. (1976) *Passages: Predictable Crises of Adult Life*, New York: Dutton,

Sherif, C. and Sherif, M. (1964) *Reference Groups: Exploration into Conformity and Deviation of Adolescents*, New York: Harper & Row.

Sherif, M. and Wilson, M. (1953) *Group Relations at the Crossroads*, New York: Harper & Row.

Shibutani, T. (1955) 'Reference groups as perspectives', in J. Manis and B. Meltzer (eds) 1972 (2nd edn) *Symbolic Interaction: a Reader in Social Psychology*, Boston: Allyn & Bacon.

Shipman, M. (1967) 'Theory and practice in the education of teachers', *Educational Research*, 9: 208–12.

Siegel, A. and Siegel, S. (1957) 'Reference groups, membership groups and attitude change', in M. Warren and M. Jahoda (eds) 1973, *Attitudes*, Harmondsworth: Penguin.

Sikes, P. (1986) 'The mid-career teacher: adaptation and motivation in a contracting secondary school system', unpublished PhD thesis, University of Leeds.

Sikes, P., Measor, L., and Woods, P. (1985) *Teachers' Careers: Crises and Continuities*, Lewes: Falmer Press.

Smith, L. and Geoffrey, W. (1968) *The Complexities of an Urban Classroom*, New York: Holt, Rinehart & Winston.

Smith, L., Kleine, P., Prunty, J., and Dwyer, D. (1986) *Educational Innovators: Then and Now*, Lewes: Falmer Press.

Spencer, D. A. (1986) *Contemporary Women Teachers: Balancing Home and School*, New York: Longman.

Sprinthall, N. A. and Thies-Sprinthall, L. (1983) 'The teacher as an adult learner: A cognitive-developmental view', in G. A. Griffin (ed.) *Staff Development*, 82nd Yearbook of the National Society for the Study of Education, Chicago: University of Chicago Press.

Stenhouse, L. (1980) 'Curriculum research and the art of the teacher', *Curriculum*, 1(1): 40–4.

Strogdill, R. (1959) *Individual Behaviour and Group Achievement*, Oxford: Oxford University Press.

Swidler, A. (1979) 'Pressures for intimacy', in S. Delamont (ed.) (1984) *Readings on Interaction in the Classroom*, London: Methuen.

Taylor, P. (1986) *Expertise and the Primary Teacher*, Slough: NFER/Nelson.

Taylor, P. H. (1975) 'A study of the concerns of students on a Postgraduate Certificate in Education course', *British Journal of Teacher Education*, 1: 151–61.

Taylor, J. and Dale, I. (1971) *A Survey of Teachers in their First Year of Service*, Bristol: University of Bristol.

Thomas, J. (1980) *The Self in Education*, Slough: NFER/Nelson.

Thomas, W. (1931) 'The relation of research to the social process', in *Essays on Research in Social Science*, Washington: Brookings Inc.

Tropp, A. (1957) *The Schoolteachers*, London: Heinemann.

Van Manen, M. (1984) 'Action research as theory of the unique: from pedagogic thoughtlessness to pedagogic tactfulness', paper presented at American Educational Research Association Conference, New Orleans.

Veenman, S. (1984) 'Perceived problems of beginning teachers', *Review of Educational Research*, 54(2): 143–78.

Vernon, M. (1955) 'The functions of schemata in perceiving', *Psychological Review*, 62(3): 180–93.

Walker, R. and Adelman, C. (1976) 'Strawberries', in M. Stubbs and S. Delamont (eds) *Explorations in Classroom Observation*, Chichester: Wiley.

Waller, W. (1961) (new edn), *Sociology of Teaching*, New York: Russell and Russell.

Winnicott, D. (1955) *The Family and Individual Development*, London: Tavistock.

Woods, P. (1977) 'Teaching for survival', in P. Woods and M. Hammersley (eds) *School Experience*, London: Croom Helm.

—— (1979) *The Divided School*, London: Routledge & Kegan Paul.

Woods, P. (1981) 'Strategies, commitment and identity: making and breaking the teacher role', in L. Barton and S. Walker (eds) *School Teachers and Teaching*, Lewes: Falmer Press.

—— (1984) 'Teachers, self and curriculum', in S. Ball (ed.) *Defining the Curriculum: Histories and Ethnographies of School Subjects*, Lewes: Falmer Press.

—— (1987a) 'Managing the primary teacher's role', in S. Delamont (ed.) *The Primary School Teacher*, Lewes: Falmer Press.

—— (1987b) 'Life-histories and teacher knowledge', in W. J. Smyth (ed.) *Educating Teachers: Changing the Nature of Pedagogical Knowledge*, Lewes: Falmer Press.

Wragg, E. (1982) *A Review of Research in Teacher Education*, Slough: NFER/Nelson.

Yeomans, R. (1985) 'Are primary teachers primarily people?' in G. Southworth (ed.) 1987, *Readings in Primary Management*, Lewes: Falmer Press.

Zeichner, K. and Tabachnick, B. (1983) 'Teacher perspectives in the face of institutional press', paper presented at the American Educational Research Association Conference, Montreal.

Subject index

Name index

344 86

Printed in the United Kingdom
by Lightning Source UK Ltd.
102638UKS00001B/91